FDI and Economic Growth in India

FDI and Economic Growth in India

Narayan Sethi
Sanhita Sucharita

RAWAT PUBLICATIONS
Jaipur • New Delhi • Bangalore • Hyderabad • Guwahati • Kolkata

ISBN 978-81-316-0590-5

Published by
Prem Rawat for **Rawat Publications**
Satyam Apts, Sector 3, Jawahar Nagar, Jaipur 302 004 (India)
Phone: 0141 265 1748 / 7006 Fax: 0141 265 1748
E-mail: info@rawatbooks.com
Website: www.rawatbooks.com

New Delhi Office
4858/24, Ansari Road, Daryaganj, New Delhi 110 002
Phone: 011 2326 3290

Also at *Bangalore, Hyderabad, Guwahati* and *Kolkata*

Typeset by Rawat Computers, Jaipur
Printed at Nice Printing Press, New Delhi

Contents

List of Tables

Preface

This book provides an overview of the foreign direct investment (FDI) and economic growth in India. Its main objectives are to examine the relationship between FDI and economic growth in India, and also to identify the motivating factors and problems of FDI inflows into India. It attempts to study and quantify the impact of FDI on selected macro-economic variables in India using time series data for the period 1974–2008. It also examines the trends and composition of FDI inflows as well as its impact on economic growth and then suggests policy implications thereof. Thus, book provides the basic ideas about the advent of FDI to students, research scholars, policy makers and academicians who have some training in basic economic theory. We believe that the book goes well in attaining its objectives, within the limitations created by an enormous earlier literature and constrains of our own knowledge and understanding. The primary target for this book is the research scholar and academician with basic knowledge of economic theory. We would like to recommend this book as a background or supplementary reading for doctoral course in economics with specialization of international finance.

The book stretches into seven chapters. It begin with an introduction (Chapter 1) discussing the significance and need of FDI, rationale and benefits of FDI and spells out the scope and objectives, methodology, and data sources of the study. Chapter 2, we reviews the existing theoretical and empirical literature on the impact and effects of FDI on economic growth. Chapter 3 discusses FDI in India and its policies and trends. This chapter also examines the economic reforms and FDI in India, different industrial policies, government policy towards FDI and recent initiatives to attract FDI. In Chapter 4, we discuss policy and incentive package for FDI by government. This chapter also highlights foreign investment and taxation policy in India and incentives. We analyse global trends of FDI flows in comparing with developing and South Asian countries.

Chapters 5–6 bring out a detailed discussion about the tools of time series and methodology used for study. The study makes use of variety of econometric models to carry out the empirical analysis. Chapter 5 describes the motives, determinants and problems of FDI. We describe the factors attracting FDI inflows and also factors discouraging FDI inflows into India. Chapter 6 empirically examines the impact of FDI on economic growth in India. We employed the variety of models for the study to bring out the empirical results. In this chapter, we discuss the model used for finding the casual relationship between FDI and economic growth in India. The chapter also empirically examines the effect of FDI on macro-economic variables, including economic growth in India.

The final and the seventh chapter summarizes the study and concludes and suggests some policy implications. The experience with liberalization of inward FDI flows in India shows close similarities with other liberalizing economies.

This book could not have been written without the support and encouragement of our friends, parents, students and colleagues. We would like to thank them all for their suggestions and comments during the writing of the book.

We would also like to record our deep appreciation to the editorial team of Rawat Publications, specifically Pranitji, for his support and help. Finally, we convey our prayer to Almighty for His grace.

1

Background, Issues and Objectives of the Study

Significance and Need for FDI

Developing countries, emerging economies and countries in transition increasingly see foreign direct investment (FDI) as a source of economic development, modernization and employment generation, and have liberalized their FDI regimes to attract investment. The overall benefits of FDI for developing economies are well documented. Given the appropriate host country's policies and a basic level of development, a preponderance of studies show that FDI triggers technology spillovers, assists human capital formation, contributes to international trade integration, helps create a more competitive business environment and enhances enterprise development. All these contribute to higher economic growth. Beyond the initial macro-economic stimulus for actual investment, FDI influences growth by increasing total factor productivity and, more generally, the efficiency of resource use in the recipient economy. Technology transfers through FDI generate positive externalities in the host country.

FDI provides financial resources for investment in the host country and thereby augments the domestic saving efforts. This contribution of FDI is, however, small for most developing countries. The share of FDI in gross domestic investment in developing countries was only 3.2 per cent in 1992 and in 2001 it stood at a staggering 27.9 per cent and the relevant ratio for some countries of the South Asian region (e.g., Bangladesh, India and Pakistan) was even less than 1 per cent. On the other hand, there are some countries in which the

Table 1.1 *FDI flows as a percentage of gross fixed capital formation (GFCF) of some Asian countries, 1981–2011*

Economies	*1981–90*	*1991*	*1995*	*2000*	*2001*	*2002*	*2003*	*2004*	*2005*	*2006*	*2007*	*2008*	*2009*	*2010*	*2011*
China	14.5	3.3	25.7	10.3	10.5	10.4	8.6	8.2	8.8	8.0	6.0	5.8	4.3	4.4	3.7
South Korea	1.9	1.0	1.1	7.1	3.1	1.9	2.1	3.8	3.0	1.9	0.9	3.1	3.1	2.9	1.5
Bangladesh	0.3	0.1	na	2.7	0.8	0.5	2.2	3.5	4.6	3.9	4.0	5.6	3.2	3.7	4.0
India	1.2	0.3	3.6	2.3	3.2	3.0	3.2	3.4	3.6	8.7	6.3	9.9	8.2	4.4	6.4
Pakistan	5.1	3.3	6.7	3.7	4.9	7.2	4.3	6.2	13.1	24.1	18.7	18.3	8.1	7.5	5.3
Sri Lanka	6.9	2.4	2.0	3.8	2.4	5.6	5.6	5.1	4.4	6.2	7.5	7.3	4.3	4.0	2.1
Indonesia	7.6	3.6	6.5	–14.3	–10.8	0.4	–1.3	1.9	12.3	6.4	6.4	6.6	2.9	6.1	7.0
Malaysia	43.7	23.8	17.9	16.5	2.5	14.5	10.8	19.1	15.2	20.1	21.3	16.5	3.7	18.9	21.4
Singapore	59.3	33.6	24.6	45.6	43.8	25.6	41.7	77.5	57.5	79.5	117.2	22.5	47.7	89.7	105.2
Thailand	10.2	4.9	2.9	12.4	14.4	3.3	5.7	2.5	17.5	16.5	17.4	11.3	7.5	12.2	10.6
Vietnam	na	na	na	15.0	13.7	11.0	11.6	11.3	11.5	12.5	24.7	30.4	23.4	22.4	22.1

Source: UNCTAD, World Investment Report.

contribution of FDI flows to gross fixed capital formation (GFCF) has been significant. For example, concerning data for some South, East and South-East Asian countries are presented in Table 1.1.

Another contribution of FDI is that it provides the much-needed foreign exchange to help bridge the balance of trade deficit. Indeed, in the wake of the debt crisis, FDI has come to be viewed as an increasingly important source of external finance for developing countries. After the financial crisis and low flow of Official Development Assistance (ODA) in India during 1990s, it has got some relief in capital crisis by getting FDI as the investable fund in their economy.

One of the more important contributions of FDI lies in raising the technological standards and levels of efficiency and competitiveness of the host country. This can occur in several ways. FDI brings with it complementary assets such as technology, management and organizational competence and there are spillover effects of these assets on the rest of the economy. As the foreign-owned enterprise comes into competition with the local firms, the latter category of enterprises are forced to improve their technology and standards of product quality. Further, the foreign-owned enterprises pressurize and assist the local related and support industries to improve the quality of their products and ensure greater reliability of delivery, both of which make it necessary for the related and support industries to upgrade their technology (Dutt, 1997).

FDI also helps the host country to improve its export performance. By raising the level of efficiency and the standards of product quality, FDI makes a positive impact on the host country's export competitiveness. Further, because of the international linkages of transnational corporations (TNCs), FDI provides the host country better access to foreign markets. Also, where the foreign investment has been made with the specific intention of sourcing parts/components (or even final products) from the host country to take advantage of low cost conditions there (e.g., low wages), FDI contributes to exports directly.

Thus, understanding the significance of FDI, especially from the viewpoint of developing countries, it is useful to make a distinction between macroeconomic and microeconomic effects. The former are connected with issues of domestic capital formation, balance of payments and taking advantage of external markets for achieving faster growth, while the latter are connected with the issues of cost reduction, product quality improvement, making changes in industrial structure and developing global inter-firm linkages.

It has been increasingly recognized that growing FDI inflows can contribute to economic development and promise a variety of potential benefits to poor country recipients. Due to the potential role FDI can play in accelerating growth and economic transformation, many developing countries seek such investment to accelerate their development efforts. Consequently, FDI has become an important source of private external finance for developing countries.

FDI can enhance growth in two ways. First, it increases total investment by attracting higher levels of domestic investment. Also, through interaction of the more advanced technology with the host country's human capital, it is more productive than domestic investment. Indeed, the most significant channel through which FDI contributes to productivity growth is perhaps increased access to technology, through market transactions such as joint ventures, licensing and goods trade. While the FDI represents investment in production facilities, its significance for developing countries is much greater. Not only can FDI add to investable resources and capital formation, but, perhaps more important, it is also a means of transferring production technology, skills, innovative capacity, and organizational and managerial practices between locations, as well as of accessing international marketing networks. In addition, the FDI can improve overall growth by promoting competition in the domestic input market. In particular, the foreign investment could increase competition in the host country's industry, and hence force local firms to become more productive by adopting more efficient methods or by investing in human and physical capital. Multinational firms' large size, advanced technology and advertising expertise often enable them to invest in industries in which barriers to entry, such as large capital requirements, coupled with trade restrictions, reduce the access of potential local competitors.

Moreover, FDI can boost domestic investment too. For instance, a recent empirical work indicates a strong link between the volume of FDI and domestic investment. Bosworth and Collins (1999) find that a dollar of FDI results in an almost similar increase in investment. In addition to the impact of FDI on the volume of investment, the presence of foreign firms can generate important benefits for domestic firms by increasing their knowledge of, and access to, advanced technology, by improving the overall skills of the workforce (through valuable training opportunities to workers), and by increasing demand for domestic firms' products and the supply of inputs.

Multinational corporations can promote the transfer of technology, with possible spillovers to the rest of the host economy or domestic firms. Technology spillover is a channel through which capital account liberalization can have a positive impact. These spillovers are most clear in the case of FDI, especially through foreign firms incorporating new technologies in their subsidiaries. As new technologies are generally developed and adapted by firms in industrial countries, FDI may be the most efficient way for developing economies to gain access to them. In addition, this knowledge may become more widely available in the country over time, as employees with experience in the techniques used in foreign companies switch to other firms.

Multinationals can also improve labour skills through on-the-job training, seminars and formal education. For example, Athukorala and Menon (1995) show that FDI to Malaysia facilitated technology transfer and improved the skills of the labour force. FDI also contributes indirectly to growth through emulation of foreign affiliates by domestic firms and diffusion of skills throughout the economy as employees move to domestically-owned firms. These spillover benefits of FDI are greatest in countries with sound investment climates marked by well-developed human capital, efficient infrastructure services, sound governance and strong institutions.

Also, the FDI spillovers appear to depend on human capital. The results from existing studies indicate that higher levels of human capital raise the benefits from FDI liberalization and flows. For example, for a country with a high level of human capital, such as Korea, increasing the openness measure by the average gap between closed and open economies can raise growth by as much as a quarter of a per cent a year (World Bank, 1999). Many studies suggest that even in poor countries with sound macro-economic policies and limited public sector interventions in competitive markets, low levels of education and skills may limit the benefits of FDI.

Recent analyses using macro-economic data suggest that FDI can have a positive impact on growth, particularly when the receiving country has a highly educated workforce (a measure of its absorptive capacity), allowing it to exploit FDI spillovers (Borensztein et al., 1998).

Furthermore, FDI can help boost host country's exports. Multinational enterprises may help developing host countries process and export locally produced raw materials, using their marketing skills, superior technology and general know-how. They facilitate the export of local production through their distribution networks, and also often account for a significant share of host country exports (Fontagne, 1997).

Meaning and Types of FDI

Meaning

Before the 1970s the debates about the roles of MNCs and FDI in development were conducted in the same way. This was because the mode for MNCs' involvement in low developing countries (LDCs) were in the form of FDI, i.e., 100 per cent foreign ownership. However, from the 1970s, MNCs started influencing development through quasi-FDI or non-FDI activities in LDCs such as buying and selling goods and services like management, technology, marketing, etc. Then, franchising, joint ventures, licensing agreements, international sub-contracting, etc., have become increasingly important. That is, FDI is only one among many alternatives of MNCs' involvement in LDCs.

Some researchers like De Mello define FDI very broadly, i.e., as a form of international inter-firm co-operation that involves equity and/or management control of foreign enterprises, quasi-investment arrangements (licensing, leasing, franchising, etc.), joint ventures and R&D co-operation.

Data on MNC activity is still very limited. The statistics that are available refer to FDI, which are very imperfect and difficult to interpret. The data most frequently used is the one provided by the IMF which defines it as: 'direct investment can be new capital, reinvested earnings or net borrowing from a parent company or its affiliates. A guiding criterion is that it is investment made to acquire a lasting interest and an effective voice in the management of an enterprise'.

FDI is the outcome of the mutual interests of multinational firms and host countries. It is generally defined as a form of long-term international capital movement, made for the purpose of productive activity and accompanied by the intention of managerial control or participation in the management of a foreign firm.

FDI is the movement of capital across national frontiers in a manner that grants the investor control over the acquired asset. Thus, it is distinct from portfolio investment which may cross borders, but does not offer such control. Firms which source FDI are known as 'multinational enterprises' (MNEs). In this case control is defined as owning 10 per cent or greater of the ordinary shares of an incorporated firm, having 10 per cent or more of the voting power for an unincorporated firm or development of a greenfield branch plant that is a permanent establishment of the originating firm.

In the years after the Second World War global FDI was dominated by the United States, as much of the world recovered from the destruction wrought by the conflict. The US accounted for around three-fourths of new FDI (including reinvested profits) between 1945 and 1960. Since that time FDI has spread to become a truly global phenomenon, no longer the exclusive preserve of OECD countries. FDI has grown in importance in the global economy with FDI stocks now constituting over 20 per cent of global GDP.

Types of FDI

Greenfield investment is the direct investment in new facilities or the expansion of existing facilities. Greenfield investments are the primary target of a host nation's promotional efforts because they create new production capacity and jobs, transfer technology and know-how, and can lead to linkages to the global marketplace. Greenfield investments are the principal mode of investing in developing countries.

Mergers and acquisitions occur when a transfer of existing assets from local firms to foreign firms takes place. Cross-border mergers occur when the assets and operation of firms from different countries are combined to establish a new legal entity. Cross-border acquisitions occur when the control of assets and operations is transferred from a local to a foreign company, with the local company becoming an affiliate of the foreign company. Mergers and acquisitions are the principal modes of investing in developed countries.

Once a direct investment enterprise has been identified, it is necessary to define which capital flows between the enterprise and entities in other economies should be classified as FDI. Since the main feature of FDI is taken to be the lasting interest of a direct investor in an enterprise, only capital that is provided by the direct investor either directly or through other enterprises related to the investor should be classified as FDI. The investment by the direct investor which are classified as FDI are equity capital, the reinvestment of earnings and the provision of long-term and short-term intra-company loans (between parent and affiliate enterprises).

According to the benchmark definition of the OECD, a direct investment enterprise is an incorporated or unincorporated enterprise in which a single foreign investor either owns 10 per cent or more of the ordinary shares or voting power of an enterprise (unless it can be proven that the 10 per cent ownership does not allow the investor an effective voice in the management) or owns less than 10 per cent of the ordinary shares or voting power of an enterprise, yet still maintains an effective voice in management. An effective voice in management only implies that direct investors are able to influence the management of an enterprise and do not have absolute control. The most important characteristic of FDI, which distinguishes it from foreign portfolio investment, is that it is undertaken with the intention of exercising control over an enterprise (OECD, 1983 and 1987).

FDI also known as foreign private investment, refers to foreign money which flows from one country to another for profit-earning purpose. FDI refers to the transfer of finance and tangible corporate assets, including global markets link, by non-residents who have an effective voice (in contrast to private portfolio investors) in the management of the enterprise in which they invest. Traditionally, such investments were in the form of whole or majority ownership. In recent times, however, there has been a proliferation of new forms of minority ownership including a variety of non-equity contractual arrangements such as licensing franchising, counter trade, co-production arrangements, managerial contracts, turn key operations, joint projects in research, production and marketing, as well as some more complex arrangements under the bilateral or multilateral government agreement (Reza and Rashid, 1997).

Another way, FDI is defined as money spent on acquiring or starting companies plus the retained earnings of foreign-owned firms. Technically, FDI requires both the transfer of capital and some degree of managerial control (UNCTAD, 1999). The suppliers of FDI are the individuals and institutions from abroad who invest in a foreign country in the hope of earning more compared to that in their own countries. 'FDI occurs when an investor based in one country (the home country) acquires an asset in another country (the host country) with the intent to manage that asset. The management dimension is what distinguishes FDI from portfolio investment in foreign stocks, bonds and other financial instruments' (WTO, 1996).

According to the World Investment Report, 2002 (UNCTAD, 2002: 291) FDI is defined as an investment involving a long-term relationship and reflecting a lasting interest and control by a resident entity in one economy (foreign direct investor or parent enterprise) in an enterprise resident in an economy other than that of the foreign direct investor (FDI enterprise or affiliate enterprise or foreign affiliate). FDI implies that the investor exerts a significant degree of influence on the management of the enterprise resident in the other economy. Such investment involves both the initial transactions between the two entities and all subsequent transactions between them and among foreign affiliates, both incorporated and unincorporated. Individuals as well as business entities may undertake FDI.

Flows of FDI comprise capital provided (either directly or through other related enterprises) by a foreign direct investor to an FDI enterprise, or capital received from an FDI enterprise by a foreign direct investor. FDI has three components: equity capital, reinvested earnings and intra-company loans.

- Equity capital is the foreign direct investor's purchase of shares of an enterprise in a country other than his own.
- Reinvested earnings comprise the direct investor's share (in proportion to direct equity participation) of earnings not distributed as dividends by affiliates, or earnings not remitted to the direct investor. Such retained profits by affiliates are reinvested.
- Intra-company loans or intra-company debt transactions refer to short- or long-term borrowing and lending of funds between direct investors (parent enterprises) and affiliate enterprises.

Portfolio investment, on the other hand, consists of investment in shares and debentures of local firms by foreigners. This type of investment is generally of renter category and need not imply management control over the firms whose shares are purchased by foreigners.

The term 'FDI' refers to investment that is made to acquire a lasting interest in an enterprise operating in an economy other than that of the investor's, the investor's purpose being to have an effective voice in the management of the enterprise. In other words, FDI is an international financial flow with the intention of controlling or participating in the management of an enterprise in a foreign country (Mamun, 2003).

From the above definitions, some characteristics of FDI come to the fore. These are:

- Investors should be transnational companies or a person who will not be a resident of host countries.

- Investors will have power to exert some control over the invested units.
- Investment would be in the form of equity participation, transferring of technology, capital machinery and equipment, reinvested retained profits, intra-company borrowings or loans, and research and development.
- Investment should be made according to the host and home countries macro-economic policies (Alam, 1998).

FDI is different from foreign investment. Foreign investment is the total investment made in the host countries covering private foreign investment and official foreign investment. The private foreign investment consists of FDI, portfolio investment and export credit. Therefore, FDI is a part of foreign private investment. On the other hand, official investment may come from grants, non-confessional flows and loans. The classification of foreign investment can be presented in the Figure 1.

Figure 1 *Classification of Foreign Investment*

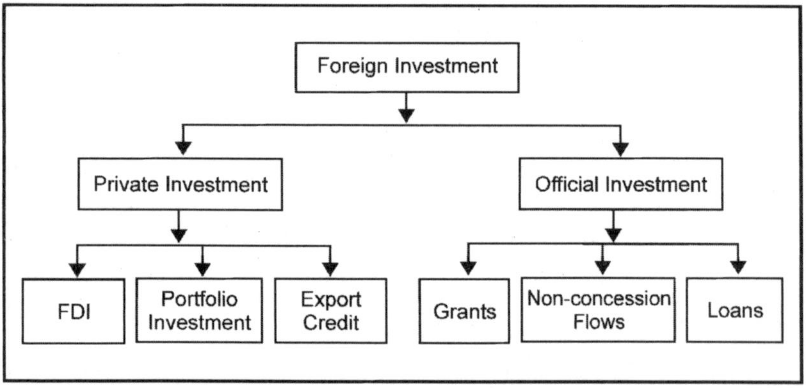

Foreign Direct Investment and Portfolio Investment

It is customary to distinguish two kinds of long-term private international capital movements—direct investment and portfolio investment. Not everyone makes the distinction in quite the same way, but there is a great deal of similarity, and basically it is a question of who controls the enterprise in which the investment is made. If the investor directly controls the foreign enterprise, his investment is called a direct investment. If he does not control it, his investment is a portfolio investment (Hymer, 1976).

As a matter of clarification, it is important to distinguish between FDI and portfolio investment. FDI is generally defined as a form of long-term international capital movement, made for the purpose of productive activity, and accompanied by the intention of managerial control or participation in the management of a foreign firm. FDI should not be confused with portfolio investment which does not seek management control, but is motivated by profit. Portfolio investment occurs when individual investors invest, mostly through stockbrokers, in stocks of foreign companies in foreign land in search of profit opportunities. That is, portfolio investment consists of investment in shares and debentures of local firms by foreigners. This type of investment is generally of renter category and need not imply management control over the firms whose shares are purchased by foreigners.

Equity inflow or FDI is the predominantly largest component of private foreign capital flow in most of the countries. FDI is comprised of direct and portfolio forms of investment. The basic difference between these two is that, in the case of direct investment, the investor who is based in one country (home country) acquires an asset in another country (host country) with an intention of managing the assets in the host country. FDI here refers to equity participation, reinvested earnings and net lending by the parent company to the affiliate. Direct investment comes in the form of financial investment and transfer of technology.

In the case of portfolio investment, the investor does not manage the assets but just invest with an intention of capital appreciation. It is thus management aspect that distinguishes direct investment from portfolio investment. This kind of portfolio investment is done through investment in foreign stocks, bonds and other financial instruments mostly by foreign institutional investors (FIIs). The portfolio investment is generally carried out by the business firms both in home country and host country, i.e., both the investor and the asset it manages abroad are business firms. This being the case, the investor in the home country is referred to as parent firm and the asset in the host country, as affiliate or subsidiary.

The main categories of direct investment, as per the World Bank, are wholly owned, majority-owned and minority-owned affiliates and joint ventures. On the other hand, portfolio investment flows are net flows and include non-debt creating portfolio equity flow (the sum of country funds, depository receipts and direct purchases of shares by foreign investors) and portfolio debt flows (bonds issues purchased by foreign investors). FDI flows are generally much less volatile than portfolio flows. FDI involves the acquisition of a business or other commercial assets in a country (the host country) by multinational enterprises, other foreign firms, or individual foreign residents with intent to manage the business or commercial assets in the host country. The management dimension is what distinguishes foreign direct investment from portfolio investment in foreign stocks, bond, and other financial instruments. FDI flows include equity investment by multinational enterprises, their reinvested earnings in foreign subsidiaries, and short-term and long-term borrowing and lending of funds between 'parent' multinational enterprises and their affiliates in foreign countries (DeRosa, 1998).

FDI can be done in the following ways:

1. In order to participate in the management of the concerned enterprise, the stocks of the existing foreign enterprise can be acquired.
2. The existing enterprise and factories can be taken over.
3. A new subsidiary with 100 per cent ownership can be established abroad.
4. It is possible to participate in a joint venture through stock holdings.
5. New foreign branches, offices and factories can be established.
6. Existing foreign branches and factories can be expanded.
7. Minority stock acquisition, if the objective is to participate in the management of the enterprise.
8. Long-term lending, particularly by a parent company to its subsidiary, when the objective is to participate in the management of the enterprise.

FDI is perceived superior to other types of capital inflows for several reasons as under:

- In contrast to foreign lenders and portfolio investors, foreign direct investors typically have a longer-term perspective when engaging in a host country. Hence, FDI inflows are less volatile and easier to sustain at times of crisis.
- While debt inflows may finance consumption rather than investment in the host country, FDI is more likely to be used productively.
- FDI is expected to have relatively strong effects on economic growth, as it provides for more than just capital. It offers access to internationally available technologies and management know-how, and may render it easier to penetrate world markets.

The risk-sharing properties of FDI are undisputed. This suggests that FDI is the appropriate form of external financing for developing countries, which have less capacity than highly developed economies to absorb external shocks. Likewise, the evidence supports the predominant view that FDI is more stable than other types of capital inflows. Moreover, the volatility of FDI remained exceptionally low in the 1990s, when several emerging economies were hit by financial crises (Sury, 2004).

Rationale for FDI

Because of the assumption that perfect competition in conventional trade theories does not permit any company-specific advantage, the theory of FDI draws specifically on the role of companies or firms as creators and exploiters of intangible assets (Hymer, 1976). From this perspective, FDI is viewed to take place only in imperfect markets and it is the firm, not the country, that is the real actor causing FDI flows across national borders (Ozawa, 1992).

The emergence of the multinational enterprise/corporation and associated internationalization of production has been viewed primarily as a response to the existence of transaction cost and factor cost incentives for global integration of related activities (Dunning, 1981; Teece, 1986; Krugman, 1990). The necessary conditions for international production have been specified as: (i) possession of owner-specific advantages by the firm (for example, a monopoly, brand name, a patent, or a superior knowledge of the market); (ii) local production under equity ownership or internationalization leading to enhanced exploitation of these advantages relative to arm's length transactions (such as licensing and exporting); and (iii) overseas location factors (such as high-quality, low-wage labour; low transportation costs; or policy-determined advantages and direct incentives), which are more favourable than domestic ones.

In a dynamic setting, the comparative advantage itself changes as in product life cycle theory of trade and investment, which explicitly brings in the factor of a hierarchy of economies as an additional element in the analysis. In this theory, new products are initially introduced in a high-income country, and then eventually introduced to the rest of the world as the products mature and become technologically standardized. Clearly, Vernon's description in terms of product cycle was a major explanation of the movement of production overseas, rather than just an explanation of international trade. According to

Kojima (1975), foreign investment is not only complementary to international trade, it also creates an enlarged basis for trade through the transplantation of intangible assets from the source country's comparatively disadvantaged industries to the host country's comparatively advantaged ones.

Conceptually, the following three types of foreign investments are possible: (a) cost-oriented, (b) market-oriented, and (c) resource-oriented. Cost-oriented investment refers to those investment arising from an acute shortage of labour, increasing cost of production and restructuring of the domestic industrial sector, all of which force investors in foreign countries to look for cheaper production bases outside of their countries. Market-oriented foreign investment arises out of the desire and need to avoid trade friction and market conflict (for example, Japanese investment in the United States, Canada and European Union countries). Locational advantages may also be used for resource-oriented investments, particularly when the host market is relatively small and there are some special considerations, such as the quota allocation under the Multi-Fibre Arrangements (MFA).

It is well-known that the movement of production overseas is carried out primarily by multinational corporations (MNCs) or transnational corporations (TNCs). Two basic factors that attract TNCs to foreign locations are safety of investment and opportunity for profit. Their objectives in crossing borders include gaining access to foreign markets, access to inputs, freedom of decision-making and operations, and reduction of risks. The objectives of host country governments, on the other hand, include the desire to gain economic efficiency, equity in TNC distribution of benefits, and participation in ownership, management, technology, and research and development (R&D). The objectives are not always conflicting; often there is similarity of interests between TNCs and host governments. Thus, there is less need for regulation or coercion by governments on TNC activities.

In fact, opinions on the desirability of FDI from the host country's viewpoint have differed among scholars in this field. In the late 1960s through the mid-1970s, TNCs often came under severe criticism in developing countries. They were viewed as 'suction pumps' in an overall imperialist design to perpetuate an exploitative economic system. Not surprisingly, therefore, this period witnessed a proliferation of restrictions on FDI inflows such as strict screening of such investments, limiting their entry into key sectors and prohibiting takeovers of local firms by foreign firms. Analysts like Caves (1982) also pointed out many social and economic costs associated with FDI in the form of transfer pricing, fictitious and irrelevant transfer of technology, excessive product differentiation, need and taste creation, the crowding-out of local capital and inhibiting the emergence and growth of domestic entrepreneurship, as well as political pressures leading to serious policy distortions. Moreover, Oman (1993) has argued that the procyclical tendency of FDI reduces its benefits to recipient developing countries.

By the early 1980s, the pendulum started to swing in the other direction when developing countries increasingly began courting FDI in the face of dramatic increases in real interest rates, the debt crisis and the virtual disappearance of voluntary bank lending. At the theoretical level, it was pointed out by Grosse and Behrman (1992) that TNCs can offer major benefits to host countries in the form of assistance in improving not only their internal balance (for instance, income and employment) by providing access to invertible funds, proprietary technology, and managerial and marketing skills, but also their external balance by providing low-cost inputs from abroad, access to export markets and import substituting production. Besides, they can also help in achieving non-economic goals through such methods as placating pressure groups by providing jobs and other benefits, and by helping the host country in dealing with the firm's home government.

Another positive point is the non-debt-inducing nature of FDI. According to some observers, the larger inflow of FDI could itself help the indebted countries overcome their debt-servicing difficulties (Agosin, 1985). In addition, there also simultaneously occurred the desire in the developing countries to set up export processing zones and eliminate anti-export policy biases. This liberalized the environment for foreign investment, particularly in the manufacturing sector. At the same time, it is worth noting that the preference of the developing countries, in general, shifted to the financial component of the traditional FDI 'package', whereas a large number of investors came to prefer the 'new' forms because of their risk-shedding advantages and their potential for greater financial leverage on certain non-financial assets (Oman, 1993).

Be that as it may, nearly every developing country today is striving to attract investment from overseas, even at the risk of excessive policy competition among themselves; fears of diversion of foreign investment to the formerly socialist countries of Central and Eastern

Europe have intensified such competition. So strong indeed is the current attitude in favour of foreign investment that 'a restrictive attitude limiting the entry of FDI is regarded as foolish' (Williamson, 1990: 7). In fact, policy on FDI has begun to contest with trade policy in importance in the arena of economic relations among countries (Chatterjee, 2003)

Benefits of FDI

The analysis of FDI is quite different from that of foreign investment. FDI may be defined as equity investment of multinational corporations in host countries. The multi national corporations (MNCs) manage foreign direct investments and have become the driving force of the international economy. FDI can brought of as trade in entrepreneurial services and ideas while foreign investment is just asset trade (Lall, 1993).

The development impact of foreign investments on host countries has always aroused great controversy, but this controversy has subsided greatly in recent years. A number of factors have led developing countries to change their earlier trade, industrialization and investment strategies. Prominent among these is the realization that FDI does not have many of the costs previously associated with it and that many developing countries have managed to industrialize successfully with FDI. It will be noted that open door policies to FDI are neither necessary nor sufficient to ensure industrial (or any other form of) development. However, in the right circumstances FDI does offer many benefits, and alternatives may not be equally open to countries in South Asia.

The contributions that foreign entry can make are well known. Apart from finance, which is increasingly an important consideration to countries with mounting debt burdens, FDI can bring in new technology and provide continuous access to changes in technology. Moreover, it can import new managerial and marketing skills; stimulate domestic competition, long constricted by import barriers and barriers to entry and exit; provide entry into export markets and help lower protective barriers in the home countries of MNCs; and help local suppliers improve their quality and competitiveness. More generally, in a world of growing technological progress and rising costs of keeping up with such progress, alliances with MNCs may be an essential requirement for developing countries to participate in sophisticated technologies.

The key advantages of FDI are that it brings in new knowledge and entrepreneurial skills. This is now keenly understood by nearly everyone these days (Ruffin, 1993). According to the endogenous growth models, the faster is technology progress, the larger is the levels of accumulated human knowledge. This is because the cost of innovation falls as the level of human knowledge increases. Therefore, income growth will be faster among countries that have relatively larger educated population and an economic environment which is favourable to the accumulation of human knowledge. FDI can also increase the rate of growth by bringing in new ideas and lowering the cost of innovation.

It is a well-established fact that developing countries suffer from a shortage of appropriate knowledge in the development process. In FDI literature, it is already recognized that FDI not only brings capital for productive development to the host economy, it also transfers a considerable amount of technical and managerial knowledge and skills, which is likely to spillover to domestic enterprises in that economy. In other words, FDI helps developing countries to reduce the 'knowledge gap' with the developed world by bringing both the managerial and technological knowledge and skill to the host countries. Thus, FDI benefits the host economy more through different channels as compared to its direct impact which are recognized as the sources of the economic growth.

The possible channels of gains from FDI inflows to the host country can be explained through its effects both directly and indirectly. It is already recognized that FDI inflow nurtures the growth process directly by increasing production resulting from the rise in the volume of investment. It also transfers technology pertaining to direct production and know-how such as managerial skills to the host country. FDI may provide a stock of knowledge to developing countries and make factors of production more productive. It can also stimulate the economic growth by augmenting trade if the inflows are channelled to the export-oriented industries. The indirect positive effects (or positive externalities) of FDI inflows include technological spillovers to local firms and workers. It may also create a competitive business environment among domestic firms and could have a positive effect on the general price level.

Supporters of FDI contend that foreign investors introduce a package of highly productive resources into the host economy, including production and process technology, managerial expertise, accounting and auditing standards, and knowledge of international markets. The challenge for the host economy is to benefit from the MNC's presence, and to appropriate some of the increased income accruing from the resultant productivity growth. The large literature on FDI impacts concludes that the host economy benefits are quite uneven, both across and within countries.

It is now generally accepted that the distinguishing characteristics of FDI are its stability and ease of service relative to commercial debt or portfolio investment, as well as its inclusion of non-financial assets in production and sales processes. Apart from increasing output and income, potential benefits to host countries from FDI inflows include the following:

Foreign firms bring superior technology

This is one of the key reasons mentioned by those advocating FDI. It is believed that with the increase in FDI, there will be a transfer of technology. Since foreign firms maintain control over the local firms, it is argued that they do not mind exporting their state-of-the art technology. Empirical studies have shown that the vertical linkage has been one of the most effective ways to transfer technologies. But, when there exist huge differences between the technologies used in the host and home countries, it might not produce desired results. This is understandable because the host country might not have the necessary skilled human resource. There are still others who go on to say that the MNCs might start using inferior technologies in the host country and thus inhibit technological progress there.

Transfer of capital

Developing countries have realized over the years that FDI might be the solution for their inadequate access to foreign capital. It could be the over the years driving force for economic growth and development. Developing countries have also that domestic savings alone might not be enough to solve their outstanding developmental needs. The problems associated with raising capital from alternative sources have been addressed in above section.

Enhance of managerial capacity and skills

Since profit maximization is the goal of MNCs, they will manage the firm efficiently. They will hire the best management staff and provide adequate training to hone their skills. All this happens in pursuit of self-interest.

Access to world market

It is generally agreed that MNCs are better positioned to penetrate foreign markets. They have subsidiaries in many countries. In addition, they also have the resources and expertise to study foreign markets and come up with excellent strategies to enter those markets. In an empirical analysis, the probability that a domestic plant will export was found to be positively correlated with proximity to multinational firms. One implication is that governments may encourage potential exporters to locate near each other by (a) creating special economic zones, or export processing zones, or promoting clusters, or by (b) conferring special benefits, such as duty-free imports of inputs, subsidized infrastructure, or tax holidays, to help reduce costs for domestic firms in breaking into foreign markets (Asian Development Bank, 2004).

Employment generation

This is one of the most debated issues. Empirical studies are not decisive about the effect on net employment. MNCs will undoubtedly hire local people. But, their activities might force some domestic firms, especially those producing similar products or services, to shut down. The net effect on employment is therefore inconclusive at best.

Foreign investment increases competition in the host economy

The entry of a new firm in a non-tradable sector increases industry output and may thereby reduce the domestic price, leading to a net improvement in welfare.

Improvement in export competitiveness

FDI can help the host country improve its export performance. By raising the level of efficiency and the standards of product quality, FDI makes a positive impact on the host country's export competitiveness. Further, because of the international linkages of TNCs, FDI provides to the host country better access to foreign markets. Also, where the foreign investment has been made with the specific intention of sourcing parts/components (or even final products) from the host country to take advantage of low cost conditions, FDI contributes to exports directly. Enhanced export possibility contributes to the growth of the host economies by relaxing demand side constraints on growth. This is especially important for those countries which have a small domestic market and must increase exports vigorously to maintain their tempo of economic growth.

Possible Costs of FDI

It is important to note at the start that the benefits of foreign investment, like those of any other investment, depend crucially on the broader economic framework in which investments are made. Where the incentive structure is distorted and competition stifled by widespread, uneconomic regulations, FDI can be inefficient. The benefits of FDI can be maximized only in a relatively free and market-oriented environment where private economic decisions do not diverge greatly from the social good.

This does not, however, mean laissez faire, completely free market without intervention. There are many cases in every economy, especially developing economies, where markets fail to give the right signals or what is termed 'market failure' by economists. Some market failures call for remedial action by the government. If the government manages such interventions correctly, including in FDI, the results can be high and sustained rate of growth. Where it does not, the result of government failure can be further distortion and poor economic performance.

The main arguments against the FDI inflows are that MNCs bring monopoly resources as FDI, supplant domestic firms, introduce production technology inappropriate to the host economy and create balance of payments crisis through repatriation of profits from the host country (Sahoo, 2006). In general, the MNCs bringing FDI have a bunch of superior resources such as technology, organization capability, managerial skills and marketing know-how, which together may have a negative externality on the domestic firms as foreign firms erode their market share (Markusen and Venables, 1997; Agosin and Mayer, 2000; Kumar and Pradhan, 2002). As a consequence, FDI may crowd out domestic investment in the relevant industries. In most of the cases, FDI inflows to developing countries utilize capital-intensive techniques in the production process, which may lower the demand for the abundant factor of production, i.e., labour, in developing countries. If this happens in a labour-abundant country, it may lower the economic growth. Since the impact of FDI on economic growth is not clear from either the theoretical or empirical perspective, and it needs to be examined in the case of South Asian countries.

Transferring technology to developing countries by all the modes of transfer, FDI carries the largest risk of creating some dependence. MNCs are the world's leading generators of new technology, but their innovative activities remain centralized in the developed world. There are sound economic reasons for this from the MNC perspective. There are large economies of scale in conducting innovative R&D, so that it is costly for MNCs to set up research activities in host economies. R&D requires advanced skills that most developing countries lack and also needs interaction with other innovators, research institutes, universities and technology infrastructure institutions—all of which also tend to be weak in developing countries. FDI then becomes a very efficient means of transferring the results of innovation rather than the innovative process itself.

This may not matter for developing countries with relatively small industrial bases and weak capabilities, such as Bangladesh or Sri Lanka. It does matter for countries such as India that have a base of innovative capabilities and can fruitfully add to it. The entry of foreign investors then has to be controlled and directed to promote the development of local innovative capabilities. FDI should be encouraged when it feeds into local innovation and should be restricted when it threatens to substitute for local innovation.

FDI and Economic Growth

Protectionist theories played a dominant role in the formation and implementation of industrialization policies, even before the 1980s, among the majority of the developing countries, which predominantly gave importance to import substitution industrialization strategies, based on advanced ideas given by Prebisch (1950) and Singer (1950). However, in the early 1980s, a group of economists recommended that development strategies should be based on market-oriented reforms, which include, among others, the reduction of trade barriers and the opening up of international trade to foreign competition. One of the most striking features of openness since the beginning of the 1980s in developing countries was the inflow of private capital in the form of FDI. Since then, FDI inflows have been considered as one of the important sources of economic growth in developing countries.

The gains from FDI inflows are unquestionable as it contributes to economic growth through an increase in productivity by providing new investment, better technologies and managerial skills to the host countries, However, the effect of FDI on domestic investment is an issue of concern as there is a possibility of displacement of domestic capital due to competition from foreign investors with their superior technologies and skills. Thus, the ultimate impact of FDI on economic growth depends on the degree of capacity of the host country to use it as efficiently as possible. Similarly, trade liberalization may facilitate economic growth through efficiency in production by utilizing the abundant factors of production more effectively and absorbing better technologies from advanced countries on the one hand, and it may harm the growth process on the other through various forms of macroeconomic instability such as terms of trade deterioration and balance of payments crisis. Thus, it is a challenge for developing countries to find out the appropriate direction of the role of FDI and trade liberalization in economic growth.

As part of developing countries, South Asian economies were also concerned with issues pertaining to foreign private capital inflows and trade liberalization initially. However, they later moved to liberalize their trade and investment policies to include various investment incentives, particularly for foreign investors. Along with these, South Asian countries have maintained high and steady economic growth, single-digit inflation rate, have a growing domestic market, a large number of low-paid workers with growing number of skilled personnel and a more favourable investment climate. As a consequence, South Asia, as a group, has been successful in attracting a significant amount of FDI and raising its volume of trade (export plus import) as percentage of GDP during the last two decades. The question which naturally arises here is whether the increase in growth was brought about by FDI inflows. Therefore, it is important to explore the impact of FDI on the growth process, quantitatively, in South Asian economies for a better understanding about the linkages among FDI and economic growth.

FDI is often seen as an important catalyst for economic growth in developing countries. Development economists have long argued that countries pursuing externally-oriented development strategies are more likely to achieve higher rates of economic growth than those that are internally focused. A number of studies have examined the relationship between inward FDI and economic growth in the developing host countries (De Mello, 1997). A generally accepted conclusion is that FDI has played a significant role in promoting economic growth in host countries because FDI represents 'the transmission to the host country of a package of capital, managerial skills, and technical skills' (Borensztein et al., 1998). An interesting finding of previous studies is that the economic and technological conditions of a recipient economy influence the extent to which FDI contributes to growth.

Today, FDI is widely viewed among the major forces as propelling the globalization of the world economy, that is, the increasing specialization of production and trade through global networks of production and distribution, pioneered, and operated by multinational enterprises (WTO, 1996). With its orientation to developing enterprises directly, FDI helps to strengthen economic potential. Empirical work on the role of FDI in host countries seems to suggest that FDI is an important source of capital, complements domestic private investment, is usually associated with new job opportunities, and in most of the cases is related to the enhancement of technology transfer and overall boosts economic growth in host countries. FDI is now becoming quite crucial for many developing countries in view of the increasing need for additional foreign capital to achieve the Millennium Development Goals (MDGs) by the year 2015. This is becoming a hot issue particularly in the case of South Asia with a very small share of FDI inflows relatively to other developing regions (WIR, 2002).

FDI can play an important role in the process of industrialization and economic growth in the developing countries too (Barro, 1991; Bashir, 1999). Most countries in the world have recognized that FDI by TNCs contribute in many ways to the process of economic growth of host countries. Since 1980s, there has been a dramatic shift in the attitude of developing countries towards FDI. The huge inflow of FDI into the Asia-Pacific regions has facilitated the growth and transition of many developing Asian economies, such as Hong Kong, China, Singapore, Malaysia, Thailand, and most recently PRC, and Vietnam. In order to augment the resource mobilization, these countries are, therefore, intensifying their efforts to attract FDI.

Like other developing countries, India also realized the importance of FDI and considered it the key to rapid economic growth. In the 1980s, not only developed but also developing countries introduced economic liberalization policies and India was not an exception. Since 1990s, the governments have opened up their economy for foreign competition and have taken a lot of structural adjustment measures. Deregulation of government enterprises has been intensified and at present, India have offered a huge number of incentives and facilities to foreign investors under the foreign investment policy framework for attracting FDI.

World inflows of FDI amounted to US$ 735 billion, of which US$ 503 billion (68.43%) went to developed economies, and US$ 205 billion (27.89%) to the developing economies in 2001. Developing countries of Asia and the Pacific received US$ 102 billion (13.87%) of world inward FDI in the same time. However, South Asian countries received only US$ 4 billion (0.54%) inward FDI in 2001. FDI inflows to South Asia was only 3.92 per cent of total FDI flows to developing Asia and Pacific countries (UNCTAD WIR, 2002). Global FDI rose modestly in 2004 following large declines in their value in 2001 (41%), 2002 (13%) and 2003 (12%). At US$ 648 billion in 2004, they were 2 per cent higher than in 2003 (US$ 632). Out of US$ 648 billion developed economies received US$ 380 billion, and developing economies received US$ 233.22 billion. Developing countries of Asia and Oceania South, East and South-East Asia have received US$ 137.7 billion. Among this region South Asian economies inward FDI flows is only US$ 7.005 billion. FDI inflows to South Asia was only 5 per cent of total FDI flows to Developing Asia and Pacific countries (UNCTAD WIR, 2005).

Significant FDI has yet to be poured in Bangladesh and India as compared to the FDI flows into South-East Asian countries like Malaysia, Singapore, China, Korea and Vietnam. Total FDI inflow in South Asia was US$ 4 billion in 2001 and it rose to US$ 4.6 billion in 2002, and 7.005 billion in 2004. FDI inflows in Pakistan, Sri Lanka and India were increased by 114 per cent, 195 per cent and 1.35 per cent respectively (UNCTAD WIR, 2003). On the other hand, FDI flows to Bangladesh were declined in 2002 to US$ 52 million, from US$ 79 million in 2001. However, in 2004 inward FDI flows rose modestly by US$ 460 million after three years of declining flows (US$ 268 million in 2003, US$ 52 million in 2002 and US$ 79 million in 2001). The record shows that FDI inflow in Bangladesh is not satisfactory according to the country's expectation compared to other SAARC members (Table 1.1). It is clear from the Tables 1.1, 1.2 and 1.3 that there is considerable variation in the magnitudes of FDI received by India and Bangladesh during 1991–2004. This proportion summarized in Tables 1.2 and 1.3 shows that generally the relative importance of FDI as a source of capital investment is much smaller in Bangladesh compared to India.

So far, no in-depth study has been conducted to find out the reasons for insignificant flows of FDI in both the countries as compared

Table 1.2 *FDI inflows in South Asian countries, 1991–2011*

(millions of dollars)

Countries/Continents	*Annual average 1991–1996*	*1997*	*1998*	*1999*	*2000*	*2001*	*2002*	*2003*
World	2,54,326	4,81,911	6,90,905	10,86,750	13,87,953	8,17,574	7,16,128	6,32,599
Developing economies	91,505	1,93,224	1,94,055	2,31,880	2,52,459	2,19,721	1,55,528	1,66,337
Developing Asia	59,411	1,09,092	1,02,209	1,12,588	1,46,067	1,11,854	92,009	1,01,278
Bangladesh	8	139	190	180	280	79	52	268
Bhutan	1	na	na	na	na	na	na	1
India	1,085	3,619	2,633	2,168	2,319	3,403	3,449	4,269
Maldives	8	11	12	12	13	12	12	14
Nepal	8	23	12	4	na	21	–6	15
Pakistan	501	713	507	530	305	385	823	534
Sri Lanka	125	433	150	201	175	82	197	229
South Asia	1,735	4,938	3,504	3,095	3,092	3,961	4,521	5,329
Countries/Continents	*2004*	*2005*	*2006*	*2007*	*2008*	*2009*	*2010*	*2011*
World	7,42,143	9,45,795	13,05,852	19,75,537	17,90,706	11,97,824	13,09,001	15,24,422
Developing Economies	2,83,003	3,14,310	3,79,078	13,10,425	10,19,648	6,06,212	6,18,586	7,47,860
Asia	1,69,994	2,08,743	2,59,438	3,49,412	3,80,360	3,15,238	3,84,063	4,23,157

Cont'd...

...Cont'd

Bangladesh	460	692	625	666	1,086	700	913	1,136
Bhutan	1	2	1	3	7	18	16	14
India	5,335	6,676	16,881	25,506	43,406	35,596	24,159	31,554
Maldives	13	9	14	126	174	152	212	282
Nepal	10	2	–7	6	1	39	87	95
Pakistan	1,118	2,201	4,273	5,590	5,438	2,338	2,022	1,327
Sri Lanka	233	278	485	603	752	404	478	303
South Asia	7,601	9,866	22,274	34,695	52,869	42,370	31,746	38,942

Source: UNCTAD, World Investment Report (WIR), various issues.

Table 1.3 *FDI inflows as a percentage of GFCF in South Asia, 1991–2011*

Countries	*Annual average 1991–1996*	*1997*	*1998*	*1999*	*2000*	*2001*	*2002*	*2003*	*2004*	*2005*	*2006*	*2007*	*2008*	*2009*	*2010*	*2011*
World	4.4	7.5	10.6	16.0	19.8	12.0	10.6	8.3	7.5	10.5	12.6	15.6	12.8	9.6	9.6	9.2
Developing economies	6.5	11.4	12.3	14.7	14.9	13.1	9.5	8.8	10.5	12.6	13.8	16.1	12.0	8.6	8.6	9.4
Asia	6.1	9.7	10.6	11.3	13.3	10.2	7.7	7.3	9.1	11.3	12.9	11.4	10.3	8	8.2	7.4
Bangladesh	0.1	1.6	2.1	1.8	2.7	0.7	0.5	2.2	3.5	4.9	3.9	4.0	5.6	3.2	3.7	4.0
Bhutan	0.6	–0.5	0.2	0.2	na	0.1	0.1	0.3	0.2	1.4	0.9	0.6	1.5	3.5	2.8	2.1
India	1.3	4	2.9	2.2	2.3	3.2	3.0	3.2	3.4	3.5	8.7	6.3	9.9	8.2	4.4	6.4
Maldives	8.5	6.5	7.1	6.7	9.8	8.6	7.6	5.8	5.0	4.6	6.4	20.8	25.1	20.7	35.6	72.4
Nepal	0.9	2.2	1.2	0.5	na	2.0	–0.6	1.3	0.8	0.2	–0.4	0.3	0.0	1.4	2.2	2.5
Pakistan	5.3	7.4	5.7	6.4	3.6	5.0	7.2	4.3	6.2	13	24.1	18.7	18.3	8.1	7.5	5.3
Sri Lanka	4.6	11.8	3.8	4.7	3.8	2.4	5.6	5.6	5.1	5.5	6.2	7.5	7.3	4.3	4.0	2.1
East & South-East Asia	7.4	10.4	11.5	12.9	15.2	10.8	8.2	7.7	9.7	10.4	11.5	11.1	8.9	7.0	8.3	7.5

Source: UNCTAD World Investment Report (WIR, Various issues).

Table 1.4 *India: Selected FDI indicators, 1985, 1990, 1995, 2000–2011*

Item	*Country*	*1985*	*1990*	*1995*	*2000*	*2001*	*2002*	*2003*	*2004*	*2005*	*2006*	*2007*	*2008*	*2009*	*2010*	*2011*
FDI inflows, BoP Net (million dollars)	India	58	169	1,929	2,319	3,403	3,449	4,269	5,335	6,676	16,881	na	na	na	na	na
Inward FDI stock (million dollars)	India	747	1,657	5,641	17,517	22,319	25,408	30,827	38,676	45,274	50,680	na	na	na	na	2,01,724
Inward FDI stock as percentage of GDP (%)	India	0.3	0.5	1.6	3.8	5.2	5.4	5.4	5.9	5.8	5.7	na	na	na	na	na
Growth of FDI inflows (annual, %)	India	na	–6.1	98.25	7.6	46.7	1.4	23.8	25.0	25.13	152.86	na	na	na	na	na
FDI inflows as percentage of GFCF (%)	India	na	0.5	2.6	2.3	3.2	3.0	3.2	3.4	3.5	8.7	6.3	9.9	8.2	4.4	6.4
GDP at current price (billions dollars)	India	257.5	311.08	379.3	479.3	487.96	518.48	635.21	698.55	645.86	698.75	na	na	na	na	na
Real GDP growth (%)	India	3.8	5.9	4.9	5.9	5.3	4.4	5.3	6.5	8.4	9.60	9.30	6.70	8.40	8.37	6.53

Sources: Author's calculation based on UNCTAD WIR.

to the other South-East Asian countries. In 1990s, there was an influx of FDI in Malaysia causing a spectacular growth of averaging 8 per cent in that period, offering not much facility for FDI attraction than those offered presently by Bangladesh and India. FDI in China is one of the most palpable outcomes of its open door policy, which was adopted in December 1978. Already, in 1993, China held a position second only to the United States as the largest host country for FDI. By the end of 2001, China had attracted US$ 46.8 billion worth of FDI—the largest FDI recipient in the region as well as in the developing world as a whole (UNCTAD WIR, 2002). It entails that the situations of an LDC like Bangladesh and those of an emerging economy like Hong Kong, China, Malaysia and South Korea differ significantly. So a systematic and comparative study on FDI attracting policies would help policy makers and planners of both the countries for better understanding of the problem. Since early to mid-1980s, there has been a dramatic shift in the attitude of developing countries towards FDI. The rapid increase in FDI in recent years has raised a number of important questions, some of which we will examine in detail in this study. First, do the countries acquire expected FDI flows into the priority sectors for economic growth? Second, what are the primary factors responsible for the upsurge in FDI in recent years? Third, what has been the effect of FDI on economic growth in India? And, finally, in which sectors has FDI contributed to growth in India in the recent (10–15) years?

Objectives of the Research

There is plenty of evidence to suggest that foreign investment has changed from investment in primary resources to manufacturing and services. The volume of the flows has increased considerably and the identities of the source and destination countries have altered as well.

In the view of the above mentioned inquiries, the following objectives can be set forth for the proposed study:

(i) To find out the trends of FDI in India.
(ii) To identify the motivating factors and problems of FDI inflows in India.
(iii) To examine the empirical relationship between FDI and economic growth in India during the study period 1974–2008.
(iv) To evaluate the existing policies and incentive packages offered by the government to securing FDI.
(v) To study the prevailing environment of FDI in India.

Research Questions

Following statements define the problem of the study more clearly, precisely and succinctly:

1. Is there any relation between FDI and economic growth in India?
2. What are the favourable factors of FDI inflows into India?
3. What are the determining factors of FDI inflows of India?
4. Is there any impact of FDI policies and incentive packages on the flows of FDI?
5. How conducive the investment environment to attract FDI of the country?
6. What are the unfavourable factors or problems relating to FDI in India?
7. What types of initiatives should be taken by the governments to attract more FDI?

Hypotheses

With the changing investment climate in the world, FDI plays an important role for transferring resources and technology. It is assumed that economic growth of India may be influenced by FDI. Economic growth also depends on domestic public and private savings and investment ratios. These factors are influenced by domestic, international and sectoral market sizes as well as their growth rates. As objective of the study is to examine the relation between FDI and economic growth of India, the main hypotheses are drawn accordingly as follows:

H_1 : GDP growth rate of India depends upon FDI inflows.

H_2 : The growth rate of the other sectors constituting the economy of India would depend upon FDI inflows.

H_3 : The larger a host country's market size, as indicated by GDP, the greater the host country's inward FDI.

Research Methodology

Sources of Data

The relationship between FDI and economic growth has been tested using data from India over the period from 1980 through 2008. Primary data has been collected from the executives of relevant organizations and foreign investors, professionals, policy makers and entrepreneurs. For this purpose a set of structured questionnaires is prepared for the respondents.

The present research work has involved a huge literature work and analysis based on various published articles and data collected mainly from secondary sources. Various journals, periodicals, reports of various organizations and books of various writers have been used for references. More specifically data used in the proposed research is collected from the documents published by the World Bank, Asian Development Bank (ADB), UNCTAD publications, Foreign Investors Chamber of Commerce and Industries (FICCI), Ministry of Finance, FIPB-India, Reserve Bank of India (RBI), Indian Investment Centre (IIC) and other relevant organizations.

Secondary data for this study is collected from Global Development Finance (GDF) and World Development Indicators (WDI) published by the World Bank, World Investment Report (WIR) published by the UNCTAD and International Financial Statistics (IFS) published by the International Monetary fund (IMF). The WDI and IFS database includes variables such as GDP, per capita GDP, GDP growth rates, FDI, trade in goods and services, domestic capital formation, human capital, market openness (data of export and import), domestic savings and investment, government expenditures, etc.

Tools of Time Series Analysis

Statistical tools were applied while analysing the data on FDI. The details of analysis carried are presented here below:

1. To identify the trend in FDI inflows, the following approach was made:
   (a) Economy-wise issue of FDI flows from 1980–1991 and 1991–2008 was analysed to examine the direction of flow of new capital.
   (b) Region and country-wise trend was analysed to compare the performance in relation to attract the FDI.
2. The problems relating to the FDI were analysed and suggestions have been given taking into account the outcomes of the analyses of the surveyed data of the study.
3. The changes in policies governing FDI was analysed by studying the policies since 1970s. This facilitated understanding of the evolution of the policies and also major shifts in policy focus over the time period.

Description of Data

The following is a description on the variable we have used in this study, and how the data has been constructed for each variable:

- *FDI inflows* are net inflows of investment to acquire a lasting management interest (10% or more of voting stock) in an enterprise operating in an economy other than the home country of the investor. The measure is the sum of equity capital, reinvestment of earnings, other long-term capital and short-term capital as shown in the balance of payments. No private portfolio investments are considered in this study.
- *GDP* in current market price and real per capita GDP data are collected from various publications of World Bank, UNCTAD and IMF.
- *Globalization index* (trade openness) is calculated as the sum of exports and imports divided by GDP. This ratio of trade to GDP provides a measure of the degree of economic openness.
- *Human capital* means (proxied) by percentage of relevant group participating in secondary or tertiary education. Secondary education completes the provision of basic education that began at the primary level, and aims at laying the foundations for life-long learning and human development, by offering more subject or skill-oriented instruction using more specialized teacher.
- *Gross domestic investment* consists of outlays on additions to the fixed assets of the economy plus net changes in the level of inventories. It is coded as percentage of GDP.
- *Gross fixed capital formation (GFCF)*: Investment has made the GFC. So we want to observed the contribution of GFC to economic growth in the next period with others variable. Savings are not considered, because, S =/= I, some portion has been invested and other portion has consumed.
- *Credit/GDP (DCR)* is domestic credit provided by banking sector to GDP.

After the 1990s, FDI and trade growth have increased rapidly in the developing countries. To see the interaction of FDI with trade, we have included FDI*XM respectively.

Past empirical studies have indicated that FDI, trade and domestic investment have positive impact on economic growth in developing countries. We expect positive interactions between FDI and trade and FDI and domestic capital investment in promoting growth. A positive co-efficient for the interaction term would suggest that FDI and domestic investment (DI) and trade openness (XM) reinforce (complement) each other in advancing economic growth (Makki and Somwaru, 2004).

An interaction term FDI and domestic investment have taken into account to see the combined impact of FDI and domestic investment (FDI*DI) on economic growth.

Another interaction term FDI and domestic investment have taken into account to see the combined impact of FDI and human capital (FDI*HC) on economic growth.

Dummy variable (Dm) (D=1 for democratic government, D = 0 for otherwise). To capture the effect of good governance in affecting the FDI a dummy variable is used. Good governance is proxied by democratic government.

Empirical Model Specification

The empirical growth literature has identified a number of variables that are typically correlated with economic growth. In the light of the above discussion in the variables definition section, initially the following regression model is specified to measure the effects of FDI on economic growth:

$$g = \alpha_o + \beta_1 (Y_o) + \beta_2 (\text{FDI}) + \beta_3 (XM) + \beta_4 (GE) + \beta_5 (HC) + \beta_6 (GFCF) + \beta_7 (GDI) + \beta_8 (DCR) + \beta_9 (FDI*XM) + \beta_{10} (FDI*DI) + D_m + \varepsilon \quad \text{.........(1)}$$

where, g = per capita GDP growth rate; Y_o = initial per capita GDP (GDP_{t-1}); FDI = net foreign direct investment inflows as percentage of GDP, XM = trade openness (the sum of total export and import as percentage of GDP); GE = government development expenditure as ratio of GDP; HC = human capital; GFCF = gross fixed capital formation to the share of GDP; DI = gross domestic investment is coded as percentage of GDP; CR = ratio of private domestic credit to real GDP; FDI*XM = interaction of FDI with trade; FDI*DI = interaction of FDI with domestic investment; FDI*HC = interaction of FDI with human capital; Dm = dummy variable and ε = error term.

Positive relationships are expected between the dependent variable and all explanatory variables. If the model specification is reasonable, the estimated coefficient of FDI will indicate the direction and magnitude of the impact of FDI on economic performance.

Appropriate statistical tools will be used for the presentation, interpretation and analysis of collected data. Granger causality tests have applied to see if there exists unidirectional or bi-directional causality between the variables in concern.

Organization of Book

This book is organized into seven chapters as under:

Chapter 1 provides the background required to understand the intricacies and complexities associated with the FDI. It also outlines the methodology adopted for the study that provides a preliminary sketch of the entire study.

In Chapter 2, we review some of the existing theoretical and empirical studies made on the relationship between FDI and economic growth.

Chapter 3 gives a brief account of Indian economy and provides background information of the FDI policies of the Indian government. It discusses the structure and nature of industrial policies of Indian government, and also the determinants of FDI of India.

Chapter 4 is a comparative study involving the review of FDI policy and incentives in India with various developing countries.

Chapter 5 is devoted to the analysis of foreign investor's motives, favourable and unfavourable factors in investing in India, the problems faced by the foreign investors and the suggestions for improving the FDI promotion in this country, based on the survey data.

Chapter 6 analyses the effects of FDI on economic growth in India with the help of secondary time series data for the period 1974–2008. It presents the econometric model specification and estimation procedure and analyses the empirical results. It begins with brief statement of previous empirical evidence and data definition and data sources, and explanation of econometric issues like unit root test, ADF test, co-integration test, Granger causality test.

Chapter 7 provides a summary of the study. It draws some conclusions from the observations and indicates some recommendations and policy guidelines. Some limitations of the study and agenda for further research are mentioned at the end of the chapter.

2

FDI and Economic Growth

A Literature Survey

About forty years ago, the first comprehensive analysis of the consequence of inbound foreign direct investment for a host country was published (Dunning, 2002). The subject of the study was the United Kingdom. Since then, similar investigations have been undertaken with varying degree of sophistication for almost every country in the world. In 1991, the UNCTAD Division on Transnational Corporation and Investment (DTCI) identified over 3,000 books, reports and articles published between 1988 and 1990. Hundreds of books, articles or government reports have been found on the topics of MNCs and their operations, and FDI and its effects in developing countries. Most of the studies cover some common areas, such as the role of MNCs in developing countries, FDI inflows and outflows in various developing regions or countries, country-specific effects, beneficial and baneful effects of MNCs, host country government policy towards FDI and incentives offered to MNCs for attracting their investment, etc. A number of studies have been conducted on FDI in developing countries and many of them somehow cover the investment activities of MNCs. For the review of literature, this study has included only those articles or books which have been written on MNCs, FDI and economic growth in developing countries like India and Bangladesh and emphasis has been put only on those studies which have been conducted recently. This chapter is divided into two sections. While the first section reviews comprehensive literatures on MNCs, FDI, determinants, spillovers and economic growth in developing countries, the second section reviews literature on MNCs, FDI and economic growth in India.

I

FDI to Developing Countries

FDI inflows have increasingly engaged the attention of national policy makers as well as the international negotiators over the past decade. The rapid growth of the magnitudes of FDI over the past decade has generated optimism among the developing countries about not only solving their resource scarcities with greater inflows but also getting along with them other critical resources for development such as entrepreneurship, technology, organizational capability and, sometimes, even market access. Therefore, most developing countries have liberalized their policy regimes governing FDI and have attracted them with incentives and other preferences. However, FDI inflows have been highly concentrated in the high- and middle-income countries. Furthermore, there is a great variation in their quality. Hence, their developmental impact has varied across countries quite widely.

FDI is becoming increasingly important to developing countries. Through FDI, individuals or corporations obtain partial or total ownership of firms located in another country. But, the foreign investor should have lasting interest and substantial control over the investment. FDI contributes to growth through several channels. It directly affects growth through being a source of capital formation. As a part of private investment, an increase in FDI will, by itself, contribute to an increase in total investment. Similarly, an increase in investment directly contributes to growth. A large number of studies have been done in the field of FDI and economic growth. Some of the major studies are reviewed and discussed below in this section.

Kyaw (2003) discussed the key issues related to FDI flows to developing countries in the globalized world. In particular, the paper focused on the recent trends and direction of FDI flows to developing countries and the uneven distribution of the flows among the countries. The study identified that despite the remarkable growth in FDI flows to developing countries as a whole, these remain highly concentrated in just a few countries.

On the basis of empirical evidence the study suggested that in order to induce more FDI to developing countries, the countries should focus on improving the investment climate for the foreign investors by paying special attention to measures that facilitate FDI. The study found that the developing countries that received the lion's share of the surge in FDI flows during the 1990s had more open door policy regimes or hospitable regulatory framework, large markets and favourable economic environment.

Waldkirch (2002) used data on FDI in a relatively skilled-labour and capital-scarced country, Mexico, at a highly disaggregated level to investigate what determines FDI flows among mostly dissimilar countries. The estimation was based on a recently developed unifying framework of multinational activity which yields clear empirical predictions.

The study examined that neither the horizontal nor the vertical model can be rejected for Mexico. It highlighted that during the last decade growth in world FDI far outpaced growth in either world production or world trade. Coincided with this growth in FDI, theoretical research on the multinational firm and its determinants has burgeoned. Yet, empirical research was lagging behind the theoretical advancements. Few studies on the determinants of FDI were based on a consistent, general equilibrium model of multinational activity. Moreover, most evidence on what determines FDI relates to developed countries, with the majority using data on US and Japanese FDI.

The study found that factor-endowment divergences between Mexico and the source countries of its foreign investments as well as joint market size are important in explaining inward FDI. Neither the horizontal nor the vertical model can be rejected. The study also found that the development of a unified theory of multinational activity with clear testable implications was an important step forward in analysing the determinants of FDI. This study had attempted to make a significant step forward by exploiting a dataset from a developing rather than a developed FDI host country, with FDI data on a much more disaggregated level than previously available. However, further testing is needed as better and more disaggregated data is becoming available for an increasing number of countries, both developed and developing.

Baniak et al. (2002) traced the trajectory of the recent flows of FDI from global and regional perspectives and to explore the reasons behind the prevailing trends and patterns. The study found that FDI has registered a tremendous growth during the last four decades. The amount of FDI reached about US$ 53.2 trillion in 1996 rising from only US$ 2 trillion in 1993 and US$I trillion in 1987. Sales and assets of TNCs are growing faster than world GDP, exports and gross fixed capital formation. The author mentioned that the increased flows of FDI indicate the growing internationalization and integration of economic activities around the globe. At the same time, with the gradual change in the motives for FDI as well as the shift of some location-specific advantages from developed to developing countries, the patterns and trends of FDI have been experiencing a significant change in recent past. The study concluded that along with the current waves of regional integration, the intra-regional FDI got its momentum in recent years and has become a bright future of the worldwide flows of finance capital. A significant shift also took place in relation to the forms of foreign investment. Conventional Greenfield investment is giving way to the merger and acquisition and many other low-equity and non-equity forms of international investment modes. The sectoral recipe of FDI also underwent a radical change. Service sector replaced the dominance of primary and manufacturing sectors as the major FDI recipient.

Gregorio (2003) analysed the role of FDI in economic growth, and discussed whether, based on these results, there was some rationale for special policies that discriminate in favour of particular sectors to attract FDI and promote growth. At a sectoral level, the study also discussed the role of natural resources in economic growth. The view that having natural resources was bad for growth and welfare was questioned.

FDI has long been a topic high on the policy agenda in emerging markets. The contribution of FDI to a country's external financing and economic growth, the behaviour of multinational corporations, and the extent of regulation of FDI and other forms of capital flows were some of the issues on which policy makers usually had to take a stand. Not coincidentally, economic research had devoted a large effort to exploring these issues.

Thus, FDI is beneficial for economic growth. But there is no solid basis for arguing that any one sector should be promoted against any other, and therefore, as a general guideline, inducements to FDI should not be made on a discriminatory sectoral basis without some clear rationale. The issue of industrial policy went beyond the purpose of this study, but there were no strong reasons to argue that developing natural resources rather than manufacturing may be detrimental for growth. It identified that countries can benefit greatly from FDI. To attract it, and to take full advantage of it when it comes, growth-promoting institutions are the essential ingredient.

Chatterjee (2003) examined whether the positive impact of FDI on development in a country depended on the quality of FDI it was receiving. It also looked at the global FDI trend, which was important to understand the debate on FDI and development. The study argued that it is difficult to predict whether FDI will promote economic development, but it can be said that if FDI adds to the productive capacity of the economy, for example, when it uses local resources, it is beneficial for the country. The country would likely to be benefited if such use of resources is market-driven. If it is policy-driven, there could be distortions outweighing benefits of FDI. Often, companies establish units in a country, import semi-processed goods and export finished goods, which is likely to add very little value to the country's productive capacity. Further, development benefits of FDI in a small country also depend on the country's absorptive capacity. This is especially true for small developing countries, which are small players in the global trade. A country can lose from FDI through the same routes by which it can benefit from FDI. It should take measures to improve its investment environment before liberalizing its FDI regime to allow more foreign investors. FDI would have a positive effect on development, if a country is able to make sure that it has adopted measures, which would maximize benefits from FDI. At the least, a country should adopt minimum regulatory measures to ensure that FDI or domestic investment does not harm its economy.

Marino (2000) investigated the possibility that the trade policy regime followed by host countries influences significantly both the amount of inward FDI received by recipient countries and the impact of FDI on growth. The author had used different indicators in order to measure the degree of openness of an economy. In this study countries were sorted according to a given variable and then qualified as 'open' or 'closed' according to a procedure similar to the regression tree methods used in recent growth empirics.

Marino (2001) reviewed the empirical evidence about the distribution of capital flows across developing countries. The study showed that when FDI was measured in per capita terms, rather than as a share of GDP as it is usually done in the empirical literature, a clear and positive correlation between income and foreign capital levels emerges. It identified that while FDI was expected to promote growth, foreign capital inflows were constrained by the development level. The study discussed that how insights offered by some recent growth models can account for this sort of development trap. It also computed the cross-country estimates of the elasticity of FDI inflows to the income level.

The study further identified that FDI inflows were a positive function of the host country income level. The econometric estimates in this study showed that the elasticity of FDI inflows over a certain period to the initial income level of the same period was positive, high and significant. The study also highlighted that the elasticity was significant when inward FDI was expressed in per capita terms, but not when it was computed as a share of GDP (coherently with the insights of the model). The study found that the relationship between income and foreign capital inflows estimated here was so strong that one may wonder whether it still makes sense to talk about 'FDI-led growth' for developing countries.

Fan and Dickie (2000) examined the contribution of FDI to economic growth and stability in the ASEAN-5 economies based upon a simple growth accounting framework. The contribution of FDI in mitigating external shock was assessed in the study by comparing the inflow before and during the Asian financial crisis. To quantify the contribution of FDI to growth, this study applied a simple growth accounting approach to analyse the importance of FDI in promoting growth through serving as a source of capital formation.

The study found that FDI had made an important contribution to the economic development of ASEAN-5 economies. FDI had been a major source of capital formation and had played a significant role in augmenting growth. The study also found that FDI had played important part in averting external shocks during the Asian financial crisis. It also found that there had been a continuation of FDI inflow in ASEAN-5 during the crisis. The study identified that FDI had reduced the economic and financial fluctuation in the ASEAN-5 countries.

This section has described another seven dimensions as stated below:

- FDI, economic growth and domestic investment
- FDI and liberalization
- Knowledge spillovers and productivity improvements
- FDI and host country market structure
- Growth models and FDI
- FDI and spillover effects
- FDI and determinants

Developing countries had a 'fear-mood' attitude towards FDI even until the mid-1980s due to open contentious debate about the unexpected costs and benefits of FDI inflows in the host countries. The debate developed due to the notion that FDI in developing countries was mostly concentrated on the low-priced primary export to developed countries and thus had a negative or insignificant impact on the host country's overall growth. In effect, a large number of developing countries adopted closed macro-economic policies during that period, which essentially encouraged import substitution industrialization policies, backed by a dominant role of the state in development policies. However, since the late 1980s, the conception started to change in favour of FDI inflows into developing countries, due to a possibly positive contribution of FDI to growth through capital formation and technology transfer, enabling them to convert their comparative advantage into a global force. The lack of available capital for rapid industrialization in developing countries also recognized the role of FDI as a channel of capital mobility in the host economy. For these reasons, the inflow of FDI increased rapidly during the late 1980s and the 1990s in almost every region of the world, lending support to the view that FDI and economic growth are positively correlated.

DeRosa (1998) examined the evaluation of foreign trade and investment policies in developing Asian countries vis-à-vis emerging market countries and other developing countries in the rest of the world since the mid-1980s. The study revealed that non-Asian emerging market countries have made appreciable progress in closing the 'trade policy gap' with leading East Asian countries. It also found that emerging market countries outside Asia are more liberal today in their policies towards FDI than many if not most East Asian countries.

The study concluded that during the mid-1980s, developing countries both within and outside Asia had widely reduced their average levels of tariff protection and also, very importantly, their average levels of NTB protection. However, the South Asian economies remained among the world's most highly tariff-protected economies. In the East Asia, there was also evidence of increased levels and dispersion of tariff across categories of commodities and manufactures in the East Asian newly industrialized economies (NIEs), albeit at still the lowest average levels of applied tariff worldwide. The People's Republic of China (PRC) continues to rely heavily on NTB protection, particularly for production of agricultural raw materials and capital-intensive iron and steel manufactures. Finally, it is concluded that in the aftermath of the Asian financial crisis and recession, the findings point to the importance of maintaining, if not also deepening, reforms to foreign trade and investment policies in developing Asia. This is important so that the region might continue to attract a commanding share of FDI flows and enjoy the related trade and other economic benefits of this investment in the increasingly more competitive global economy.

FDI, Economic Growth and Domestic Investment

Although a number of studies have analysed the relationship between FDI inflows and economic growth, the issue is far from settled in view of the mixed findings reached. A number of early studies have generally reported an insignificant effect of FDI on growth in developing host countries. For instance, Sinha (1994) found the FDI penetration variable to have little or no consequence for economic or industrial growth in a sample of 73 developing countries and reported an insignificant effect of FDI inflows on medium-term economic growth of per capita income for a sample of 41 developing countries.

The relationship between FDI and economic growth has received a great deal of attention from economists in the past two and half decades, particularly in relation to least developed countries (LDCs). However, the results of numerical empirical studies have yet to provide a coherent, unified explanation as to whether FDI has any effect, positive or negative, on levels of economic growth.

Either neo-classical growth models or endogenous growth models are considered as the theoretical basis for empirical studies on FDI and growth. Most of the empirical studies which tried to investigate the relationship between growth and FDI used either of these growth models as the basis using both the cross-country and country-specific data for the analysis. These studies systematically incorporated FDI as one of the determinants of economic growth with other determinants of growth such as growth of labour, education and technological progress as suggested by the standard growth models. The incorporation of FDI in the growth models opened the door for discussion about the possible role of knowledge capital in economic growth, especially of the developing countries.

It is a well-established fact that developing countries suffer from a shortage of appropriate knowledge in the development process. In FDI literature, it is already recognized that FDI not only brings capital for productive development to the host economy, it also transfers a considerable amount of technical and managerial knowledge and skills, which is likely to spillover to domestic enterprises in that economy. In other words, FDI helps developing countries to reduce the 'knowledge gap' with the developed world by bringing both the managerial and technological knowledge and skill to the host countries. Thus FDI benefits the host economy more through different channels as compared to its direct impact which are recognized as the sources of the economic growth.

Blomstrom et al. (2003) found that FDI inflows had a significant positive effect on the average growth rate of per capita income for a sample of 78 developing and 23 developed countries. However, when the sample of developing countries was split between two groups based on level of per capita income, the effect of FDI on the growth of lower-income developing countries was not statistically significant, although still positive. They argue that least developed countries learn very little from MNEs because domestic enterprises are too far behind in their technological levels to be either imitators or suppliers to MNEs.

Borensztein et al. (1995), for a sample of 69 developing countries for the period 1970–89, find that the effect of FDI on host country's growth is dependent on the stock of human capital. They infer that the flow of advanced technology brought along by FDI can increase the growth rate only by interacting with country's absorptive capability. They also find FDI to be stimulating for total fixed investment more than proportionately. In other words, FDI results in domestic investment. However, the results are not robust across specifications. Balasubramanyam and Mahambare (2003) find the effect of FDI on average growth rate for the period 1970–85 for a cross-section of 46 countries as well as the sub-sample of countries that are deemed to pursue an export-oriented strategy to be positive and significant, but not significant and sometimes negative for a sub-set of countries pursuing inward-oriented strategy. Pradhan (2004) finds a significant positive effect of lagged FDI inflows on growth rates only for Latin American countries in a panel data estimation covering the 1975–95 period for 71 developing countries. The effect of FDI was not significantly different from zero for the overall sample also for other regions.

De Mello (1997) has conducted time series as well as panel data estimation for a sample covering 15 developed and 17 developing countries for the period 1970–90 of the relationships between FDI, capital accumulation, output and productivity growth. The time series estimations suggest that the effect of FDI on growth or on capital accumulation and total factor productivity (TFP) varies greatly across countries. The panel data estimation suggests a positive impact of FDI on output growth for developed and developing country sub-samples. However, the effect of FDI on capital accumulation and TFP growth varies across developed (technological leaders) and developing countries (technological followers).

FDI has a positive effect on TFP growth in developed countries but a negative effect in developing countries, and the pattern is reversed in case of effect on capital accumulation. De Mello (1977) infers from these findings that the extent to which FDI is growth enhancing depends on the degree of complementarity between FDI and domestic investment. The degree of substitutability between foreign and domestic capital stocks appears to be greater in technologically advanced countries than in developing countries. Developing countries may have difficulty in using and diffusing new technologies of MNEs.

Agosin and Mayer (2000) analysed the effect of lagged values of FDI inflows on investment rates in host countries to examine whether FDI crowds in or crowds out domestic investment over the 1970–95 period. They find that FDI crowds in domestic investment in Asian countries and crowds out in Latin American countries, while in Africa the relationship is neutral (or one-to-one between FDI and total investment). Therefore, they conclude that the effects of FDI are by no means always favourable, and simplistic policies are unlikely to be optimal.

Similarly, Chakraborty and Basu (2002) explored the two-way link between FDI and growth for India using a structural co-integration model with vector error correction mechanism. The study, focusing on the relationship between FDI and growth in India, found the existence of two co-integrating vectors between GDP, FDI, the unit labour cost and the share of import duty in tax revenue, which captured the long-run relationship between FDI and GDP. A parsimonious vector error correction model (VECM) was estimated to find the short-run dynamics of FDI and growth. In this study, the co-integration approach was used to study the short-run and long-run relationship between FDI and growth for India. The author reviewed some empirical literature on FDI and growth which was made some basics of this study. The study highlighted some basics concepts of co integration and VECM model that increased the readability of the article. The study also found the shortcomings of Engle-Granger single equation-based co-integration tests. It examined the FDI flows for the Indian economy over the period 1974–1996.

The study found that FDI was related positively to GDP and inversely to import duties in tax revenue (IMPDT). The second co-integration relationship in this study represents a long-run technological relationship between GDP and ULC that holds up independently of the foreign investment flows as well as changes in the policy regime. It also found that while there was strong evidence of GDP causes FDI flows for India, there exists no significant role in the short-run adjustment process of GDP.

Frey (1984) examined the role of FDI in promoting growth in the framework of a macro-model for a pooled time series cross-section of 16 developing countries for the 1966–1988 period. The countries included in the sample are Argentina, Brazil, Chile, Egypt, India, Mexico, Nigeria, Pakistan, Sri Lanka, Turkey, Venezuela and five Pacific basin countries—Indonesia, Korea, Malaysia, the Philippines and Thailand. From the sample, he did not find that FDI exerted a significantly different effect from domestically financed investment on the rate of economic growth. Rather, he found that FDI had a significant negative effect on domestic investment, suggesting that it crowds out domestic investment. Hence, FDI appears to have been immiserizing. However, this effect varies across countries and in the Pacific basin countries FDI seems to have crowded in domestic investment.

Liu et al. (2002) investigated the causal links between trade, economic growth and inward FDI in China at the aggregate level. The integration and cointegration of properties of quarterly data analysed. Long-run relationships between growth, exports, imports and FDI were identified in a cointegration framework, in which this study found bi-directional causality between economic growth, FDI and exports. The study revealed that economic development, exports and FDI appeared to be mutually inforcing under the open door policy.

The study examined the causal relationships between economic growth, trade and FDI in China by using multivariate Granger causality tests in a co-integration framework. The study further tested the integration properties of the data, then employed the Johansen procedure to detect the number of co-integrating vectors, and then tested causality in the resulting restricted VECM. The study considered the four variables—GDP, FDI, imports and exports—to set the scene and considered a VAR involving four variables. The study tested for unit roots, fits a VAR, selecting lag length through the usual combination of residual diagnosis and coefficient *F*-tests, test for co-integrating rank, and finally tests for causality that was pioneer.

The study found that two-way causal connections exist between economic growth, FDI and exports, with rather weaker evidence of feedback from imports to the other three variables. The study also found that failure to account for interaction between FDI, growth and external trade can produce spurious results in the analysis of the relationships between above four variables.

Townsend (2003) made a study to investigate the relationship between FDI and economic growth in least developed countries (LDCs). The study investigated whether differences in the datasets used in previous research account for the disparate findings. In order to investigate the relationship between FDI and growth in LDCs data were collected on only LDCs. The study examined whether the disparate results can be explained by differences in the data used within the studies. Two well-established model were used to analyse the impact of different datasets on FDI and economic growth. Focusing the investigation on the recent Carkovic and Levine (2002) results, the study found that differing datasets do not account for the disparate findings.

Dutt (1997) examined the relationship between the sectoral pattern of direct foreign investment (DFI) and growth using theoretical and empirical analysis. The author, citing Singer (1950), stated that DFI from developed economies—collectively referred to the North—to LDCs or the South has a detrimental effect on the development of LDCs and leads to uneven global development. The purpose of the study was to examine the validity of one possible explanation of the change in different views regarding FDI and economic growth, which argues that there had been a change in the sectoral pattern of DFI into LDCs, which had strengthened the positive development effects of DFI flows while it had weakened the negative effects.

The study investigated whether the growth effects of DFI from rich to poor countries depend on the sectoral pattern of DFI. In the study the author argued that there are good theoretical reasons to expect that the growth consequences of DFI on LDCs depend on what kinds of sectors receive it, because of the differential effects of such DFI on North-South terms of trade and on the nature of technological development of countries of south. On the empirical front the author had attempted to use cross-country growth equations to see whether the pattern of DFI can explain rates of growth across countries. The study had not been able to detect any empirical regularities in the above regard either in terms of primary and secondary sector distinctions, or taking into account high or low technology sectors.

Although the relationship between the sectoral pattern of DFI, growth and structural change is a complex one, case studies of fast and slow-growing LDCs, examining the sectoral pattern of DFI and government policies regarding such patterns, can be expected to yield rich dividends on the quest of the relationship between the pattern of DFI and growth.

Moore (1993) explored the relationship between FDI and economic growth in eight transition countries of EU in the period 1994–2001. Surprising statistically robust negative causal relationship between FDI and growth emerged implying that FDI hampered their real convergence with EU, the study found. The study explained the amazing results by the form of FDI. In the study period, acquisitions were the predominant form and the proceeds of the sales were spent on consumption and imports rather than enhancing productive assets. Indeed, current account and FDI were strongly linked: the bigger the inflow of FDI into a country, the higher its current account deficit and foreign debt.

The study concentrated on a very narrow sample both regarding the set of the countries and the period included. The sample consists of eight EU countries, viz., Czech Republic, Estonia, Hungary, Latvia, Lithuania, Poland, Slovakia and Slovenia in the post-transition period, which was also the period of their gradual accession to EU and high reliance on FDI.

Positive spillovers of FDI can promote growth and national welfare but while 'the studies provide detailed information about the various channels for spillovers, they said little about the importance of such spillovers' (Blomstrom, and Kokko, 2003: 11). Indeed, arguments for positive spillovers through a particular channel were not stronger than arguments for negative spillovers. The study found that the productivity spillovers could be weakened by small size of the countries and concentration of FDI in trade and finance. It also indicated that increased efficiency of the restructured firm acquired by MNC could be more than offset by its inclusion into MNC structure and resulting decrease of economic links with local firms.

Similarly, Chowdhury and Mavrotas (2003) examined the causal relationship between FDI and economic growth by using an innovative econometric methodology to study the direction of causality between the two variables. The researchers applied a new methodology, based on the Toda-Yamamoto test for causality, to time-series data covering the period 1969–2000 for three developing countries, namely, Chile, Malaysia and Thailand—all of them are the major recipients of FDI with a different history of macro-economic episodes, policy regimes and growth patterns. Empirical findings of the study clearly suggested that it was GDP that causes FDI in the case of Chile and not vice versa, while for both Malaysia and Thailand, there was a strong evidence of a bi-directional causality between the two variables. The robustness of the above findings was confirmed by the use of a bootstrap test employed to examine the validity of the results.

Bengoa and Sanchez-Robles (2003) designed and discussed a simple model in which FDI generates endogenous, non-zero growth. The researchers considered the FDI as one of the channels by which technology may diffuse from developed to developing countries. It identified that FDI, in particular, brings about growth because it offsets the tendency to decreasing returns to domestic capital exhibited by the production function.

The study presented some empirical evidence obtained by exploiting a panel data from 18 Latin American countries over the period 1970–2000. Regressions of the growth rate of GDP per capita on FDI and a set of control variables seem to confirm the hypothesis that FDI promotes growth. The researchers pursued an empirical exercise in order to test the connection between FDI and growth. They described why the study focused on the analysis of the Latin American countries. On the theoretical level, the nations belonging in this region are developing countries but have already a minimum level of social capacity, in terms of human capital, financial intermediaries and a certain level of institutional stability, as compared, for example, to Africa. It further argued that the sample offers enough variability in order to capture the impact of different degrees of the considered variables.

Carkovic and Levine (2002) investigated the potential relationship between economic growth and FDI using new statistical techniques and two new databases. Based on a recent World Bank dataset the study constructed a panel data set with data averaged over each of the seven 5-year periods between 1960 and 1995. The authors also confirmed the results using new FDI data from the International Monetary Fund (IMF).

This study estimated the effects of FDI inflows on economic growth after controlling other growth determinants and the potential biases induced by endogeneity, country-specific effects and the inclusion of initial income as a regressor. Moreover, the study examined whether the growth effects of FDI depend on the level of educational attainment, economic development, financial development and trade openness of the recipient country. The study also assessed whether the impact of FDI on growth depends primarily on the stock of human capital. Finally, the researchers examined the importance of human capital using an alternative specification. This specification also indicated that the impact of FDI on growth does not robustly vary with the level of educational attainment.

Thus, the study found that the exogenous component of FDI does not exert a robust, positive influence on economic growth. By accounting for simultaneity, country-specific effects and lagged dependent variables as regressors, the researchers reconciled the micro-economic and macro-economic evidence. However, this is a well written paper on relation between FDI and economic growth though it did not discuss the determinants of FDI.

Borensztein et al. (1998) examined the effect of FDI on economic growth in a cross-country regression framework, employing a dataset of FDI flows from industrial countries to 69 developing countries over the last two decades. The purpose of this study was to examine empirically the role of FDI in the process of technology diffusion and economic growth in developing countries. The researchers conducted the empirical work by a model of endogenous growth, in which the rate of technological progress was the main, but not the only, determinant of the long-term growth rate of income.

The study found a robust relationship between economic growth, FDI and human capital. The researchers also investigated the effect of FDI on domestic investment, namely, whether there was evidence that the inflow of foreign capital crowds out domestic investment. The results of the study were supportive of a crowding-in effect, that is, a one-dollar increase in the net inflow of FDI was associated with an increase in total investment in the host economy of more than one dollar, but does not appear to be very impressive. The most important finding of this paper was that the effect of FDI on economic growth was dependent on the level of human capital available in the host economy. However, there was a strong positive interaction between FDI and the level of educational attainment.

Kumar and Pradhan (2002), in a recent quantitative study analysing relationships between FDI, growth and domestic investment for a sample of 107 developing country's for the 1980–99 period, postulated a dynamic nature of the effect of FDI on host country's growth with an initial generally adverse competitive effect and a subsequent usually more favourable effect through backward linkages with the net effect, depending on the quality of FDI. Panel data estimations in a production function framework suggest a positive effect of FDI on growth. However, tests of causality find that in a majority of cases the direction of causation is not pronounced, and in a substantial number of cases the direction of causation actually runs from growth to FDI. Further estimations corroborate the proposition that FDI affects domestic investments in a dynamic manner with a negative initial effect and the subsequent positive effects for the panel data as well as for most of the countries individually. Although FDI appears to crowd out domestic investments in net terms, in general, some countries have experienced a favourable effect of FDI on domestic investments in net terms, suggesting a role for host country policies. Therefore, they inferred that policy flexibility is important for developing countries for benefiting from FDI.

Bruee (1983) in his study argued that current FDI must be understood as a largely sequential process stemming from the advantages of flexibility of a multinational system.

Kumar (1994) has examined the trends and patterns of FDI inflows into India over the emergence of Indian enterprises as direct investors abroad against the background of a changing policy regime. He found that the sectoral pattern of FDI in India reveals a shift in favour of more technology and skill-intensive industries as the country industrialized itself. The Indian government's policies appear to have played an important role in shaping this pattern by affecting the relative configuration of ownership, internationalization and location advantages of foreign investors in the country. The study revealed that the recent liberalization of the policy regime has not yet succeeded in attracting efficiency seeking FDI in a considerable manner. In the current environment of intense competition among developing countries to attract such FDI, just the liberalization of policies may not be adequate. More effective use of India's bargaining advantages with respect to MNEs, such as the large domestic market, abundant supply of skilled labour and technical professionals as well as low wages, may be desirable to attract a greater proportion of such FDI.

Ruffin (1993) in an article examined the role and flow of foreign investment to Asia-Pacific region of the world. He pointed out that among both developing and developed countries, Asian countries are the 'superstars' of economic growth. The developing countries in Asia and the Pacific produced 25 per cent of world output in 1988—the same as the United States. The countries in the region range from tiny and prosperous Hong Kong to India with a huge population but having one of the world's smallest per capita gross domestic products (GDP). The author stated that FDI can increase the rate of growth by bringing in new ideas and lowering the cost of innovation. He argued that a product or process is just an idea.

FDI and Liberalization

Foreign investment, if it is not heavily subsidized, pays by raising wages in the capital-importing country. More foreign investment today benefits future generations because higher wages stimulate capital accumulation. But this is just a once-and-for-all change. According to the new theory of endogenous growth, FDI can increase the rate of growth by bringing in new ideas and lowering the cost of innovation. Of course, spillover effects may not always occur. But ideas have the property of being non-rival in consumption and good ideas are contagious. The policy of reserving the home market for its own entrepreneurs fails to take into account the enormous gains from trade in ideas, which may far exceed the usual gains from trade. This hypothesis helps explain the rapid growth of the developing countries in the Asian and Pacific region (Ruffin, 1993).

Knowledge Spillovers and Productivity Improvements

The other stream of studies has related the productivity levels across industries or firms within a country to the extent of foreign presence in an attempt to evaluate the presence of knowledge spillovers, following Caves (1982). These studies have also had mixed findings. Blomstrom and Kokko (1996), for example, has found a strong positive association between the labour productivity of local enterprises and the foreign share in employment in 1970 in Mexican manufacturing industries. However, foreign entry was not found to be related to changes in the technological frontier or labour productivity of the least efficient plants.

A simple relationship between productivity levels and foreign ownership as examined by these studies has the limitation of the potential overestimation of the positive impact of foreign presence if the FDI was concentrated in more productive industries. Blomstrom and Kokko (2003), in a further work on 20 two-digit Mexican industries for the period 1965–1984, found increasing convergence of the productivity levels of locally owned firms and those of foreign-owned firms, suggesting the presence of knowledge spillovers. Holland et al. (2000), in the case of Morocco's manufacturing sector using a firm level panel data set for 1985–1989, discovered no significant relationship between higher productivity growth in domestic firms and greater foreign presence in a sector. Athukorala and Menon (1995) in a similar exercise for Venezuela, learnt that foreign ownership affected the productivity of domestically owned plants adversely and that negative effects of FDI were large and robust. Similar results were reported for Indonesia, where negative effect on productivity of domestic plants was slightly weaker. Therefore, the authors inferred that the benefits of FDI are limited to direct effects on productivity improvements with improved technology by enterprises receiving foreign participation, and that the spillovers to other local enterprises are negligible and do not justify the incentives granted by host governments to foreign investors.

Kojima (1975), by examining Mexican data, found no evidence of spillovers in industries where the foreign affiliates had a much higher productivity and larger market shares than local firms. In other industries, there appeared to be a positive relationship between foreign presence and local productivity. This result suggests that spillovers from foreign enterprises are dependent upon the local capability in the industry. If the local firms are too weak they will not be able to absorb spillovers and might vanish in the face of competition from foreign firms. Similar finding was obtained by Kathuria (1998) in India.

Inter-industry spillovers and vertical inter-firm linkages

The vertical inter-firm linkages created by foreign enterprises could not only be an important externality for the host economy but also sources of diffusion of knowledge from them. Kyaw (2003), for instance, noted that the inflow of FDI into the Argentine manufacturing sector in the 1950s had a significant impact on the technologies used by local firms. The technical progress took place not only in the MNEs' own industries, but also in other sectors, because the foreign affiliates forced domestic firms to modernize by imposing on them minimum standards of quality, delivery schedules, prices and so on in their supplies of parts and raw material. The volume of vertical backward linkages generated is determined by two decisions concerning the sourcing of raw materials and intermediate products of the firm: 'import or procure locally' and 'make or buy'.

A number of studies have compared the dependence of foreign and local firms on imported raw materials in order to get an idea of the extent of linkages generated in the domestic economy, as the local content in production is an indicator of the strength of local linkages. Foreign affiliates can be expected to import a higher proportion of their raw materials and other inputs than local firms, because of their familiarity with foreign suppliers and the alleged inadequacies of local producers, and sometimes to provide a market for the products of their associates elsewhere. Foreign firms have been found to depend more on imports than their local counterparts in studies by Balasubramanyam and Sapsford (2007) for India. Lall and Streeten (1997) in a study of six countries including India, however, did not find any significant difference between the import dependence of foreign and local firms. Kumar (1994) also did not observe a statistically significant difference between the import dependence of foreign and local firms across 43 branches of Indian manufacturing.

The make or buy decision actually relates to the degree of vertical integration. The latter is inversely related to sub-contracting parts of the production run to unassociated vendors. In countries such as India, which have evolved a strict trade and exchange control regime that restricts the freedom of firms to import, sub-contracting may be an important aspect of a firm's decision-making concerning the sourcing of intermediates and raw materials. A number of market failures may tempt a firm to internalize the manufacture of intermediate inputs, so as to ensure the certainty of delivery schedules and quality standards. A certain monopoly rent may also be associated with vertical integration. On the other hand, firms can internalize a part of the scale economies in the manufacture of intermediates and can escape problems of industrial relations by sub-contracting their production to other firms. Marino (2000) and Willmore (1986) found a reverse pattern in the case of Brazil. Lall (1993), however, did not find any significant difference between the extent of sub-contracting of a foreign subsidiary and a local company in India both producing trucks. Kumar (1994) noted foreign-controlled firms to have a greater extent of vertical integration than their local counterparts in 43 Indian manufacturing industries even after controlling for firm size, profitability and financial variables in the framework of multivariate analysis.

On the basis of analysis of patterns of FDI by US and Japanese MNEs in developing countries, Kumar (1998) has noticed a slow progress with respect to generation of backward linkages by either US or Japanese MNEs in developing host countries. In this context, it may also be useful to keep in mind the strategy of multinational companies, especially those from Japan, which tend to transplant their traditional Keiretsu links existing in the home country to their host countries. This generally takes the form of vendors of the Japanese parent company in Japan following the overseas production strategy of the parent. This tends to limit the diffusion of knowledge brought in by the MNEs in the host country through vertical inter-firm linkages. The extent of these practices for MNEs from other home countries is not clear.

Training and employee mobility

Some studies have documented the spillovers from FDI to local economies in the form of on-the-job training provided by MNE affiliates to their personnel and through the mobility of trained personnel. Gregorio (2003) examined detailed career data for 72 top and middle-level managers in 41 manufacturing firms and concluded that MNE affiliates offer more training to their managers than local private firms, although the mobility seemed to be lower for managers employed by MNEs than for those in private local firms.

FDI and Host Country Market Structure

The studies analysing the impact of MNEs or FDI on host country's market structures, conduct and performance have confined themselves to an examination of relationships between FDI and the level of concentration, advertisement and R&D intensities or performance in terms of profitability. Lall (1993) provides an early survey of the literature, whereas Caves (1982) and Kumar (1997) provide a more up-to-date survey.

Market structure can be affected by the relative scale of operation of enterprises. A number of studies have provided evidence on the larger scale of operations of foreign enterprises than that of their local counterparts, for instance, Moore (1993) for Mexico and Brazil and Lall and Streeten (1977) for India and Willmore (1986) in Guatemala have found a significant correlation between the degree of the presence of MNEs and seller concentration. Evans (1998) and Willmore (1986) for Brazil, Lall (1977) for Malaysia and Blomstrom (1996) for Mexico observed a positive influence of foreign ownership on industry concentration even after controlling for entry barriers.

Market structures or the level of concentration could also be affected by the relative conduct of MNEs, such as their behaviour in terms of advertising and R&D behaviour. Caves (1982) found the foreign share in industry sales to have a significant positive influence in explaining the proportion of advertising expenditure in Canadian manufacturing industries. Wallace (1990) noted that foreign enterprises spent a higher proportion of sales on advertising than their local counterparts in Brazil even after controlling for firm size and industry.

Feldstein (2000) in Latin American countries and Kumar (1997) reported that the local firms had a greater inclination to do in-house R&D than their foreign-controlled counterparts. Lall (1993) found a positive relationship between foreign ownership and R&D in the Indian engineering industry but a negative one in the chemical industry.

Kumar (2002) attempted to provide a framework explaining behavioural differences between foreign and local enterprises in a country. He contends that in order to maximize the revenue productivity of their dowry of intangible assets such as internationally recognized brand names, captive access to technology and reservoirs of technical, managerial and organizational skills, MNE affiliates are more likely to pursue non-price modes of rivalry than their local counterparts. Non-price modes of rivalry involve product differentiation accompanied by extensive advertising and marketing campaigns to highlight the unique features of the product and thus obtain monopolistic advantage in the market. The study found that, the comparison of the behaviour of two groups of firms in 49 Indian industries in the framework of both univariate as well as multivariate discriminant analyses, showed that the MNE affiliates operate at relatively larger scales because of the economies of scale involved in advertising and marketing, and are more vertically integrated because of greater proprietary element in product specifications. Because of their monopolistic hold over the markets through brand and trade name goodwill they are able to charge higher prices, and concentrate on the upper ends of the markets with relatively inelastic demand curves. Hence, they are found to enjoy higher profit margins even after controlling for extraneous factors. With regard to advertising and R&D, they also benefit from the global expenditures of their associates.

The tendency of MNE affiliates to opt for non-price modes of rivalry has important implications for the market structure and competitive situation in the host developing countries. MNE affiliates' preference to operate on a larger scale, and to depend more heavily on marketing, advertising and R&D activity to differentiate their products, raises barriers to the entry of new firms. Hence, they tend to perpetuate the concentration of market structures and the level of competition is affected adversely.

These 'contrived barriers' to entry perhaps explain the continued domination by MNE affiliates of several brand-sensitive consumer goods industries despite the instruments of the government's policy, which sought to curb monopolies as observed in India (Kumar, 1994).

Furthermore, the recent global trend for the restructuring of the global industry through mergers and acquisitions (M&As) between large MNEs results in a consolidation of their market position. Besides the consolidation of the market power of affected companies, M&As between large MNEs could have more direct adverse effects on the market structures in their host countries. For instance, the global pharmaceutical industry is being consolidated, with the mergers of Ciba-Geigy and Sandoz to form Novartis, Glaxo, Wellcome and Smith Kline and Beecham, and Pharmacia and Upjohn among others; the automobile industry with the takeover by BMW of Rover, the merger of Daimler-Benz and Chrysler, takeovers of Mazda and Volvo cars by Ford; and with the takeover of Brooke Bond by Unilever, which already owned Lipton, two of the largest packaged tea companies in the world thus came under common control. The recently strengthened and harmonized international regime of intellectual property protection under the TRIPS agreement also fortifies the monopolistic hold of MNEs on technologies. While the EU and the USA are equipped with effective anti-trust regulations to deal with the possible abuse of monopoly power of patent-holders and anti-competitive effects of international mergers, most developing countries lack anti-trust legislation designed to deal with such situations.

The exiting literature, therefore, suggests that the host country may not benefit from knowledge spillovers when the technology gap between foreign and domestic firms is too wide, as is generally the case in poorer countries. The literature also found the effect of FDI on growth to be dependent on the presence of skills that facilitate the absorption of new knowledge. In view of the relatively low levels of skill accumulation, poorer countries are not able to experience more favourable effects of FDI. Some studies have observed an insignificant or adverse effect of FDI on low-income countries and a more favourable effect on middle-income countries. Therefore, not only is FDI concentrated in relatively richer countries, these countries are also able to experience its more favourable effects than poor countries. FDI also often generates fewer linkages and tends to crowd-out domestic investments in net terms in more countries than it crowds-in. The fact that some countries have experienced a favourable effect of FDI on domestic investments in net terms suggests a role for host country's policies. Therefore, policy flexibility is important for developing countries for benefiting from FDI. Given the tendency of MNEs to operate at larger scales and pursue non-price modes of rivalry, FDI could also have an adverse impact on competition in domestic industries and may perpetuate concentration. Furthermore, the ongoing global industrial restructuring in the industry leading to consolidation of market power of large MNEs is also leading to further concentration in the host countries where the corporations involved in these deals have operations.

Growth Models and FDI

De Mello (1997) provides a survey of the literature relating the effects of FDI on economic growth. The early neo-classical approach to FDI was based on capital arbitrage (capital flows result from interest rate differentials) and the beneficial effects for the host country arise from a larger capital stock, increased tax revenues, increased labour income (or employment) and favourable externalities (diffusion of technology and training). Long-run growth can only arise because of technological progress and/or population growth both considered exogenous. That is, FDI will only be growth enhancing if it affects technology permanently and positively.

Endogenous growth models: FDI can affect growth endogenously if it generates increasing returns in production via externalities and productivity spillovers. Moreover, policy changes might induce permanent increases in output growth by providing incentives to host FDI. Specifically, FDI is thought to be an important source of human capital accumulation and technological change.

Capital accumulation: FDI encourages the incorporation of new inputs and technologies in the production function of host countries.

Technological change: FDI transfers knowledge from technological leaders to followers, promotes the use of advance technologies by domestic firms and provides increasing labour training and skill acquisition and diffusion, introduces new management practices and organizational arrangements, etc.

Thanks to the externality effect, the social return to investment exceeds the private rate of return. This discrepancy occurs because individual acts of private investment add to the stock of knowledge and, hence, the productivity of the capital stock. Therefore, in the aggregate term, the return to capital stock does not diminish although returns to single acts of investment might diminish.

Balasubramanyam and Mahambare (2003) analyses the relation between trade strategy, FDI and growth in developing country in the context of endogenous growth theory. For a sample of LDCs, they show that the effects of FDI, in terms of enhanced growth, is stronger in those countries that pursue export promotion (EP) than in countries pursuing an inward-oriented (IS) policy.

The model is an augmented production function, which includes exports as the ancillary variable:

$$Y = f\,(L,K,F,X,t) \quad (1)$$

where y is output, L is labour force, K is domestic capital stock, F is the stock of foreign capital, X is exports and t is a time trend capturing technological changes. Take logs and difference over time to obtain:

$$y = \alpha + \beta l + \gamma k + \psi f + \phi x \quad (2)$$

where lower case indicate rate of growth of the individual variables and β, γ, Ψ, and φ are elasticities.

They approximated domestic and foreign capital stock by the ratio of domestic and foreign direct investment to GDP respectively. Then equation (2) becomes:

$$y = \alpha + \beta + \gamma(I\,/\,Y) + \psi(FDI\,/\,Y) + \phi x \quad (3)$$

where the elasticity of output with respect to foreign capital is of particular interest. They expect not only a $\psi > 0$ but to be larger in EP countries relatively to IS countries. Also, because of the spillover effects and the externalities associated with FDI, they predict that the elasticity of output with respect to foreign capital exceeds to that of domestic capital. The importance of domestic and foreign investments in terms of their individual contribution to output growth can be measured by 'beta' or standardized regression coefficients (relevant regression coefficient multiply by the ratio of the standard deviation of the relevant regressor to that of the dependent variable).

Testing their hypothesis for a cross-section of 46 LDCs using annual averages over 1970 to 1985, they acknowledged the problem of FDI data reporting as well as the difficulties to find a criterion to split the sample in EP and IS groups. They classified them according to their ratio of imports to GNP and assumed that countries with higher M/GNP are likely to be EP because a high ratio indicates low level of protection.

To rank the sample, they applied Brown et al's, test of structural stability and classified 28 LDCs as IS and 18 LDCs as EP. They also used the classification provided by the World Bank (34 countries in the sample were divided into 10 EP and 14 IS).

They estimated equation (3) for the whole sample, for each sub-sample (based on M/GDP and World Bank) using OLS and generalized instrumental variables to offset the possibility of simultaneous equation bias arising from the endogeneity of FDI and exports.

Borensztein et al. (1998) examine empirically the role of FDI in the process of technology diffusion (transmission of ideas and new technologies) and on economic growth. MNCs spend substantially in R&D and are among the most technological advanced firms, so FDI by MNCs is considered one of the channels for access to advanced technologies by LDCs. The sample consists of FDI flows from industrial countries to 69 LDC during 1970–89.

An endogenous growth model motivates the empirical work where the rate of technological progress is the main determinant of long-run growth. Technological process takes place through 'capital deepening', i.e., introduction of new varieties of capital goods. MNCs possess more advanced 'knowledge' and are able to introduce them at lower cost. The application of this new technology requires a sufficient high stock of human capital in the host country. The stock of human capital reflects the capabilities of the host country and limits the transmission of technology.

They estimated the following regression model to find the effect of FDI on economic growth:

$$g = c_0 + c_1(FDI) + c_2(FDIxH) + c_3(H) + c_4(Y_0) + c_5(X)$$

where FDI is foreign direct investment, H is the stock of human capital, Y_0 is the initial GDP per capita and X is a set of variables often included in long-run growth studies (government consumption, black market premium as a proxy for exchange market distortions and dummies for Latin America and Sub-Saharan Africa).

The regressions are based on panel data for two decades (1970–79 and 1980–89). They applied seemingly unrelated regressions equations (SURE) technique because the disturbances of the regressions include factors that are common to all countries as well as factors that are specific to the country (i.e., equations are linked by their disturbances). Also, because the set of equations has the same parameters and estimating the equation separately will waste information (Greene, 2011), they did not report the cross-section regressions that yield similar results as the panel estimation. They also performed in the growth per capita regression to correct for endogeneity of FDI and overall, the results were qualitatively similar to the ones obtained with SURE.

The results show that FDI has a positively insignificant effect on growth. Once the product of FDIx schooling replaces the FDI variable, it yields a significantly positive coefficient. If FDI and the product of FDIxs chooling are added, the effect of FDI on growth is negative and insignificant while the interaction term is positive and significant. The values of these coefficients indicate that countries with secondary school attainment above 0.52 will benefit positively from FDI. In their sample, 46 out of 69 countries satisfy this benchmark. The black-market premium (proxy for distortions in the trade regime), the dummies for Africa and Latin America, political instability are negatively correlated with growth. The measure of financial development (M2/GDP) and the proxy for quality of institutions (Knack and Keefer's measure from the International Country Risk Guide) had also the expected signs.

The contribution of FDI to growth could come from complementing or adding to domestic capital and/or being more productive or efficient than domestic investment. They analysed the effects of FDI on total fixed investment and the results suggest that FDI increases investment more than one for one but the interaction FDI-human capital was insignificant. This suggests that the complementarity between foreign and domestic investment is not sensitive to the productivity of FDI. Note that the complementarity effect is not robust to different regression specifications. In fact, except for the baseline specification, the estimated coefficients are insignificant. To explore possible higher efficiency, they regress growth after controlling for aggregate investment and show that the effect of FDI on growth is significant once the interaction FDI and H is included. The value of the educational attainment threshold is 0.88 and is satisfied by 29 countries in the sample.

They found that FDI is an important vehicle of technological transmission, contributing more to economic growth than domestic investment when the host country has a minimum threshold stock of human capital. The study revealed that the effect of FDI on growth depends on the level of human capital available in the host country. There is a strong and positive interaction between FDI and the level of educational interaction (proxy for human capital). The same interaction is not significant in the case of domestic investment. They also found some evidence (not robust) of 'crowding-in', i.e., FDI is complementary to domestic evidence. The paper has not explored the effects of FDI on the level of human capital (training, etc.).

FDI and Spillover Effects

The issue that arises is whether FDI leads to spillover effects of the kind envisioned by the theory of endogenous growth. Do the ideas stay with the company or do they spillover into the rest of economy? This is a difficult question to answer because the spillover effects may be quite general and not limited to the industry. Many have found that industries that have been recipients of FDI have higher rates of technological progress. For example, one found a positive association in Hong Kong. But, recently, another study noted that proximity to FDI had weak effects on domestic firms but strong effects on domestic firms that were foreign-owned at one time. Of course, when one looks at a particular industry, he is never quite sure whether the FDI caused the technological progress or that foreign investors simply located in the more productive industries.

Baniak et al. (2002) explored two hypotheses of the export-spillover hypothesis: (1) all export activities generate spillovers, and (2) only the export activity of multinational firms generates spillovers. Spillovers make take different forms, for example, geographic concentration of exporters and facilities in terms of communication, storage facilities, etc. In the case of MNCs, they are 'conduits' of technology, information of foreign market, etc.

They used panel data of 2104 Mexican manufacturing plants over the period 1986–1990 and test if a firm is more likely to export the larger is the concentration of export activity or if there are spillovers associated to specific activities of MNCs. Their empirical model assumes that the probability of exporting is a function of domestic and foreign final-goods prices, cost variables common to both markets, market specific cost variables, and the local concentration of export activity (from total export activity and a from export activity of MNCs in the regional industry to which the firm belongs). Using probit technique they found that the probability of domestic firm exports is positively correlated with the proximity of multinational firms but that the plant export decision was not correlated with the local concentration of overall export activity. That is, the evidence suggests that export spillovers are restricted to multinational activities.

Baniak et al. (2002) examined (a) the extent to which joint ventures or wholly owned foreign subsidiaries, (i.e., foreign firms) exhibit higher level of productivity than their domestic counterpart, and (b) the evidence of technological spillovers to domestically owned firms from foreign firms. They used the following equation:

$$Y_{ijt} = \beta_0 + \beta_1 DFI\_Plant_{ijt} + \beta_2 DFI\_Sector_{ijt} + \beta_3 DFI\_Plant_{ijt} *DFI\_Sector_{ijt} + \beta_4 X_{ijt} + \varepsilon_{ijt}$$

where Y_{ijt} is the (log) of output for plant i in sector j at time t, X_{ijt} are (log) inputs for production (skill labour, unskilled labour, capital), DFI_Plant_{ijt} is the share of equity participation at the plant level (which ranges from 0 to 100) and DFI_Sector_{jt} measures the presence of foreign ownership in the industry (proxy by foreign equity participation averaged over all plants in the sector, weighted by each plant's share in sectoral employment). If positive spillovers were present, the estimated coefficient of DFI_Sector_{jt} would be positive. The interaction term *DFI_Plant *DFI_Sector* helps to examine if the effects of presence of foreign firms on foreign firms is different than the effect on domestic firms. To the extent that foreign firms benefit from the presence of other foreign firms, β_3 would be positive. However, if joint ventures are affected negatively by the presence of foreign firms, then β_3 would be negative.

Hassan (2003) in his paper examined whether policies to promote FDI make economic sense. The study focused on the specific issue of whether spillovers related to production by multinational firms are sufficient to justify subsidies to FDI. It found that many developing countries offer a wide variety of tax breaks to FDI. The available evidence suggests that FDI is quite sensitive to host country's characteristics. Higher taxes deter foreign investment and a more educated workforce and larger consumer and industrial markets attract FDI. There is weak evidence, at best, that FDI generates positive spillovers for host economies. A commonly mentioned possibility is that FDI raises the productivity of domestic agents. While multinationals are attracted to high-productivity countries, and to high-productivity industries within these countries, there is little evidence at the firm or plant level that FDI raises the productivity of domestic enterprises. Plants in industries with a larger multinational presence tend to enjoy *lower* rates of productivity growth over time. Using a simple theoretical model, the study revealed that subsidies to FDI are more likely to be warranted where multinationals are intensive in the use of elasticity-supplied factors, the arrival of multinationals to a market does not lower the market share of domestic firms, and FDI generates strong positive productivity spillovers for domestic agents. On the basis of case studies, it is concluded that the existing empirical research suggests the first and third conditions are likely to hold.

FDI and Determinants

Davidson (1980) reviewed the role of host country's characteristics or determinants of FDI location pattern. The researcher analysed the effect of corporate experience on location decisions. Prior experience in a host country has found to be increased the firm's priority for projects in that country relative to other investment options. In addition, the experience level of the firm influenced the relative importance of different country characteristics in determining factor patterns. The study revealed that inexperienced firms exhibit greater preference for near, similar markets than firms with broader international experience. Market size and growth are widely associated with investment pattern. Tariff and non-tariff barriers to trade, input costs and geographic proximity affect the economics of direct investment. Legal, political and economic conditions are considered important in investment decisions. As firms gain experience, the location of foreign investment activity will increasingly represent an efficient response to global economic opportunities and conditions.

FDI is the investment decision of profit-maximizing firms facing world-wide competition and where significant differences in cost structures (due to, say, factor productivity, wage differential) justify cross-border investment and production. Some common determinants are as follows:

(a) *Institutional features of the host country:* degree of political stability and government intervention in the economy; the existence of property law legislation; the property and tax system; adequate infrastructure, etc.

(b) *Economic factors:* trade and investment regime; the degree of 'openness' of the host countries; the absorptive capacity and growth prospects of the host country; fix and variable costs of production relocation; the degree of monopolistic competition which prevents the entry of other (domestic and foreign) firms; general macro-economic performance (inflation, monetary and fiscal policy) etc.

(c) *Policy-related factors:* fiscal (tax rebates and exemptions) and financial incentives (subsidised loans); laws that restrict FDI in certain sectors on the ground of political sensitivity of certain industries (oil, broadcasting, etc.); policy that restricts the degree of foreign ownership (temporal or permanent), the remittance of interest, dividends and fees for technology and the shares allowed to foreign-owned firms through limits on capital repatriation, minimum investment, etc.

(d) *Characteristics of the labour force:* education, skills, etc.

Edwards (1990) analysed the determinants of OECD foreign direct investment into LDCs during the period 1971–81. The researcher used two groups of variables to explain DFISH (total OECD direct foreign investment distributed across countries), and DFI/GDP (average level of DFI relative to the average GDP during 1971–1981 in a specific country). The first group relates to economic variables that summarize the structure of each country. The second group captures political and institutional characteristics of each country.

Edwards postulated that FDI was affected by:

(–) Real per capita income as a proxy for (the inverse) return on capital. According to the theory, DCs will invest in LDCs that have higher return on capital. Therefore, countries with lower income per capita will tend to receive a higher share of FDI.

(+) The ratio of foreign trade to GDP as a measure of degree of openness of the host country.

(+) Country's real GDP as a proxy for large markets. It was included in the DFISH regressions to account for size of the economy and potential extent of economies of scale.

(+) Domestic investment ratio which was assumed to complement FDI.

(–) The share of government consumption in GDP as a proxy for size of government. This variable reflects the host country's stance towards the private initiative.

(+) The Summer and Heston measure of the real exchange rate as a proxy of the country's degree of international competitiveness.

(?) Different measures of each country's structure production (shares of manufacture, mining and agriculture relative total GDP). The sign of their coefficient was not determined apriori.

(?) Dummy variables for Latin America and Asia.

Edwards dealt with data availability by constructing proxies or excluding the variable if it was not possible to construct the appropriate proxy. No variable indicative of policy legislation (say, tax inducement) was included due to the lack of comparable data across countries.

Because of the presence of heteroscedasticity, the different equations were estimated using OLS with each country's population used as a weight. The results showed across regressions that, real

GDP, domestic investment ratio, the size of the government, and the international competitiveness indexes had the expected signs and were significant at conventional levels. The results suggest that structural reforms were likely to affect FDI.

After controlling for the economic variables, Edwards postulated that FDI was also affected by:

(–) The degree of political instability, which was proxied by the Cukierman-Edwards-Tabellini (CET) index. This index was constructed by fitting a probit equation for government changes in 79 countries over the period 1948–82. The explanatory variables included were significant political events which signal crisis and structural variables that accounted for country differences. The CET index was estimated for each country in the sample during 1971–82 and then, averaging the estimated probabilities of government change during that period.

(–) The degree of political polarization and violence. This variable was constructed as the sum of the yearly frequency of political assassinations, violent riots, protests and political attacks, and political motivated strikes.

The econometric results showed that most of the economic variables have the expected sign and are significant. The joint test of significance on all the economic variables as a group (F-test) indicates that the null hypothesis was rejected at a high level of significance. The proxy for degree of political instability had always the expected sign but was significant in three out of five regressions. The index of political violence was never significant and sometimes had the wrong sign. Again, joint test of significance on all the political variables indicates that the null hypothesis was rejected at high levels of significance.

Therefore, Edwards concluded that economic and political variables explain the distribution and magnitude of FDI. In order to assess the relative importance of these variables, Edwards constructed standardized estimates of each coefficient. He found that the relative importance of the political instability variable was not very high compared with other regressors suggesting that a better political environment would not increase FDI as much as structural reforms (change in government size,, increasing the degree of openness, etc.).

Balasubramanyam and Mahambare (2003) analysed the determinants of FDI and its efficacy in promoting development in India. The study examined the various reasons for the relatively low volumes of FDI in India. It argued that the volume of FDI a country was able to attract was a function of its structure, stage of development, sources of FDI it had access to and the volume of co operant factors it possesses. The study discussed the India's foreign trade and FDI regimes in two distinct phases: the pre-1991 phase and the post-1991 phase. It also discussed the reasons for India's poor performance in attracting FDI in comparison to China. The study found that the volume of FDI in India was much lower than that in other developing countries, and was well below the government's target of US$ 10 billion of FDI inflows per annum.

The researcher argued that although FDI was a superb catalyst of development, large volumes of it alone may be ineffective in promoting growth in the absence of preconditions necessary for efficient operations of foreign affiliates. For these and other reasons, discussed in the study, exhortations that India should throw open all doors to FDI may be misplaced. And China, which had been attracted relatively large volumes of FDI, may not be a role model for India.

The study only considered the overall policy framework and product market as the determinants of attracting FDI. However, there were no established determinants to the foreign investors to invest their capital in other countries.

Baniak et al. (2002) carried out a study on determinants of FDI in transition economies. According to them, 'FDI brings host countries capital, productive facilities, and technology transfers as well as new jobs and management expertise. Thus, it is important to understand why in many countries FDI inflow is lower than expected.' The goal of the study was to explore some important factors determining flow of FDI into transition countries. In particular, they analysed the legal environment for FDI in some transition economies. The study modelled the impact of stability of the economic and legal environment on the pattern of FDI. The study found that (i) higher variability of basic macroeconomic fundamentals reduces the flow of FDI; (ii) high volatility of fiscal and business regulations makes the inflow of FDI smaller; and (iii) macro-economic and legal instability leads to adverse selection of the investors. Based on theoretical findings, the researchers formulated a clear message for policy makers stating that in order to expect significant flow of long-term and non-speculative foreign capital, first of all, a stable economic and institutional environment is needed.

Using a panel data of 95 countries and eight MENA countries over the 1980–2001 period, Hassan (2003) examined the important factors that contribute to FDI and economic growth in the world and compares them with those of MENA countries. The eight MENA countries covered in this study were Egypt, Iran, Jordan, Saudi Arabia, Morocco, Tunisia, Turkey and Yemen. This study was in line with previous studies investigating how country factor conditions affect the amount of FDI. It provides a special contribution to FDI theories by focusing on technological, particularly communications, infrastructure, an area of increasing importance in global competition, and by comparing MENA economies to developed ones. The purpose of the study was to investigate the differences between the world and the MENA countries in market-factor determinants of FDI inflows. The central theme of the study was to ascertain whether FDI enhances or retards economic growth with special reference to information technology.

The study identified that FDI brings host countries capital, productive facilities, new technology and modern management know-how. It identified that information and communication technology (ICT) was essential to not only a country's growth, but also to develop its productive capacity in all sectors of the economy, and links its with the global economy and ensures competitiveness. The study found both growth and FDI were related to a host of macro-economic variables like ICT and globalization. The study also provided some policy recommendations for improving FDI inflows with special focus on trade facilitation, export processing zones, investment promotion agencies, export performance requirements and WTO rules and incentives.

The contribution of this study was that it went beyond the standard Granger causality econometric techniques employed in previous econometric work, and adopted a panel data approach within the framework of economic growth model, which was more comprehensive than others.

Lensink and Morrissey (2001) in a study examined the factors influencing FDI in lesser developed countries. The study intended to measure the magnitude and the direction of suspected determinants that heavily influence a firm's decision to invest in FDI in a least developed country (LDC). By utilizing the World Bank's World Development Data from 1997 in an OLS regression model, the study also demonstrated the nature of key determinants of FDI. It also examined why firms decide to invest in an LDC. In order to maximize FDI, it highlighted to make policy changes in the host country with necessary information for the investors.

In this study FDI has been considered as a dependent variable and GDP and other endogenous factors as independent variables. Besides, FDI has been measured as a percentage of GDP. The study identifies that the relationship between FDI and GDP is positive. It also suggests that MNCs are attracted to areas that contain large amounts of people.

The most important finding of this study is that the education in a country plays an important role in attracting FDI. While the urban population and past economic performance are important, the human capital of a nation is equally essential in attracting FDI. Education, especially in technical disciplines, provides the people with the skills that are demanded by the MNCs, this study highlighted. The study also found that LDCs that have highly limited resources should invest in the education of the people first in order to increase their probability of attracting FDI.

Liu et al. (2002) investigated the contribution of FDI to economic growth in Arabian developing countries. Using data from an Arab country, the study showed that FDI contributes to higher growth both directly and indirectly through its effects on exports. Knowledge of the positive influence of FDI on growth could enable businesses to have a stronger negotiation position vis-à-vis the host country. Drawing on the findings and the methodology in the study, business decision-makers could enhance their measurement of expected risks by estimating the effects of increased FDI to the host country. The results also highlighted the potential for FDI to contribute to political stability through efficient allocation of corporate resources.

For international financial institutions, politicians and the vast majority of economists FDI appears to be a sort of panacea for every economic problem in the emerging market economies; its positive impact on economic growth has acquired the status of conventional fact. Economic theory suggests that unfettered international capital inflows foster efficient allocation of resources, which by itself should promote growth. The economic benefits of FDI are considered to be two-fold: first, it can help countries if domestic savings are insufficient to finance economic expansion; and secondly, a foreign corporate presence is associated with positive externalities. The almost desperate efforts of many countries to attract as much FDI as possible indirectly support the theory. However, substantial gains of inward FDI for the host countries have been much more asserted than confirmed by empirical evidence. The results of a rapidly growing number of empirical studies on the relation between FDI and economic growth differ, although most studies start with essentially the same benchmark cross-country growth model. In many studies dealing with subsets of the countries, FDI or FDI in combination with some other factor(s) is positively related to growth, while several studies have found no significant relationship between FDI and growth. Most studies have stressed the differences among the sets of countries included regarding their trade policies, institutional characteristics, or level of development. More than two decades ago Bhagwati (1978) suggested that the impact of FDI on growth depends on the trade policy of a host country: in export-promoting countries FDI would increase growth, while it would have no impact in a country with an import substitution trade policy. This hypothesis was also tested by Sapsford and Balasubramanyam (2003) and the outcome that came was mixed. Blomström et al. (1999) found that FDI only promotes growth in higher-income developing countries. Empirical studies on the subject have therefore not refuted the statement that 'in general, the results of these studies indicate that the size of inward FDI stocks or flows, relative to GDP, is not related in any consistent way to rates of growth' (Lipsey, 2002).

The next set of studies examined deals with FDI in developing countries. Nunnenkamp and Spatz (2002), studying a sample of 28 developing countries during the 1987–2000 period, find significant Spearman correlations between FDI flows and per capita GNP, risk factors, years of schooling, foreign trade restrictions, complementary production factors such as administrative bottlenecks, cost factors, population, GNP growth, firm entry restrictions, post-entry restrictions and technology regulation all proved to be non-significant. However, when regressions were performed separately for the non-traditional factors, in which traditional factors (i.e., population and per capita GNP).

Holland and others (2000) reviewed several studies for Eastern and Central Europe, searching for evidence of the importance of market size and growth potential as determinants of FDI. Townsend (2003) analysed the decades of 1970 and 1980 and addressed the endogeneity problem between FDI and growth by developing a system of simultaneous equations. Also, FDI was alternately measured as a flow, and as a stock. Market size turned out to be more important for

FDI flows than growth. The trade surplus presents a negative sign and is significant for FDI, while the flow of FDI decreases as the nominal wage decreases. On the other hand, the impact of FDI on economic growth is quite limited.

Campos and Kinoshita (2003) used panel data to analyse 25 transition economies between 1990 and 1998. They reached the conclusion that for said set of countries FDI is influenced by economy clusters, market size, the low cost of labour and abundant natural resources. Besides all these factors, the following variables presented significant results: sound institutions, trade openness, and lower restrictions to FDI inflows.

Garibaldi and others (2001), based on a dynamic panel of 26 transition economies between 1990 and 1999, analysed a large set of variables that were divided into macro-economic factors, structural reforms, institutional and legal frameworks, initial conditions and risk analyses. The results indicated that macro-economic variables, such as market size, fiscal deficit, inflation and exchange regime, risk analysis, economic reforms, trade openness, availability of natural resources, and barriers to investment and bureaucracy all had the expected signs and were significant.

Causality between FDI and Economic Growth

The linkage between FDI and economic growth has been the subject of considerable research for many decades. However, the link between FDI and economic growth, which has been subjected to empirical scrutiny, remains the subject of debate. There is renewed interest in this area of research is recent years largely due to the globalization of the world economy and to the recognition that multinational corporations play an increasingly important role in trade, capital accumulation and economic growth in developing countries. Three developments have added an additional twist to the literature on the FDI-led growth study, particularly in the area of empirical studies. First, previous econometric studies based on the assumption that there is one-way causality from FDI to GDP growth have been criticized in more recent studies. In other words, not only can FDI 'Granger-cause' GDP growth (with either positive or negative effects), but GDP growth can also affect the inflow of FDI. Failure to consider either direction of such causality can lead to an inefficient estimation of the impacts of FDI on economic growth and hence is subject to the problem of simultaneity bias. Second, the so-called 'new growth theory' has resulted in some reappraisal of the determinants of growth in modelling the role played by FDI in the growth process. Third, new developments in econometric theory, such as time-series concepts of co-integration and causality testing, have further expanded the debate on the FDI-growth relationship.

Empirical studies on the FDI-growth nexus can be categorized into two broad groups: (i) the studies which focus on the role of multinational firms and on the determinants of FDI; and (ii) the studies which very recently, applied causality tests based on time-series data to examine the nature of causal relationship between FDI and output growth.

In the second group of studies on the FDI-growth nexus, some scholars have applied time-series data analysis and directed their FDI-led growth studies towards the use of the Granger no-causality testing procedure. However, one of the problems with these studies is their arbitrary choice of the lag length used for causality test. Furthermore, these studies have applied F-test statistics for the causality test (United Nations, 2002). It is now well established in the econometric literature that the F-test statistics is not valid if times-series data are integrated as argued by Gujarati (1995).

Some empirical studies have examined the FDI-led growth hypothesis in the case of the Chinese economy. However, these studies suffer from two major problems. First, none of them have tested for the direction of causality between GDP growth and FDI inflow; they have implicitly assumed a one-way causality running from FDI to GDP growth and estimated impacts of FDI based on such a causality which cannot yield reliable conclusions. Second, most of these studies have used cross-section data, the validity of which is also subject to debate.

The main arguments against the use of cross-section data and in favour of the use of times-series data have been that cross-country studies implicitly impose or assume a common economic structure and similar production technology across different countries which is most likely not true; and further, the economic growth of a country is influenced not only by FDI and other factory inputs, but also by a host of domestic policies such as monetery fiscal and external policies. Finally, the significance of the conclusions drawn from cross-section data is claimed not to be sufficient in finding a long-run causal relationship (Enders, 2002). Some studies have attempted to overcome the problems with cross-section data analysis and the simultaneity bias by using a simultaneous equations model.

As far as the model specification is concerned, most of these studies have used a simple two-variable relationship. It should be pointed out that the approach of using a two-variable framework in the causality test without considering the effects of other variables (such as export, import and investment growth) is subject to a possible specification bias. It is established in the econometric literature that causality tests are sensitive to model selection and functional form (Gujarati, 1995). Reza and Rashid (1997) have pointed out an important finding that omitting the import variable in the VAR estimation process can result in both 'type I' and 'type II' errors, that is, spurious rejection of one causality as well as spurious detection of it.

Another problem that has often been ignored and/or has not been dealt with adequately in the literature, yet far more important, is the endogenous nature of a production function as argued by Greenway and Sapsford (1994). Therefore, studies, which do not consider the endogenous nature of the growth process, are subject to a simultaneously bias. The use of a VAR model has proved to generate more reliable estimates in a endogenous context (Gujarati, 1995).

Although the choice of the optimal lag length in the causality test has been noted in some studies, very few studies have considered the problem of the sensitivity of the causality test results under different lag structures. It is vital to obtain consistent causality results for least some consecutive lag structures along with the optimal choice of the lag, using some conventional criterio such as Akaike Information Criteria (AIC) and/or the Schwartz Criterion (SC).

Theoretically, the causality between FDI and GDP growth could run in either direction: FDI could promote further GDP growth as postulated, among others. Recently, some economists, in the line with the 'new growth theory', argue that through the capital accumulation in the recipient economy, FDI is expected to generate non-convex growth by encouraging the incorporation of new inputs and foreign technologies in the production function of the recipient economy. Further, through knowledge transfers, FDI is expected to augment the existing stock of knowledge in the recipient economy through labour training and skill acquisition, on the one hand, and through the introduction of alternative management practices and organizational arrangements, on the other (De Mello, 1997). As a result, foreign investors may increase the productivity of the recipient and economy and FDI can be deemed to be a catalyst for domestic investment and technological progress.

However, the causality could also run the opposite way: rapid GDP growth could induce the inflow of FDI. This is because rapid GDP growth will usually create a high level of capital requirement (and a resource gap) in the host country, and hence the host country will demand more FDI by offering concessional terms for FDI to attract overseas investors. Further, rapid economic growth in the host country (for example, in China) will build up the confidence of overseas investors investing in the host country. More importantly, rapid economic growth, accompanied by an increased higher per capita income, will create huge opportunities for FDI to invest industrial sectors, consumer durable goods production and infrastructure in the host country.

It should be pointed out that direction of the causality between FDI and GDP growth depends on many economic as well as political and cultural factors, such as the level of economic development, the productivity of FDI and the policies shaping FDI inflow. Since the adoption of the open-door policy, China has achieved high rates of economic growth. Some sectors, such as the infrastructure, became a serious bottleneck to further economic development, which has become available for the introduction of foreign capital. During the 1990s, China's rapid economic growth was increasingly dependent on the huge FDI inflow, while its rapid economic growth also attracted more capital form overseas.

II

Literature on MNCs, FDI and Economic Growth in India

A large number of articles, books and reports have been published on the topic MNCs and FDI in India. Some institutions or government organizations, especially RBI, have also conducted studies on investment by MNCs and their operations on a regular basis. Although most of these studies have been conducted from perspectives of MNCs some of them have been undertaken to judge the impact of MNCs operations on technology transfer, balance of payment problem and export performance in the context of liberalization programme introduced by the Government of India in 1991. This section reviews some of the important studies on MNCs, FDI and economic growth in India.

Kishor (2003) analysed the trends of global FDI inflows into India and some other selected countries. The author evaluated the sector-wise, country-wise and state-wise inflows of FDI in India as percentage of GDP and gross fixed capital formation. In the study the author examined the conceptual definition of FDI and economic growth and development and the benefits of FDI to developing countries. The study revealed that developed countries received major share of the world FDI inflows over the decade.

The researcher examined the prospects and challenges of FDI in India at a greater length and some policy measures are suggested to enhance FDI inflows into India. The study was made on the basis of secondary data sources that will help to other researchers and policy makers to take further decisions regarding FDI in India.

A study was conducted by Pant (1989) on a financial model of MNCs to explore the impact of tax rate or currency devaluation on investment or employment of MNCs affiliates. At the beginning of the study, the author explains the model in details and then shows its application. The model presented in the study shows that an increase in tax rate by home country of MNCs would promote investment and employment in a host country at the expense of the home country. Similarly, an increase in the host country's tax rate would reduce investment and employment in the host country. The study also shows that a devaluation of host country's currency reduces the outflows of repatriated earnings from subsidiary company (host country) to parent company (home country). As a result of this, devaluation of host country's currency would increase reinvestment of repatriable earnings in the host country.

Pant (1993) examined the export performance of MNCs in India. To measure the export performance of MNCs, the researcher also examined the export performance of Indian local companies in manufacturing sector and compares between the two groups. The results of the comparative analyses indicated that there was no significant difference in export efforts of MNCs and local companies with the sole exception of the pharmaceutical industry. The study results also indicated that MNCs orientation towards the domestic market is even greater than that of local companies. Based on the results, the author concluded that India's ardent efforts in the recent years to attract MNCs for its export effort are unlikely to produce fruit.

Chakraborty and Nunnenkamp (2006) observed that FDI has boomed in post-reform India. Moreover, the composition and type of FDI has changed considerably since India has opened up its market to world. They assessed the growth implications of FDI in India by subjecting industry-specific FDI and output data to Granger causality tests within a panel co-integration framework. The study found out that the growth effects of FDI vary widely across sectors. FDI stocks and output are mutually reinforcing in the manufacturing sector. In sharp contrast, any causal relationship is absent in the primary sector. Most strikingly, the researcher find out only transitory effects of FDI on output in the services sector, which attracted the bulk of FDI in the post-reform era. By using industry-specific FDI and output data and applying a panel co-integration framework that integrates long-run and short-run dynamics of the FDI-growth relationship, the study revealed important gaps in the earlier literature. For the Indian economy, as a whole, the study found that FDI stocks and output are co-integrated in the long run. The authors examined, at the aggregate level, Granger causality tests to point to feedback effects between FDI and output both in the short and the long run. However, the impact of output growth in attracting FDI is relatively stronger than that of FDI in inducing economic growth. They pointed out that causation is mainly running from output growth to FDI stocks.

The study mentioned that it may be tempting to conclude from the sector-specific results that the pre-reform approach to FDI in India was not so bad after all. Traditionally, selective approval procedures and performance requirements were meant to promote FDI in technologically advanced and more export-oriented manufacturing industries, and to discourage FDI in the tertiary sector where foreign investors might replace local service providers. However, such a conclusion would be misconceived. The results of the study supported the view that the quality of FDI matters at least as much as the volume of FDI for the growth implications in host economies. The study identified that growth implications depend on various factors, including absorptive capacity and local skills, technological spillovers and linkages between foreign and local firms, and export orientation—all of which may differ across industries and sectors in the host economy. They suggested that all this does not speak in favour of selective FDI policies and policy makers attempting to target preferred types of FDI in specific industries. For such an approach to be successful in attracting growth-promoting FDI, policy makers would have to know exactly about the quality of each FDI proposal and its effects on the local economy. The study concluded that differences in the FDI-growth relationship suggest that FDI is unlikely to work wonders in India if only remaining regulations were relaxed and still more industries opened up to FDI.

Kumar (1994) made a well-documented case study to contribute to the current debate on the role of MNCs in the context of the ongoing economic reforms. At the beginning of the study, Kumar stated a brief summary of the history of foreign investment regulation introduced by the Government of India and argued that foreign investment policy was more restrictive during 1970s and 1980s. For instance, the author pointed out that by introducing FERA in 1973, the government forced foreign companies in India to reduce their foreign equity holdings to 40 per cent.

Goyal (1995) in his study examined the role of MNCs in the Third World countries with a special reference to India. The author argued that MNCs are interested in only those businesses, which generate maximum surpluses for themselves, and it is none of their concern to promote development of the host countries. However, MNCs do not hesitate to project themselves as the real promoters of development in the country of their operations. Throughout the article, the author produced many examples and data by which he tried to prove that the existence of MNCs in the developing countries like India is another obstacle to development. The researcher indicated that MNCs' export efforts were mostly in the nature of inter-branch transactions, which gave them a unique opportunity to conceal actual profits through transfer pricing mechanism. Dividend remittances and payments for technology fees have further worsened the already adverse trade balance of the country. Criticizing the ongoing privatization policy of the Government of India, he indicated that it has increased the scope of take over of public sector companies by MNCs. Commenting on the foreign portfolio investment, the researcher stated that portfolio investment with the regime of free convertibility has made the stock exchanges a major field for MNCs operations and consequently foreign portfolio investment far outstripped FDI. In the concluding section, the author emphasized formulating appropriate policy framework best suited to the conditions of the developing countries. However, what type of policy framework would be appropriate for developing countries like India is not indicated by the author.

Varshney (1995) in his study evaluated the impact of the New Economic Policy (NEP) introduced in India in 1991. In the opening discussion the author explains how MNCs help developing countries including India in locating and exploiting their natural resources, in establishing new industries, and in stimulating capital formation. In the middle part of the article, he has narrated a brief history of India's policy towards foreign investment. In the last part, the author has highlighted regulation under the NEP and has shown the trend of MNCs to invest in India before and after the liberalization. Showing a very impressive growth of foreign investment in India after the liberalization period, the author concludes that the changes in the foreign investment policy made in India in 1991 have created a favourable impression among the foreign investors.

Chaudhuri (1995) focused on the impact of MNCs operating in Indian manufacturing sector in the context of the NEP. In the article, the government policies on FDI since 1991 are discussed and their implications are analysed. The researcher especially highlighted the response of MNCs to the NEP and its impact on indigenous firms. He shows that MNCs have reacted favourably to the NEP to enter and grow in India. A large number of MNCs have acquired Indian companies or increased their equity stake in the existing companies and have edged out the Indian partners. The author also attempts to probe whether MNCs are responding to the NEP by investing primarily in the export market or the domestic market. On this issue, data produced by the author reveals that they (MNCs) are still primarily interested in the domestic market, and it is doubtful whether export-oriented investments by MNCs will increase in future. Finally, the author proposes to change the present economic policies saying, 'a strategic intervention on the part of the government is required to take care of the negative features of the operations of TNCs and to ensure that the country gains from their investment'.

Globerman et al. (1996) examined MNCs' responses to economic reforms introduced in the early 1990s in India. The authors at first outline India's recent reforms particularly as they affect MNCs operations, and then they examine how the reforms have influenced the behaviour and performance of Swedish multinational affiliates operating in India. The study shows that after the introduction of the reforms, investment and productivity of the selected companies have increased; however, the liberalization policy failed to increase employment. It is because it provided MNCs with an opportunity to move towards more efficient capital-intensive technology that helps increase productivity at the cost of employment. The study also indicated that their response in terms of export was also relatively weak, whereas attracting export-oriented investment was one of the primary goals of the newly introduced reforms. The study is unable to offer any explanation as to why the selected companies did not respond by increasing exports even after enjoying many incentives through the reforms.

Chugan (1997) conducted a comparative study on export performance of MNCs affiliates and local enterprises in Indian automobile ancillary industry. The study pointed out that export performance of Indian local companies is relatively poor on account of the unavailability of complex machinery required for producing high quality products for export. Hence, it is expected that the MNCs affiliates with the latest equipment and technology will have relatively greater hold over exports. But, the results of the study indicated that in spite of access to foreign technology and global market, the export performance of MNCs affiliates is not better than that of selected local companies. In the light of the results, the researcher concluded that MNCs, which supply better technology to their affiliates, are interested more in the host country's domestic market than the export market.

Conclusion

Thus, the relationship between FDI and economic growth has long been a subject of great interest in the field of international development and has attracted attention from the economists in the last two decades. In the era of volatile flows of global capital, the stability of FDI emerges as an effective channel to faster growth in developing countries, particularly in relation to least developed countries (LDCs). The neo-classical models of growth as well as endogenous growth models provide the basis for most of the empirical work on the FDI-growth relationship.

3

Foreign Direct Investment in India

Policies and Trends

An Overview of Indian Economy

India is the second largest country in the world, both in terms of population and area. It has 16 per cent of the world's population and roughly 12 per cent of the world's land mass. It is also the sixth largest economy in terms of gross domestic product (GDP).

India is, without doubt, a key player in the world economy. The Indian economy is extremely diversified, ranging from technology to agriculture. Agricultural activity in India contributes only 23 per cent to the GDP, but employs approximately 65 per cent of the workforce. This places a burden on the Indian economy. On the other hand, India has the comparative advantage in terms of the considerable command of the English language and the technological abilities in certain sections of the population.

Some of the problems faced by the economy like inadequate employment opportunities, inequalities in the socio-economic status and poverty can prove disastrous to any globalizing economy. Some of the other concerns regarding the Indian economy are poor infrastructure, fiscal deficit and a large amount of non-performing assets (NPA).

India has changed from public sector domination in industries to an increasingly liberalized system, with both domestic and foreign players. It has also changed from a sellers' market with limited competition to a buyers' market with increased competition, from a country with quantitative restrictions and tariffs to quota-free and open economy and from a restricted financial market to a liberalized financial market with prudential norms. These changes are a testimony to the dynamic nature of the Indian economy. Some key strengths that India can leverage upon in creating its own indigenous industries can be its vast pool of human resources, natural resources and entrepreneurial talent. It should be noted that the country has a rich pool of skilled workers with the world's third largest reservoir of engineers and a handful of quality educational institutions.

Table 3.1 *GDP Growth in India (%) (calculated at 1999–2000 prices)*

Five year plans/FY		2000–2001	4.0 (7.7)
First Plan (1951–56)	3.6	2001–2002	5.8 (8.5)
Second Plan (1956–61)	4.2	2002–2003	4.0 (7.8)
Third Plan (1961–66)	2.7	2003–2004	8.5 (12.5)
Fourth Plan (1969–74)	2.05	2004–2005	6.9 (13.1)
Fifth Plan (1974–79)	4.83	2005–2006	9.4 (14.1)
Sixth Plan (1980–85)	5.54	2006–2007	9.6 (15.0)
Seventh Plan (1985–90)	6.02	2007–08	9.3
Eighth Plan (1992–97)	6.02	2008–09	6.7
Ninth Plan (1997–02)	5.35	2009–10	8.4
Tenth Plan (2002–07)	7.7	2010–11	8.3
Eleventh Plan (2007–12)	7.9	2011–12	6.5
Twelfth Plan (2012–17)	7.5 (p)	2012–13	7.5 (p)

Note: 1. Figures in parentheses have been calculated at current market prices.
2. P: Projected.

Source: Economic Survey 2011–2012, Government of India and Tenth Five-Year Plan document.

The Indian economy achieved a growth rate of above 7 per cent in the recent past. This robust performance of the economy was due to high growth rates in service sector and an economic environment that provided a backdrop conducive to the Indian economy. Another factor that led to this upswing in the economy was the continued maintenance of relative stability of prices.

A strong Balance of Payment (BoP) position in recent years has resulted in a steady accumulation of foreign exchange reserves. The level of foreign exchange reserves crossed the US$ 100 billion mark on December 19, 2003 and was in the range of US$ 130 billion to US$ 140 billion in 2005. Capital inflows, increased exports and the valuation gains arising from appreciation of the major non-US dollar global currencies against US dollar contributed to such a rise in forex reserves.

The current account of BoP has been in surplus since 2001–02. While the trade deficit increased, the deficit was neutralized by a higher surplus in the 'invisibles' contributed mainly by software service exports and private transfers. Growth momentum in exports has been maintained; India has registered a growth of 20 per cent in exports in the last few years. Despite a higher value of total imports in the last few years, mainly due to the petroleum and oil imports, India did not suffer a negative trade balance as it was highly compensated by the service exports. The main contributors to capital account surplus were the banking capital inflows, foreign institutional investments and other capital inflows. However, the latest statistics of Reserve Bank of India shows that the country has again slipped into current account deficit in 2005–06.

Indian economy is considered as a 'developing economy' based on its characteristic features but it is also called an 'underdeveloped economy' mainly because of the its low per capita income, low literacy rate and rapid population growth. The salient features of Indian economy can be specified as:

(i) Predominance of agriculture
(ii) Rapid population growth
(iii) Low per capita income (GDP per capita)
(iv) Unemployment
(v) Capital-scarce economy

In 1991, Indian economy faced a severe crisis. The symptoms of the crisis were evident in the second half of eighties itself in the form of macroeconomic imbalances. Pressures generated by the large and persistent fiscal deficits and foreign exchange crisis, high tariffs and the inefficiencies generated by the industrial licensing system have led to a huge deficit in the balance of payments position. Adverse global developments in 1990–91, i.e., the slowdown in world trade following recession in the industrial world, the disruption in Eastern Europe and the Gulf crisis of August 1990, aggravated the crisis. The current account deficit soared to a level of 3.2 per cent of GDP in 1990–91, which by all means was unsustainable. There was a massive shortage of the foreign exchange reserves. Despite withdrawal of US$ 2.5 billion from the International Monetary Fund (IMF) under the Contingency and Compensatory Financing Facility, the foreign currency assets dipped from US$ 3.4 billion at the end of March 1990 to a very low level of US$ 975 million on 12 July 1991. The amount was equivalent to barely a week's value of import bills. India responded to the crisis by simultaneously implementing measures for stabilization and structural reforms.

The Government of India implemented the following stabilization measures in 1991 in order to correct the imbalances in the Indian economy:

(i) Devaluation of the currency followed by partial or full convertibility in current account.
(ii) Cut in government expenditures to bring about reduction in budget deficit. For instance, budget deficit reduced from 9 per cent of GDP to 6.5 per cent of GDP during 1991 to 1992.
(iii) Liberalization of domestic markets, which included elimination of price controls and cutting down subsidies on agricultural inputs and products.

Apart from the above, the government also took following measures as part of the economic reforms:

(i) Liberalization of trade and the elimination of the protective entry barriers into industry with a view to make the industry more competitive. This meant delicensing and deregulation of industry, trade and commerce.
(ii) Liberalization of banking system and reducing the role of the state or public sector banks.
(iii) Lessening the control of the monetary authorities on policies such that the rates of interest in money market would be determined by market forces (and not by the Reserve Bank of India, in exercising the powers vested on it as the central bank of the country) and reduction in Statutory Liquidity Ratio (percentage of aggregate demand and time deposits that the commercial banks are required to invest in specified government securities).
(iv) Gradual privatization of commercial, financial and industrial enterprises.
(v) Reduction in the role of the state in the social sectors as well, like that in the education and health sectors, besides gradual move in the direction of the principle of cost recovery.
(vi) Tax reforms for rationalization of the tax structure.
(vii) Poverty alleviation programmes through the creation of social development fund.

It is clear from the above measures that the new industrial policy of 1991 has effected some very fundamental policy changes such as near abolition of licensing, easing of the rigors of MRTPA (Monopoly and Restrictive Trade Practices Act) and FERA (Foreign Exchange Regulation Act), reduced list of industries for the public sector, automatic approvals of foreign technology agreements and for 51 per cent foreign equity participation, private investment in infrastructure, liberal location policy for industry, freer import of capital goods, deregulation in small-scale industrial units and liberal policy measures for attracting foreign direct investment (FDI), and non-resident Indian investment. The main objective of the liberalized policy measures was to enhance the productivity and competitive efficiency in the industrial sector.

India's economy encompasses traditional village farming, modern agriculture, handicrafts, a wide range of modern industries, and a multitude of support services. Government controls have been reduced on foreign trade and investment, and privatization of domestic output has proceeded slowly. The economy has posted an excellent average growth rate of 6 per cent since 1990, reducing poverty by about 10 percentage points. India has been capitalizing on its large numbers of well-educated people skilled in the English language to become a major exporter of software services and software workers. Despite strong growth, the World Bank and others worried about the continuing public sector budget deficit, running at approximately 10 per cent of GDP as per various estimates.

Economic Growth and Indicators

India recorded one of the highest growth rates in the world in the past two years, second only to China, among the emerging market economies. According to the World Development Indicators 2004, India became the fourth largest economy in terms of purchasing power parity, after the US, China and Japan. Domestic developments—largely immune to the global business cycle—powered a surge in real GDP growth to 8.2 per cent—the highest in 15 years. This is the growth trend India was looking for becoming on par with China and developed nations. The trend shows, after 1991 reforms, the growth has been consistently good.

Growth Sectors

The main contributing factors for India's GDP are services, agriculture and industrial output. Currently, services sector dominates with a contribution of 57.5 per cent to the overall GDP. Agriculture and industry sectors contribute 20.5 per cent and 22 per cent respectively. Year-wise trend of percentage contribution by each sector shows that service and industry sectors are increasingly contributing to the GDP while the percentage relevance of agriculture is coming down in spite of the fact that 65 per cent of the Indian population is employed in agriculture (Economic Survey, 2006–07).

External Sector

Buoyant software exports and record workers' remittances led to a current account surplus during the past few years even as the merchandise trade deficit expanded due to the strong industrial recovery underway. The sustained buoyancy in merchandise exports was led by manufactures, reflecting structural changes and the growing competitiveness of the industrial sector. The exports now stand at US$ 57.24 billion and imports at US$ 74.15 billion.

The external sector plays a key role in enabling the conditions to accelerate the pace of the external liberalization process. Despite the international uncertainties, Indian external sector is in a strong position and driving the macroeconomic strength of the country. Global imbalances and their disruptive impact on currency markets, hardening of interest rates, volatility in crude oil prices, etc., continue to be some of the major uncertainties and risks faced by the economy. The economic survey of the year 2004–05 had hinted that the balance of payments (BoP) scenario appears to be resilient and strong even after the increase in the imports. The sustained momentum of the manufacturing sector has helped greatly in the growth of exports. The export of services like software, business and other commercial services has also been playing a significant role in improving the BoP situation in the country. The forex reserves position is also very comfortable due to the increasing capital inflows into the country. The image of India from a land of farmers has changed to that of a technology hub and the country is seen as an international destination for R&D, engineering designs and telecommunications, superspeciality health care and a manufacturing hub for high technology products. In the area of biotechnology, India has tremendous potential to become a global R&D player with the changed patent laws. The high skilled Indian workforce has also imparted a comparative advantage for the country's software industry increasing the software service exports, thereby carving a niche for the country in IT and IT-enabled services. The global demand for Indian exports had witnessed a rise of 20 to 25 per cent during last four years and has been witnessing a consistent upward rate (26% in 2004–05). Further export growth is possible if it is supported with an increase in the FDI limits in export-oriented sectors. An increase in the FDI would bring with it better technology, human capital formation, exports and increased productivity. The country also witnessed the appreciation in the value of the rupee with respect to the US dollar in the recent past.

There was a rise in the case of imports in the country; this growth in the imports was also a broad-based one with a surge in import of food, capital goods, raw materials, intermediates and consumer goods. Imports of capital goods accelerated from 6.3 per cent in 2001–02 to above 20 per cent in 2002–03. This rose further to 27.3 per cent in

2003–04 and 35 per cent in 2004–05 led by import of transport equipments, machinery and manufacture of metals. Trade is important for the economy of any country and the opportunities for the improvement in trade are further aided by the formation of trade groups like SAFTA (South Asian Free Trade Association) with the SAARC nations. Even though trade prospects will be high in the coming years, there are certain threats like firmness of the global oil prices, volatility of major currencies and the risk of interest rate hikes in developed countries. India also needs micro-strategies to put export growth on priority. There is also a need for sustained efforts towards the service sector in which the country has the potential to emerge as a major player.

Balance of Payments

The overall strengthening of the BoP situation was reflected in an unprecedented accretion to India's foreign exchange reserves, which, by March 2004, touched US$ 113 billion, the sixth highest in the world. The BoP scenario has been showing a less negative trend over the recent years due to reduction in imports relative to exports.

Exchange Rate

Over the past two decades, rupee has dropped consistently vis-à-vis the dollar but during the past few years, it has strengthened due to consolidating Indian economy and global weakening of US dollar. The expected deregulation of the Chinese currency in the coming years would further strengthen the rupee.

Industrial Sector

Industrial sector in India contributes a meagre 27 per cent of the country's GDP. This is mainly because of the fact that India's competency lies in the services sector. In 2003–04 and 2004–05, the Index of Industrial Production (IIP) grew by 6.9 per cent and 8.4 per cent respectively with the manufacturing sector being the driving force behind this growth with a contribution of almost 80 per cent. In the last 10 years, the highest growth rate of the IIP was achieved in 1995–96 with 13 per cent and the lowest being 2.7 per cent in 2001–02 (Economic Survey, 2005–06, 2006–07).

Agricultural Sector

More than 65 per cent of the country's population depends on the agricultural sector, which ironically produces only 23 per cent of the

GDP. In India, around 45 per cent of the total land is cultivated. Rice, wheat, pulses and oilseeds dominate the agricultural production in India. Besides, crops like millet, corn (maize) and sorghum are also grown in large quantities. India is the largest producer of tea, jute and fibres like jute. Among livestock, cattle and buffalo are found in great numbers in India. Indian total milk production is the highest in the world. In terms of area, India tops the list of total irrigated land in the world. Among cereal production, India is placed third, being the second largest producer of wheat and rice and the largest producer of pulses. Dairy farming, fishing and forestry are important fields of agricultural sector. However, the potential of the Indian agriculture as a profitable activity has not been realized as yet.

Infrastructure Sector

For the development of any country, infrastructure comprising transportation (railways, roads and civil aviation), communication, water supply and sanitation forms one of the most critical aspects. Infrastructure is one of the most important factors for high and sustained growth as well as alleviation of poverty. India has been actively engaged in chalking out the appropriate policy framework which gives the private sector enough confidence in investing in the infrastructure sector, but simultaneously keeps adequate checks and balances through competition and regulation. Several fiscal incentives were announced by the government to boost investment in infrastructure projects. Ten-year tax holiday offered to projects in core sectors like roads, highways, waterways, water supply, sanitation and solid waste management systems can now be availed of during the initial 20 years. Projects in airports, ports, inland ports, industrial parks and generation and distribution of power can now avail of 10 year tax holidays during the initial 15 years.

Social Sector

Though the economy has been doing well over the past decade, the percentage population below poverty line still remains at a high 25 per cent and the unemployment rate is at a high 9.5 per cent. The growing concern for India is its large population and a still growing population rate of 1.44 per cent. India is stated to overtake China as the country with the largest population by 2010. The illiteracy percentage remains at a high 40.5 per cent with the male and female percentage illiteracy at 29.8 and 51.7 respectively. The HDI rank of India reported by UNDP is at 127.

As per the Human Development Reports, published annually by the UNDP, India has consistently improved its position on the human development front and is grouped among the countries registering 'medium human development'. However, some components of human development indicators for health and income continue to lag behind. India's rank in Gender Development Index continues to be low. High regional disparity across the states is also a cause for concern. Ongoing economic reforms and the national common minimal programme (NCMP) attach high priority to the development of the social sectors and encourage people to participate in the development process. Social sector programmes and their implementation largely come under the purview of the state governments. However, the Central Government augments the effort of the state governments by extending adequate resources to them. The total Central Government spending in the social sector has increased from ₹ 18,240 crore in 1995–96 to ₹ 52,090 crore in 2004–05.

Service Sector

The service sector now accounts for more than half of India's GDP: It has gained at the expense of both the agricultural and industrial sectors throughout the 1990s. The rise in the service sector's share in GDP marks a structural shift in the Indian economy and takes it closer to the fundamentals of a developed economy (in developed economies, the industrial and service sectors contribute a major share in GDP while agriculture accounts for a relatively lower share).

The service sector's share has grown from 43.69 per cent in 1990–91 to 55 per cent in 2003–04. In contrast, the industrial sector's share in GDP has declined from 25.38 per cent to 21 per cent in 1990–91 and 2003–04 respectively. The agricultural sector's share has fallen from 30.93 per cent to 24 per cent in the respective years.

Some economists caution that if the service sector bypasses the industrial sector, economic growth can be distorted. They say that service sector growth must be supported by proportionate growth of the industrial sector, otherwise the service sector growth will not be sustainable. It is true that in India, the service sector's contribution in GDP has sharply risen and that of the industry sector fallen.

Economic Reforms and FDI in India

Major economic reforms in India have been associated with crises. For example, after nearly two decades of industry-oriented planning, India accorded due importance to the agricultural sector in the late 1960s in response to massive rood shortages. The consequence of this policy shift was the Green Revolution in the early 1970s. The balance of payments crisis of the early 1980s, together with the stagnation that had become known as the 'Hindu rate of growth', precipitated the 'new' economic policy of 1984–85, in which lay the genesis for the economic reforms of the 1990s. The reforms process in the 1980s was aimed mostly at opening up the economy to import competition, and at streamlining the process of tax administration.

The condition of Indian economy in mid-1991 was like that of a patient in the intensive care canopy. It was beset with crippling crises on all fronts—precarious forex position, untamed inflationary pressures, unbridled government expenditure, soaring fiscal deficit, sagging industrial production and, above all, an all-time low of the country's economic standard in the international arena. Against this backdrop of cumulative economic maladies, launching of a series of structural adjustment programmes by the Narasimha Rao-Manmohan Singh combine had certainly created a new economic environment in India.

The objectives of reforms were: (1) to rescue the state from potentially devastating financial crisis because it was perpetually living beyond its means; (2) to dismantle that entire gamut of regulations which, taken together, added up to such a system, of perverse incentives that it dampened growth and much else; (3) to slowly integrate Indian into the world economy. While FDI would still be only a small part of India's growth, the cumulative impact of this integration would be beneficial both for growth and for making India a more significant player in world politics; and (4) the most important, achieving the first three objectives to be a more secure and widely shared economic prosperity With growth, there should be greater revenue, and this revenue could be, through appropriate measures, used to provide better basic services such as health and education, on the one hand, and compensate for areas where there were market failures, on the other. The success of the reforms was always premised upon the reform of the state itself. The state would be compelled to end less on itself, or on unproductive activities; it would not act as a source of perverse incentives that protected only special interest groups and it would refocus its attention on those core areas where its intervention was actually needed (Gandhi, 2005).

The much discussed economic reforms of the 1990s, the first sustained effort at restructuring the economy, came in response to another BoP crisis in 1991, when India was left with only two weeks' import cover. The government reacted by ushering in sweeping macroeconomic and structural changes. Direct tax rates were reduced for both individuals and corporate entities, with the expectation that reduced rates would lead to greater compliance. Tariff rates too were reduced, and the peak tariff rate came down from 350 per cent in 1990–91 to 35 per cent in 2000–01. The structure of the other indirect taxes was rationalized, and a process was put in place to enable the introduction of value added tax in the foreseeable future (Meyer, 2003).

Licensing was eliminated, and firms in all but a few sectors were allowed to start operations with government approval. The impact of de-licensing was most evident in sectors like steel, automobiles, FMCG and consumer electronics which witnessed a surge in entry of new firms. Over time, capital account restrictions were eased to allow Indian companies to raise capital abroad, by way of Eurobonds and GDR/ADR, and acquire firms in other countries. The domestic capital market was restructured with the Securities and Exchange Board of India (SEBI) and the National Stock Exchange as the driving forces, and interest rates were liberalized. In brief, market forces were unleashed both in the product and, by and large, in the factor markets, and firms were given much more freedom to realize gains associated with allocational efficiency.

The government also made is easier for MNCs to invest in India. Today, India welcomes foreign investment in virtually all sectors except defence, atomic energy, retail and lottery business (recently, in retail sector, it has been allowed). Recently government approved 51 per cent FDI in multi-brand retail and 49 per cent in aviation industry. In sectors like road and port infrastructure, mining of gold and minerals, and pharmaceuticals, MNCs can own up to 100 per cent of their Indian affiliates without government approval. In certain other lines of business like generation of power and development of integrated townships, 100 per cent foreign ownership is possible with government approval. In activities like exploration for petroleum reserves, development of marketing infrastructure for petroleum products, and exploration and mining of coal, MNCs are allowed majority stake in the affiliates, usually varying between 51 per cent and 74 per cent. In most cases, however, their stakes in SOEs are restricted to 26 per cent. Finally, in sectors like pension and insurance, MNCs are restricted to minority stake, and are permitted 26 to 49 percent. FDI upto 100 per cent is allowed in most of the sectors, more specifically, film industry upto 100 per cent, radio industry upto 20 per cent, and print media upto 74 per cent (i.e., magazines, periodicals, journals etc.) and upto 26 per cent in publishing newspapers.

Economic reforms started in the early eighties, but a comprehensive liberalization and privatization process started only in July 1991 in the backdrop of the BoP and foreign exchange liquidity crises faced by the economy. Since then, there have been attempts to integrate the Indian economy with the rest of the world in a variety of ways, i.e., the removal of quantitative restrictions, reducing tariffs and exchange rate flexibility.

Economic reforms were indeed critical at the first phase of transforming the economy. The most important changes implemented in the new economic reform package have been in the sphere of industrial policy, removing several barriers to entry in the earlier economic system. In the earlier system the industrial licence was prevalent which required governmental permission for new investments and there was not much scope for the expansion of the existing capacity. In the new policy, licencing is now required only for a small list of industries, only because of environmental and pollutional considerations. The separate controls over investment and expansion by large industrial houses through the MRTP Act also have been eliminated. Only one area where licencing controls untouched, relates to the list of industries reserved for the small-scale sector, because of government's policy to promote the small-scale sector for social reasons.

The list of industries reserved for public sector has been drastically changed and many critical areas have been opened up to private sector participation. Thus, sea changes have taken place in the industrial sector since 1991 on account of the new economic policy.

The Government of India has initiated major structural changes in its economic policy since July 1991. The main aim of the policy is to make Indian industry more competitive. These changes include some critical reforms in its industrial policy, trade policy, policy towards financial markets and institutions and towards FDI. The role of FDI has been clearly mentioned in the process of economic development of India. Till 1991, the FDI has played only a marginal role in Indian economy in financing country's external needs. However, since the structural adjustment programmes of July 1991, a much larger role has been envisaged for FDI in India. The government has taken active steps for the reduction of administrative and regulatory barriers to FDI, providing various fiscal incentives and other measures aimed at improving the climate for FDI. The changes made in FDI policy that the government was implemented since July 1991 can be broadly classified into four categories as follows:

1. *Choice of product:* The number of products, where FDI was not permitted under the previous policy framework has been reduced.

2. *Choice of market:* The foreign investors are permitted to compete in the domestic market.
3. *Choice of ownership structure:* In most cases, the foreign investors are free to own a majority share of the firm's equity, if they wish so.
4. *Simplifications of procedures:* Most of the procedures relating to applications and approvals of foreign investment-based business ventures have been greatly simplified. India was also signed Multilateral Investment Guarantee Agency Protocol for protection of foreign investments.

Stabilization Measures

The government implemented the following stabilization measures in 1991 in order to correct the imbalances in the Indian economy:

(i) Devaluation of the currency followed by partial or full convertibility in current account.
(ii) Cut in government expenditures to bring about reduction in budget deficit. For instance, budget deficit reduced from 9 per cent of GDP to 6.5 per cent of GDP during 1991 to 1992.
(iii) Liberalization of domestic markets, which included elimination of price controls and cutting down subsidies on agricultural inputs and products.

The Government of India implemented the following structural adjustment measures as part of the economic reforms:

(i) Liberalization of trade and the elimination of the protective entry barriers into industry with a view to make the industry more competitive. This meant delicensing and deregulation of industry, trade and commerce.
(ii) Liberalization of banking system and reducing the role of the state or public sector banks.
(iii) Lessening the control of the monetary authorities on policies such that the rates of interest in money market would be determined by market forces (and not by the Reserve Bank of India, in exercising the powers vested on it as the central bank of the country) and reduction in statutory liquidity ratio (percentage of aggregate demand and time deposits that the commercial banks are required to invest in specified government securities).
(iv) Gradual privatization of commercial, financial and industrial enterprises.
(v) Reduction in the role of the state in the social sectors as well, like that in the education and health sectors, besides gradual move in the direction of the principle of cost recovery.

(vi) Tax reforms for rationalization of the tax structure.
(vii) Poverty alleviation programmes through the creation of social development fund.

It is clear from the above that the new industrial policy of 1991 has effected some very fundamental policy changes such as near abolition of licensing system, easing of the rigors of MRTPA (Monopoly and Restrictive Trade Practices Act) and FERA (Foreign Exchange Regulation Act), reduced list of industries for the public sector, automatic approvals of foreign technology agreements and for 51 per cent foreign equity participation, private investment in infrastructure, liberal location policy for industry, freer import of capital goods, deregulation in small-scale industrial units and liberal policy measures for attracting FDI and NRIs investment. The main objective of the liberalized policy measures was to enhance the productivity and competitive efficiency in the industrial sector.

Exchange Market Reforms

The Eighth Five-Year Plan in India had envisaged exchange rate reforms as part of the general trade policy reforms, and in March 1993 the exchange rates were unified and transactions on the trade account were freed from foreign exchange control. Further measures were taken to simplify procedures related to the purchase of foreign exchange so as to enhance current account convertibility. These included permission to Exchange Earrier's Foreign Currency (EEFC) account holders to use these funds for business-related current account transactions. Authorized dealers were allowed to export surplus currency to private moneychangers abroad, besides their own branches and correspondents. Monetary ceilings on remittances fora wide range of purposes were also removed.

Reforms in the Infrastructure Sector

Removing infrastructure bottlenecks has been another key component of the trade reforms package. In the telecommunications sector, significant progress has been made in involving the private sector in value-added services, such as cellular, mobile and paging services. The Telecom Regulatory Authority of India (TRAI) was established in 1997, which is responsible for separating the regulatory functions from policy formulation and operational functions. The government is also planning to establish similar authority for other infrastructural areas like power. New guidelines to allow private participation in ports and fresh guidelines for private investment in the highway sector have been introduced.

Also, procedures have been simplified and equity participation made easier. Major improvements in the public transport system through the introduction/augmentation of rail-based transit systems in cities like Delhi, Bangalore, Hyderabad, Mumbai and Kolkata have been made.

Tariffs and Trade Reforms

Since 1993, tariff reform has brought down the simple average of all rates to a level lower than 15 per cent, with most of the goods having a ceiling of 35 per cent duty (which was 71% in 1993–94). The process of tariff reform and reduction is ongoing and has been pursued by successive governments since the establishment of World Trade Organization (WTO) in 1995. However, the structure of the tariffs remains complex with a large number of bands in several industries, notably that of paper and paper products, printing and publishing, wood and wood products, food, beverages and tobacco. Reforms in the system of restrictive import licensing have moved ahead steadily. In general, products were first shifted to a Special Import Licence (SIL) list, (here producers were exposed to limited foreign competition) before being moved to the list of freely importable goods.

There has always been an emphasis in India to provide a large number of incentives for exports. These include income tax exemptions, subsidized credit, export insurance and guarantees, export promotion and marketing assistance schemes and access to certain imports that are normally subject to restrictive licensing. The scope of such incentives has been enhanced, orienting India's overall policy stance more explicitly towards exports.

With increased liberalization and globalization of trade, India's focus is on areas of its strength and advantage to meet global competition. This rationale behind this is the impetus for considerable shortening of the negative list of imports and expanding the freely importable list. As per the commitment to WTO, the country abolished the quantitative restrictions on import of most of the items on 1 April 2001.

Since 1995, India has initiated a wide ranging programme of trade liberalization and economic deregulation with the objective of integrating the Indian economy more closely with the world economy. The principal objectives of India's trade policy are: (a) to accelerate the country's transition to a globally-oriented economy with a view to deriving maximum benefits from expanding global market opportunities; and (b) to stimulate sustained economic growth by providing access to essential raw materials, intermediates, components, consumer goods and capital goods required for augmenting production.

The new policy framework attempts to raise FDI flows into India by expanding the number of investors, who consider India as a favourable industrial location. Procedural simplifications, along with several of the other policy reforms that have been initiated, serve to reduce the cost of choosing India as a host country (Saramma, 2005).

India launched its second-generation reforms in 2002, with a focus on reducing the fiscal deficit, improving infrastructure, reforming labour laws and energizing the states to participate actively in stepping up the pace of reforms. India raised its FDI limits in many important sectors including infrastructure, telecommunication, banking and insurance and civil aviation. The ongoing economic reforms process should be reappraised and revitalized to give the entire national development effort a more humane face.

Industrial Policies of Indian Government

Industrial policy is an important document which not only lays a wide canvas and sets a tone for implementing promotional and regulatory roles of the government but also indicates the relationship between government and business. The document is helpful to planners and administrators in the government, inasmuch as it gives clear guidelines for promoting and regulating industries. It is equally helpful to industrialists and others for deciding areas and priorities of their investments.

After independence, the Government of India has formulated policies for industrial growth and development. Industrial policy statements have been announced from 1948 onwards. We examine the following industrial policy resolutions and the important aspects involved in the industrial policies:

- Industrial Policy Resolution of 1948
- Industrial Policy Resolution of 1956
- Industrial Policy Statement of 1973
- Industrial Policy Statement of 1977
- Industrial Policy Statement of 1980
- The New Industrial Policy of 1991
- Industrial Policy Resolution of 1948

The Government of India announced its first Industrial Policy Resolution on 6 April 1948. The resolution laid stress on the role of the state in the development of industry. The policy aimed at 'promoting a rapid rise in the standard of living of the people by exploiting the latent resources of the country, increasing production and offering opportunities to all for employment in the service of the community'. The cardinal aim of the 1948 policy was represented in the proposition that the state must play a progressively dominant role in the development of industry. It was, at the same time, recognized that private enterprise, properly directed and regulated, should continue to play an important part in the industrial development of the country.

In pursuance of the 1948 policy resolution, a series of steps were taken by the government. Several tax concessions were allowed to industry. The Industrial Finance Corporation was set up in July 1948 to provide finance to large industries. The Fiscal Commission was constituted in 1949 to recommend a suitable fiscal policy. Following the recommendations of the Commission, the Indian Tariff Commission was set up in 1952. Topping all, the Industries (Development and Regulation) Act was passed which came into effect in 1951.

It was only after the Industrial Policy Resolution of 1948, the government recognized the need for a mixed economy and reserved national monopolies only for atomic energy, and rail and road industries. While many industries held by private firms could continue, the government had the exclusive rights to initiate projects in six other industries—coal, iron and steel, aircraft manufacturing, ship-building, telephone and telegraph, and minerals. Yet it could seek the aid of the private sector if necessary. Moreover, the government could regulate and licence 18 other industries of national importance.

Thus, the 1948 policy resolution visualized a mixed economy. It aimed at laying the foundation for India's economic and industrial development through such an economy which was guided by the desire for establishing a strong industrial base in India.

Though foreign investment, know-how and technology were regarded to be necessary for building up a proper industrial base, it was felt that as a rule the major interest in ownership and effective control should always be in Indian hands.

Industrial Policy Resolution of 1956

After the adoption of the 1948 resolution, significant development took place in India. Economic planning proceeded on an organized basis and the First Five-Year Plan was completed. Also, the nation accepted 'the socialist pattern of the society' as the basic aim of social and economic policy. These important developments necessitated a fresh statement of industrial policy. Hence, a second Industrial Policy Resolution was adopted in April 1956 replacing the resolution of 1948.

The Industrial Policy Resolution of 1956 gave the broad policy framework of industrial development in India. In spite of considerable changes which took place from time to time, this resolution remained the Magna Carta for Indian industry till its replacement by the July 1991 industrial policy, which in many respects sought to return to the spirit of 1956.

In a nutshell, the Industrial Policy of 1956, for the first time, emphasized on the role of small-scale industries in the development of the national economy. The statement pointed out the importance of the SSI sector in providing employment. It also laid emphasis on the equitable distribution of national income and the effective mobilization of resources. The industrial policy, therefore, recommended the development of ancillary industries in areas where large industries were to be set up.

Industrial Policy Statement of 1973

An industrial policy statement was made in a press note on 2 February 1973. It was an extension of the Industrial Policy Resolution of 1956. The main features of Industrial Policy Statement of 1973 were as under:

1. It declared that the state would be directly responsible for the future development of industries.
2. The role of public sector was further stressed in attaining a socialistic pattern of society. Both the public and private sectors were assigned specific roles.
3. As an initiative towards the development of joint sector units, they were supposed to function under the direction of the government.
4. Foreign investment was allowed only in specific industries. All foreign investment proposals were screened with special reference to technological expertise, export possibilities, and overall effect on the balance of payment position, subject to FERA and MRTP restrictions.
5. Small-scale and cooperative sectors were assigned a special role to play. Small and medium sectors were given preferential treatment.
6. In the area of agricultural produce, co-operative enterprises were encouraged. Thus, a fresh approach to industrialization was made in industrial policy statement of 1973 within the framework of the Industrial Policy Resolution of 1956.

Industrial Policy Statement of 1977

In December 1977, the Central Government announced a new industrial policy by way of a statement in the parliament. The industrial policy, despite some desirable elements, resulted in certain distortions, viz., 'unemployment increased, rural-urban disparities widened and real investment stagnated. On an average, the growth of industrial sector was not more than 3 to 4 per cent per annum. The incidences of industrial sickness also become widespread'.

The thrust of the Industrial Policy Statement of December 1977 was on effective promotion of cottage and small industries widely dispersed in rural areas and small towns. It emphasized that 'whatever can be produced by small and cottage industries must only be so produced'.

The focal point of development of small-scale industries was taken away from the big cities to districts. The concept of District Industries Centres (DICs) was introduced for the first time. Each district would have such a district centre which would extend all the support and services required by small entrepreneurs. These included economic investigation of the districts, supply of machinery and equipment, raw material and other resources, arrangement for credit facilities, call for quality control, research and extension, and so on.

To ensure that no unit of business group acquired a dominant or monopolistic position in the market, large industrial houses were to rely on their own internally generated resources for financing new projects or the expansion of the existing ones.

Within the SSI sector, a new concept of tiny sector was introduced. It was defined as an industrial unit with investment in machinery and equipment of up to ₹ 1 lakh and situated in a town with a population of less than 50,000 as per the 1971 census. This tiny sector was to be given special attention and helped by way of provision for margin money assistance.

The policy statement considerably expanded the list of reserved items for exclusive manufacture in the small-scale sector. This concept, recommended by the Karve Committee, was introduced in 1967 with 47 products. The list of such reserved items was 504 till 1977. The 1977 policy expanded this list to 807.

Industrial Policy of 1980

The Industrial Policy Statement of 1980 focused on the need for promoting competition in the domestic market, technological upgradation and modernization. It laid the foundation for an increasingly competitive export base and for encouraging foreign investment in high-tech areas. The policy, therefore, suggested the following measures:

- Effective operational management of the public sector.
- Integrating industrial development in the private sector.

- Regularization of unauthorized excess capacity installed in the private sector.
- Encouragement of merger and acquisition of sick units.

The 1980 industrial policy was guided merely by considerations of growth. It liberalized licensing for large and big businesses but by blurring the distinction between small-scale and large-scale industries. It sought to promote the latter at the cost of the former. Broadly speaking, the policy chose a more capital-intensive path of development and thus, it underplayed the employment objective.

Thus, the industrial policy of 1980 made a sea change in terms of liberalization of licensing policy in favour of large business houses, particularly in terms of making them free from the provisions of MRTP Act. The major changes introduced were as follows:

- Liberalization of licensed capacity.
- Relaxation of industrial licensing.
- Industrialization of backward areas.

The Industrial Policy Statement of 1980 was a growth-oriented industrial policy. The factors considered by this policy were import-export, labour relations, pollution control, ecological balance, merger and amalgamation, correcting industrial sickness, pricing policy, takeover of sick units, foreign collaboration and investment. It was a balanced industrial policy aimed at developing the industrial sector in India.

New Industrial Policy of 1991

The central government led by P.V. Narasimha Rao announced the new industrial policy in July 1991. As an aftermath of previous policies and some unstable politics, India's economy was on the verge of collapse at that point of time. It must be noted that the reforms announced in 1991 were not completely contradictory to the general trend in policy. Concerns about the lack of competitiveness of Indian industry and consequent poor export performance (and poor growth record compared to the East Asian economies that had focused on export-led growth) had led to some liberalization of both the licensing and trade policies in the late 1970s and 80s. However, the reforms in 1991 did make significant changes in industrial, trade and public sector policies. Some significant changes in industrial policies announced in July 1991 are summarized below:

- Abolished licensing for all projects except in 18 industries.
- MRTP Act amended to eliminate prior approval to large companies for capacity expansions.

- The requirement of Phased Manufacturing Programmes (PMP) discontinued for all new projects.
- Schedule 'A' of industries reserved exclusively for state enterprises cut down from 17 to 8.
- Schedule 'B' of industries, where state enterprises were to acquire a dominant position, abolished.
- Small-scale enterprises allowed offering up to 24 per cent of shareholding to large enterprises.

As far as foreign direct investment (FDI) regulations were concerned, following changes were made:

- Limit on foreign equity holdings raised from 40 per cent to 51per cent in a wide range of industries.
- Foreign equity proposals need not be accompanied by foreign technology transfer agreement.
- Procedures for FDI streamlined by creating a Foreign Investment Promotion Board to consider individual applications case by case.
- Technology imports liberalized by increasing royalty limits.
- The new industrial policy does not restrict the extent of foreign equity holdings or sectors eligible for foreign investment. The policy leaves all such decisions, including selection of technology and the terms negotiated for transfer, to the commercial judgement of the entrepreneurs. Therefore, while the facility of automatic approval for FDI can be availed from the Reserve Bank of India (RBI) much quicker, other proposals for direct investment are equally welcome. The Government of India would consider all FDI proposals including those for 100 per cent foreign equity holdings for setting up wholly owned subsidiaries.
- In the case of 100 per cent export-oriented units and units in the free trade zones/export processing zones, foreign participation may go to 100 per cent of equity.

From public sector policy point of view, following changes were made:

- List of industries reserved for the public sector (Schedule 'A') reduced from 17 to 8.
- List of sectors reserved for dominance by public sector (Schedule 'B') effectively abolished.
- Disinvestment in selected public sector enterprises to raise finances for development, bring in greater accountability and help create a new culture in their working for improved efficiency.

- Government equity ranging from 5 per cent to 20 per cent in 31 PSEs (public sector enterprises) with 'good track record' disinvested to public sector mutual funds and financial institutions.

As far as trade policy is concerned, following changes were made in the 1991 Industrial Policy:

- Administered licensing of imports replaced by import entitlements linked to export earnings. These entitlements called exim scrips made freely tradable.
- Exim scrips can be used for all open general license (OGL) items for actual users, limited permissible list, non-sensitive canalised list and non-OGL capital goods not in the restricted list.
- Permission to import capital goods without 'indigenous clearance' provided import covered by foreign equity or was 25 per cent of the value of plant and machinery (subject to a limit of ₹ 200 million).
- Scope of canalization narrowed.
- Short-term import compression measures (such as interest surcharge on bank credit and cash margin on import payments) introduced.

As far as environmental issues are concerned, following changes were brought about in India:

- Pollution control has assumed a significant role and commensurates with industrial expansion, and now a strong regulatory mechanism is required to ensure minimum environment standards to achieve this objective. A total of 2,155 pre- and post-1991 units of 17 categories have been identified for this purpose by the Central Pollution Control Board (CPCB).
- In order to strengthen the environmental management capacity at national, state and local levels, the ministry had launched an environment capacity building project in 1997.
- The government has also come up with a comprehensive national environment policy. The policies of the government are being implemented through various Acts.

The liberalization process in India started in 1973 and was carried forward in 1985, 1988 and 1990. It culminated in a manner of opening up of the economy with the industrial policy of 1991, in consonance with the globalization process emerging all over the world. A formidable number of MRTP and FERA restrictions were liberalized in order to cope with the need for integrating the Indian economy with the world economy. The investment limit of MRTP companies was removed and many of bureaucratic restrictions done away with. In the face of acute shortage and scarcity of foreign exchange, it was thought proper on the part of government to lay down all-out policy measures to strengthen the inflow of foreign capital. While investments from non-resident Indians, foreign corporate bodies and foreign investors were encouraged, foreign equity participation in Indian companies up to 51 per cent was normalized. Meanwhile, foreign investment up to 100 per cent stood permissible in export-oriented units and sophisticated technology-based industries. This was a welcome sign for foreign investors.

Government Policy towards FDI in India

FDI policy, as a part of Indian industrial policy, has gone through a number of phases. Though these are not strictly separable, these can be divided into three phases for the sake of convenience.

Phase 1: 1950–1980

At the time of independence, policy towards FDI was largely conditioned by two factors: the Industrial Policy Resolutions of 1948 and 1956 and the foreign exchange crisis, especially in the late 50s. That this conditioning continued throughout the period is clear from the preamble to the Foreign Exchange and Regulation Act (FERA), 1973. In the first phase government policy was largely determined by the struggle between the state and monopoly foreign interests. In the late 40s the primary TNCs were the oil companies. The large companies, in particular, imported crude oil from the parent companies and shipped it in their own tankers. This strategy was useful in transfer pricing and profit shifting from subsidiaries to the head office. When the Indian government made a lucrative deal with the Soviet Union for import of crude under the better trade agreement, they were faced with the refusal of the oil companies to refine Soviet crude in India. Not possessing any oil refining capacity (government or private) the government held to relent in their efforts to Indianize the oil companies and even agreed in 1967 to a substantial increase in their refining capacity. The government failure to control TNCs led to the formation of the ONGC and the IOC in 1959 primarily with the objective of reducing the monopoly stronghold of the oil companies. This policy of state intervention also conformed to 'commanding heights' objective of the 1956 industrial policy. Subsequently, the oil companies were nationalized in the seventies. However, it must be pointed out that by this time oil companies the world over were getting out from natural resource-based industries. Therefore, it is debatable whether the oil companies left under duress or not. The experience, however, altered the government of the dangers involved in giving TNCs monopoly control over an industry which is critical for the economy.

Except for legal oil companies and, as we will see later on, the tea plantations, the policy towards FDI was quite pragmatic and flexible. This is clear from the statements made by Pt. Jawaharlal Nehru on the floor of parliament. Nehru, in particular, clearly recognized the role TNCs could play in India's industrialization. In fact, except for FERA companies, there has been no discrimination between Indian and foreign controlled companies from the point of view of laws and taxation.

In 1965 and 1972 the Free Trade Zones (FTZs) were set up in Kandla, Gujarat and Santa Cruz, Bombay. Like in other Asian countries, a host of tax and other concessions were given to companies investing here for the export market. The concession ranged from liberal depreciation allowances to complete tax exemptions. However, it is now well known that the experiment was a failure (as, in fact, it was in China). The main problem was that the policy towards FDI was being determined on a case by case basis. Except in the case of the oil companies, the view was that the 1965 industrial policy resolution was unfavourable to FDI. However, as the foreign exchange crisis developed towards the late 50s, some degree of pragmatism came in as TNCs began to be viewed as owners of technology and net foreign exchange earners through exports (Kyaw, 2003).

Consequently, in 1969, a more precise policy towards FDI was evolved. This consisted of setting out three groups of industries where (i) there would be FDI without technical collaboration, (ii) only technical collaboration, and (iii) no foreign participation. Second, the foreign exchange crisis, particularly Article 29 which specified that any foreign owned firm with more than 40 per cent of equity held abroad had to apply to the RBI for approval in cases relating to expansion, mergers, purchase of share in other firms, etc. FERA came into force in 1974 and all applications had been dealt with by 1979.

The government also issued Industrial Policy in 1973. For one the policy specified the precise areas in which non-FERA companies could operate. As we noted above, this policy statement was mainly involved in specifying the detailed list of industries in which foreign firms could participate with or without FDI (that is only technical collaborations). It is clear that the idea to restrict foreign firms to sectors producing basic intermediate and capital goods. However, realizing the need for larger foreign involvement, the policy allowed for up to 49 per cent foreign equity in high technology, priority sectors which usually involved large investments. But here foreign participation was restricted to joint ventures with the government. In general, the government feeling was that the Indian private sector was ill-equipped to handling large TNCs.

How successful was FERA? In actuality there were a lot of exemptions from FERA. One, in the case of firms exporting more than 60 per cent of output, 74 per cent of equity could be held abroad. Second, up to 51 per cent foreign equity was permissible if 60 per cent of the firm's turnover was in core sector activities and it exported 10 per cent of production. The same level applied to firms exporting more than 40 per cent of their turnover. For a 100 per cent export-oriented firm, 100 per cent foreign equity was permitted.

As argued in Martinussen (1997), there was some degree of success in the equity dilution objective. Thus, the number of foreign branches came down from 500 in 1974 to about 300 in 1980. It may be remembered that a foreign branch is not incorporated under the Indian Companies Act and hence falls outside the control of local taxation in the sense that its tax burden is completely determined by the tax rate in the parent country. The essential message of FERA was that no such firms could exist after 1974. Second, and more important, as late as 1983 there were 249 companies that were exempted from the provisions of FERA. As shown in Martinussen (1997), most of these firms belonged to three industry groups, tea plantations, drugs and pharmaceuticals and subsidiaries of large TNCs. Thus, tea companies were permitted to retain upto 74 per cent foreign equity without any export commitment. Presumably, the Indian government felt that if the foreign firms withdrew, they might refuse to market Indian tea under their brand name and thus a vital foreign exchange earning industry would be destabilized.

Similarly, the exemption granted to the drug companies reflected the fact that in 1976 foreign controlled companies accounted for 42 per cent of the production of bulk drugs and formulations. Once again, if these companies wound up then precious foreign exchange would be lost in imports. In fact, it was only in the late 70s, after the development of important public sector units like IDPL that the government was able to enforce FERA. In all fairness to the foreign drug companies, the option of diluting foreign shareholding by selling shares to the Indian public was not open to them: they could only sell to the public sector companies. This clearly smacked of backdoor nationalization which had been clearly ruled out in 1953. However, their clout in policy making was undeniable.

The same point is illustrated by the considerable economic clout of Hindustan Levers which explains why, even as late as 1980, it had not conformed to FERA with the government classifying its activities as 'core sector' activities.

The essential point brought out by Martinussen (1997) is that a large number of exemptions from FERA were given by a rather liberal interpretation of what constituted 'core sector' activities. Thus, while achieving very little in the context of existing TNCs, FERA was effective in scaring away potential investors. To the mafia of Indian monopolists was added the mafia of large TNCs.

The period from 1970–80 can be then considered the most restrictive from the point of view of FDI mainly because implementation of FERA was the principal item on the agenda of policy makers. However, in terms of the general attitude towards FDI we can really think of the whole period from 1949 as one of cautious encouragement followed by strong reaction. The main drawback of the system of control through FERA was that it failed to control the large TNCs for whom it was intended. At the same time it sent negative signals to prospective investors thus perpetuating the monopoly control of foreign and local capital. Like the industrial licensing system FERA was an instrument of control rather than an incentive.

Phase 2: 1981–1990

A more liberal attitude towards foreign investment emerged after about 1980 or so. This phase begins with the Industrial Policy Statements of 1980 and 1982 and, more importantly, the Technology Policy Statement of 1983. For one, the policy statements began the process of delincensing and, to some extent, reversing the negative effects on growth and competition of the Industrial Policy Resolutions of 1948 and 1956. At the same time, some of the restrictive features of the MRTP Act were sought to be done away with (Kumar, 1997).

More specific to FDI, it was proposed to set up four new Export Processing Zones (EPZs). There was also a relaxation of the equity restriction under FERA for 100 per cent export-oriented firms. Finally, this was also the period when there was a considerable degree of trade liberalization by tariff reductions and shifting of a large number of import items from import licensing to open general license (OGL). The general mood of this period distinguishes it from the earlier one.

However, in one sense, there was little change from the earlier period in that the general fear of large volume flows of foreign equity persisted. The liberalization in this period extended mainly to collaborations with little or no equity component. This aspect will be elaborated in the next section. However, an example is very illustrative.

Thus, power to establish a foreign collaboration not involving an outflow of more than ₹ 5 million and with no foreign equity was delegated to the administrative ministries. Otherwise, if a substantial foreign equity component existed, the powerful Foreign Investment Promotion Board (FIPB) and the Cabinet Committee on Economic Affairs were to be the final authority. In general, administrative complexity increased with the level of foreign equity. As argued below, this period led to a radical change in the nature of foreign involvement in the economy.

Phase 3: 1991–2006

The New Industrial Policy of 1991 may be the starting point of a new phase in FDI in India. Let us see the salient features of the new policy as it affects FDI. For one the policy states for the first time that 'Direct Foreign Investment has always been preferred to loans and other forms of assistance'. Accordingly, upto 51 per cent foreign equity is permissible with automatic approval in specified industries producing intermediate and capital goods. Hence, although the administrative hassles have been removed, the list of industries is more or less the same as in the past.

Second, in high priority areas, 51 per cent equity is permissible with the necessary amendment of FERA to follow. Third, in a recent notification, the balancing of dividends and export earnings is no longer to be insisted upon except in the case of consumer goods. Fourth, in a break from the past, a foreign equity proposal need not have a technology import component. Fifth, permission is no longer required to bring in foreign technicians and, finally, a specially empowered board, the Foreign Investment Proposals Board (FIPB), has subsequently been set up with the objective to negotiate directly with foreign investors for large volume equity involvement in select areas like telecommunications, power, etc.

The most welcome feature of the policy is its emphasis on reduction of bureaucratic interference in commercial matters.

In the fast changing world of technology the relationship between the suppliers and users of technology must be a continuous one. Such a relationship becomes difficult to achieve when the approval process includes unnecessary governmental interference on a case by case basis involving endemic delays and fostering uncertainty. The Indian entrepreneur has come of age so that heno longer needs such bureaucratic clearance of his commercial technology relationship with foreign technology suppliers.

This is a welcome feature of the new policy. As we have seen, the discretionary case by case system of approval was the bane of the foreign investment policy in the first phase. In addition, this led to a lack of transparency which gave negative signals to new FDI.

What have been the major procedural changes following the 1991 industrial policy? The most novel feature has been the granting of automatic approval up to 51 per cent foreign equity in selected industries. This is done directly by the RBI in 15 days. For approval of foreign equity over 51 per cent or in industries not covered by automatic approval, the proposal has to be approved by the FIPB if investment required is less than ₹ 300 crores. In other cases the approval of the Cabinet Committee is required. The FIPB is made up of the Principal Secretary to the Prime Minister (Chairman), the Finance Secretary, the Commerce Secretary and the Industry Secretary. Approvals normally take about 30–45 days. Third, in cases of investment proposals in the FTZs and 100 per cent export-oriented units, the respective Development Commissioners are the arbiters subject to the requirements of value-addition, financing of equipment imports thorough equity inflows and the ₹ 1 crore limit on lump sum payments. Here, of course, 100 per cent foreign equity is permissible as long as the items produced are not subject to compulsory licensing as specified in the 1991 policy.

Hence, it would be reasonable to say that after 1991 some concrete steps have been taken to debureaucratize the process of approval of foreign investment proposals. What is probably more heartening is the recognition that foreign equity proposals (in contrast to proposals involving only foreign technical collaborations or loans) are more beneficial to the country. In this light, the Economic Survey, 1993–94 notes, 'the efforts at mobilising non-debt creating foreign capital flows has now begun to yield results'.

According to the Economic Survey, 1993–94, there has been a sharp jump in FDI approvals under the automatic route from US$ 0.2 million in 1991–92 to US$ 42.6 million in 1992–93 to US$ 50 million in the period April–December 1993. Total FDI flows in the period April–December 1993 (including the non-automatic route and NRI investment in the 40 per cent and 100 per cent foreign equity schemes) were of the order of US$ 425.3 million. Hence, there does seem to be an upswing in the flows of equity-based FDI as compared to the past and a major factor must be the attempt at reducing unnecessary bureaucratic intervention.

Although the time period is too short for any analytical study, some inferences can be drawn. One, reduction of bureaucratic procedures is not enough to attract FDI. This is evidenced by the fact that foreign investors have not been making use of the automatic approval route for FDI. The difference in the automatic and the non-automatic route lies in the industries covered and the extent of foreign ownership permissible. It is clear that if foreign control is the principal requirement of foreign investors, then 51 per cent ownership is adequate even in closely held companies. What is probably the greater deterrent to foreign investors is that the list of industries where automatic approval is permissible excludes consumer goods. It is thus clear that a major motivating factor behind FDI is the size of the domestic market. The Economic Survey for 2004–05 notes that 80 per cent of approvals have been in the priority sectors. These include power equipment and similar infrastructural facilities where the domestic demand is expected to show phenomenal growth. Second, it is also clear that export markets are not a major attraction despite the low costs of the Indian operations. Finally, the flows of FDI in the form of portfolio capital are still dominant. Since portfolio capital flows are short-term, speculative flows may not lead to an increase in productive capacity and hence cannot be of as much benefit to India as FDI flows in the form of long-term equity.

Recent Initiatives to Attract FDI

Policy Initiatives during 2002–13

Continuing with its policy to further liberalize the FDI sector, the government announced another set of sector-specific initiatives to attract larger volumes of foreign investment. Highlights of the few policy reforms undertaken are as below:

- FDI up to 100 per cent permitted under the automatic route in advertising sector. FDI under the automatic route up to 100 per cent is available for film sector and will not be subject to conditions about debt equity ratio, minimum level of equity investment, etc.
- FDI up to 100 per cent allowed in tea sector, including tea plantations, permitted subject to compulsory disinvestment of 26 per cent equity in favour of an Indian partner within a period of five years and prior approval of the state government in case of any future land use change.
- FDI in print media sector is allowed up to 26 per cent of paid-up equity capital of Indian entities publishing periodicals and newspapers dealing with news and current affairs.

- Re-issuance of ADR/GDR permitted to the extent of ADRs/GDRs which have been redeemed into underlying shares and sold in the domestic market.
- FDI up to 100 per cent permitted with prior approval of the government for development of integrated township, including housing, commercial premises, hotels, resorts and regional level urban infrastructure facilities such as roads and bridges and mass rapid transit system, subject to the guidelines of the Government of India.
- Automatic route of FDI up to 100 per cent allowed in all manufacturing activities such as arms and ammunitions, explosives and allied items of defence equipment, defence aircraft and warships, automatic substances, narcotics, distillation and brewing of alcoholic drinks and cigarettes and cigars.
- The government relaxed FDI regime in sectors including multi-brand retail, single-brand retail, commodity exchanges, power exchanges, broadcasting, non-banking financial institutions (NBFCs) and asset reconstruction companies (ARCs) in 2012.
- FDI cap was also raised from 49 to 74 per cent in broadcasting and ARCs, with an aim to bring foreign expertise in the segments. Foreign investment has also been allowed in power exchanges while foreign institutional investors (FIIs) have been allowed to invest up to 23 per cent in commodity exchanges without seeking prior approval from the government.
- India received FDI worth US$ 30.82 billion from April 2012 to January 2013 while FDI equity inflows during January 2013 stood at US$ 2.16 billion, according to latest data released by the Department of Industrial Policy and Promotion (DIPP).
- India's foreign exchange (forex) reserves stood at US$ 292.64 billion for the week ended March 29, 2013, according to data released by the Reserve Bank of India (RBI). The value of foreign currency assets (FCA) - the biggest component of the forex reserves – stood at US$ 259.72 billion, according to the weekly statistical supplement released by the RBI.
- The Indian Government, in consultation with the Foreign Investment Promotion Board (FIPB), has recently cleared 12 FDI proposals amounting to Rs 2, 609 crore (US$ 478.47 million). These included the proposal of Decathlon Sports India's proposal for infusion of foreign equity worth Rs 700 crore (US$ 128.37 million) to engage in single-brand retail. The biggest proposal cleared was Ahmedabad-based Claris Otsuka Ltd's plan to accumulate its infusions in business into a new joint venture (JV) with FDI worth Rs 1,050 crore (US$ 192.56 million).

- Japanese firm Mitsubishi has formed a joint venture with Dubai-based ETA Group to set up Mitsubishi Elevators ETA India Pvt Ltd., to manufacture, distribute, instal and maintain elevators for premium residential apartment complexes and industrial buildings in India. The company, which was already present in India focusing on the premium commercial segment, will now focus on the premium residential segment and the middle segment in Tier 2 and 3 cities.
- Meanwhile, French companies are showing keen interest to park their investments in India, pertaining to segments like defence, space, urban development and infrastructure.
- Investment proposals falling under the automatic route and matters related to FEMA are dealt with by RBI, while the government handles investment through approval route and issues that relate to FDI policy per se through its three institutions, viz., the Foreign Investment Promotion Board (FIPB), the Secretariat for Industrial Assistance (SIA) and the Foreign Investment Implementation Authority (FIIA).
- FDI under the automatic route does not require any prior approval either by the government or the RBI.
- The investors are only required to notify the concerned regional office of the RBI within 30 days of receipt of inward remittances and file the required documents with that office within 30 days of issuance of shares to foreign investors. Under the approval route, the proposals are considered in a time-bound and transparent manner by the FIPB. Approvals of composite proposals involving foreign investment/foreign technical collaboration are also granted on the recommendations of the FIPB.

Recent Initiatives

The government has permitted, except for a small negative list, access to the automatic route for FDI. The automatic route means that foreign investors only need to inform the RBI within 30 days of bringing in their investment, and again within 30 days of issuing any shares. The negative list includes: (i) all proposal that require an industrial licence because the activity is licensable, cases where foreign investment is more than 24 per cent in the equity capital of units manufacturing items reserved for small-scale industries, and all activity that requires an industrial licence in term of the locational policy; (ii) all proposals in which the foreign collaborator has a previous venture/tie-up in India; (iii) all proposals relating to acquisition of shares in an existing Indian company in favour of a foreign/non-resident Indian/overseas corporate body investor; and

(iv) all proposals falling outside notified sectoral policy/caps or under a sector in which FDI is not permitted and/or whenever any investor chooses to make an application to the FIPB and not to avail of the automatic route.

Non-banking financial companies (NBFCs) may hold foreign equity up to 100 per cent if these are holding companies. The minimum capitalization norms for fund-based NBFCs are: (i) for FDI up to 51 per cent—US$ 0.5 million to be brought upfront; (ii) for FDI above 51 per cent and up to 75 per cent—US$ 5 million to be brought upfront; and (iii) for FDI above 75 per cent and up to 100 per cent—US$ 50 million out of which US$ 7.5 million to be brought upfront and the balance in 24 months.

For non-fund-based activities, the minimum capitalization norm of US$ 0.5 million is applicable in respect of all permitted non-fund-based NBFCs with foreign investment. Foreign investors can set up 100 per cent operating subsidiaries (without any restriction on the number of subsidiaries) without the condition to disinvest a minimum of 25 per cent of its equity of Indian entities, subject to bringing in US$ 50 million, out of which US$ 7.5 million has to be brought upfront and the balance in 24 months. Joint venture-operating NBFC's that have 75 per cent or less than 75 per cent foreign investment will also be allowed to set up subsidiaries for undertaking other NBFC's activities, subject to the subsidiaries also complying with the applicable minimum capital inflow. FDI up to 49 per cent from all sources is permitted in the private banking sector on the automatic route subject to conformity with RBI guidelines. In the process of liberalization of FDI policy, the following policy changes have been made: (i) 100 per cent FDI permitted for B to B e-commerce; (ii) condition of dividend balancing on 22 consumer items removed forthwith; (iii) removal of cap on foreign investment in the power sector; and (iv) 100 per cent FDI permitted in oil refining.

The automatic route is available for proposals in the IT sector, even when the applicant company has a previous joint venture or technology transfer agreement in the same field.

FDI limit under automatic route in the advertising sector has been raised from existing 74 per cent to 100 per cent. FDI up to 100 per cent in the film sector, which is already on automatic route, now will not be subject to conditions. FDI up to 100 per cent in the tea sector, including plantation, has been allowed with prior approval of the government and would be subject to the following conditions: (i) compulsory divestment of 26 per cent equity of the company in favour of an Indian partner/Indian public within a period of five years; and (ii) prior approval of the state government concerned in case of any future land use change. Automatic route of FDI up to 100 per cent is allowed in all manufacturing activities in Special Economic Zones (SEZs), except for the activities related to security, strategic or environmental concerns.

FDI up to 100 per cent is allowed with some conditions for the following activities in the telecom sector: (i) ISPs not providing gateways (both for satellite and submarine cables); (ii) infrastructure providers providing dark fibre (IP category I); (iii) electronic mail; and (iv) voice mail. FDI up to 74 per cent is permitted for the following telecom services subject to licensing and security requirements (proposals with FDI beyond 49 per cent shall require prior government approval): (i) internet service provider with gateways; (ii) radio paging, and (iii) end-to-end bandwidth.

FDI in print media sector is allowed up to 26 per cent of paid-up equity capital of Indian entities publishing periodicals and newspapers dealing with news and current affairs. FDI in print media sector is allowed up to 74 per cent of paid-up equity capital of Indian entities publishing Indian editions of foreign, technical, scientific, specially magazines and journals. Payment of royalty up to 2 per cent on exports and 1 per cent on domestic sale is allowed under the automatic route on use of trademarks and brand name of the foreign collaborator without technology transfer.

Payment of royalty up to 8 per cent on exports and 5 per cent on domestic sales by wholly owned subsidiaries to off-shore parent companies is allowed under the automatic route without any restriction on the duration of royalty payments. Off-shore venture capital funds/companies are allowed to invest in domestic venture capital undertakings as well as other companies through the automatic route, subject only to SEBI regulations and sector-specific caps on FDI. Existing companies with FDI are eligible for the automatic route to undertake additional activities covered under this route. FDI up to 26 per cent is eligible under the automatic route in the insurance sector, as prescribed in the Insurance Act, 1999, subject to their obtaining a licence from the Insurance Regulatory and Development Authority (IRDA). FDI up to 100 per cent is permitted in airports, with FDI above 74 per cent requiring prior approval of the government. FDI up to 100 per cent is permitted with prior approval of the government in courier services subject to existing laws and exclusion of activities relating to distribution of letters.

FDI up to 100 per cent is permitted with prior approval of the government for the development of integrated townships, including housing, commercial premises, hotels, resorts, city and regional-level urban infrastructure facilities such as roads and bridges, mass rapid transit systems and manufacturing of building material in all metros, including associated commercial development of real estate. Development of land and providing allied infrastructure will form an integral part of township development subject to guidelines. FDI upto 100 per cent is permitted on the automatic route for mass rapid transport system in all metropolitan cities, including associate commercial development of real estate.

FDI up to 100 per cent is also permitted in drugs and pharmaceuticals (excluding those which attract compulsory licensing or are produced by recombinant DNA technology and specific cell/tissue targeted formulation) placed on the automatic route. The defence industry sector is opened up to 100 per cent for Indian private sector participation with FDI permitted up to 26 per cent, both subject to licensing. This will be subject to guidelines. FDI up to 100 per cent is permitted on the automatic route in the hotel and tourism sector.

NRI investment in foreign exchange is made fully repatriable whereas investments made in Indian rupees through rupee account shall remain non-repatriable. International financial institutions like ADB, IFC, CDC, DEG, etc., are allowed to invest in domestic companies through the automatic route, subject to SEBI/RBI guidelines and sector-specific caps on FDL industrial licences/letters of intent issued by the Secretariat for Industrial Assistance (SIA). In the past, carrying the condition of export obligation have been exempted from the operation of this condition for items which stand dereserved by an appropriate notification. Investment limit raised to ₹ 5 crore for 41 SSI reserved items by amending the IDR Act, 1951. The government has deleted 51 items reserved for exclusive manufacture in the small-scale sector.

These are highly significant concessions. All the restrictions of the past on foreign investment seem to have been cleared up and in that process attempt has been made to integrate the Indian economy with the global economy in a way it never was after the 1950s.

The government realizes the fact that domestic resources alone may not be adequate to sustain the required expansion in infrastructure for development. Thus, it has followed a strategy to create incentives for FDI. India, today, has an extremely liberal regime for FDI in terms of entry norms. International experience shows that there can be a number of other barriers for those willing to invest in infrastructure projects. The government has taken systematic initiatives to address these problems largely through comprehensive reforms in sectors like power and telecommunications. The combination of domestic private foreign investment and multilateral investments is likely to propel India's economic growth momentum in future.

Investment Environment

India is the second most populous country and the largest democracy in the world. The far-reaching and sweeping economic reforms undertaken since 1991 have unleashed the enormous growth potential of the economy. There has been a rapid, yet calibrated, move towards deregulation and liberalization, which has made India a favourite destination for foreign investment. The mood is upbeat and the signals strong. In a nutshell, the following features make India as one of the most vibrant and dynamic of the developing economies:

- One of the largest economies of the world, fourth largest economy in terms of purchasing power parity.
- Large and rapidly growing consumer market with more than 300 million people for branded consumer products.
- Easy access to markets of the other nations belonging to the South Asian Association for Regional Cooperation (Bangladesh, Bhutan, Maldives, Nepal, Pakistan and Sri Lanka).
- Large and diversified infrastructure spread across the country.
- Promising future in the IT industry.
- Large manufacturing capability, spanning almost all areas of manufacturing activities.
- Well-developed research and development (R&D) infrastructure and technical and marketing services.
- Well-established knowledge industry.
- Abundance of natural resources (has a rich mineral base), and agricultural self-sufficiency.
- Developed banking system with commercial banking network of over 93,000 branches supported by a number of national and state level financial institutions.
- Vibrant capital market consisting of 23 stock exchanges with over 19,000 listed companies.
- Skilled manpower and professional management, including engineers, managerial personnel, accountants and lawyers, available at competitive costs.
- Conducive foreign investment environment that provides freedom of entry, investment, location, choice of technology, import and export.

- The policy environment provides clear guidelines for entry, freedom of location, choice of technology, production, repatriation of capital, dividends, etc., which is specifically aimed of enhancing the flow of FDI.
- Well-balanced package of fiscal incentives.
- Stable democratic environment fostered by 65 years of independence.
- Established, independent judiciary.
- English the preferred business language.

As a part of the economic reforms programme, policy and procedures governing foreign investment and technology transfer have been significantly simplified and streamlined. Today, foreign investment is freely allowed in all sectors including the services sector except in cases where there are sectoral ceilings. All items/activities except the following are under the automatic route for FDI:

1. All proposals that require an industrial licence. An industrial licence is mandatory if:
   - the item involved requires on industrial licence under the Industries (Development & Regulation) Act, 1951; or
   - the foreign equity portion is more than 24 per cent of the equity capital of units manufacturing items reserved for small scale industries; or
   - the item concerned requires on industrial licence in terms of the locational policy.
2. All proposals in which the foreign collaborator has a previous venture or tie-up in India (excluding IT sector).
3. All proposals relating to the acquisition of shares in an existing Indian company in favour of a foreign investor.
4. All proposals outside the notified sectoral policy/caps, or under sectors in which FDI is not permitted.

Investment in public sector units as also in export-oriented units (EOUs), and units in EPZs, SEZs, Software Technology Parks (STPs) and Electronics Hardware Technology Parks (EHTPs) also qualify for the automatic route.

FDI in the insurance sector is allowed upto 26 per cent under the automatic route subject to licence from the IRDA for undertaking insurance activities. Recently, it has been hiked to 49 per cent.

In addition to automatic approval for new companies, such approval can also be granted for existing companies proposing to induct foreign equity, and with an expansion programme. The additional requirements would be:

1. the increase in equity level must result from the expansion of the equity base of the existing company;
2. the money to be remitted should be in foreign currency; and
3. the proposed expansion programme should be predominantly in the sector(s) under automatic route.

For existing companies without an expansion programme, the additional requirements for eligibility for automatic approval are:

1. they should be engaged predominantly in industries under the automatic route;
2. the increase in equity level must be from expansion of the equity base; and
3. the foreign equity must come in foreign currency.

Otherwise, the proposal would need government approval through the FIPB. Investors coming through the automatic route are required to file relevant documents with the RBI within 30 days after the issue of shares to foreign investors.

The reform process has deregulated the economy and stimulated domestic and foreign investments, taking India firmly into the forefront of investment destinations. The government, keen to promote investment in the country, has radically simplified and rationalized policies, procedures and regulatory aspects. Foreign investment is welcome in almost all sectors, except those of strategic concern (for instance, defence and atomic energy).

A series of incentives has been announced to promote investments. These include import of capital goods at concessional customs duty (subject to fulfilment of certain export obligations), liberalization of external commercial borrowing norms, tax holiday and concessional tax treatment for certain sector. In addition, several state governments offer incentives, such as subsidy on fixed capital, loans at concessional rates of interest and attractive power rates. While several incentives are project-specific, a number of firms have been successful in negotiating favourable investment terms with the state government concerned.

Since the initiation of the economic liberalization process in 1991, sectors such as automobiles, chemicals, food processing, oil and natural gas, petrochemicals, power, services and telecommunications have attracted considerable investments. Today, in the changed investment climate, India offers exciting business opportunities in virtually every sector of the economy. Towards this end, the FDI policy has been constantly reviewed and necessary steps have been taken to make India a most favourable destination for FDI.

Agenda to Improve FDI Environment

There has been a considerable change in policies and attitudes towards FDI on the part of most developing countries in recent years. In the year 1991, India too liberalized its highly regulated FDI regime, in place for more than three decades. With the virtual abolition of the industrial licensing system, controls over foreign trade and foreign investment were considerably relaxed, including the removal of ceilings on equity ownership by foreign firms. The reforms did result in increased inflows of FDI during the decade of the nineties. There has been a huge increase in the number of FDI approvals and the amount of FDI received. The FDI inflows have increased from US$ 155 in 1991 to US$ 38 billion during April–September 2006. Even so, the volume of FDI in India is relatively low compared with that in most other emerging economies like China, Singapore, Malaysia, etc. The relatively low volume of FDI in India, especially so in comparison with that in China, i.e., US$ 4,366 million in 1991 and US$ 69.47 billion in 2006 respectively (WIR, 2007; Economic Survey, 2006–07), has attracted widespread comment. The meagre share of India in FDI inflows is a cause for concern and underlines the need for even greater policy reforms in the FDI regime.

The reasons for low inflows are attributable to a host of factors such as procedural disputes regarding land availability, environmental clearance, and delays at state level in getting power and other infrastructural back-up. These bottlenecks result in delays in the commencement of many projects. The inability to start due to policy uncertainty and implementation issues are also hurdles in attracting the foreign investors. Also, red-tapism, antiquated labour laws and flawed policies contribute to the investor's woes.

If India has to achieve its desired goals as laid down in the Tenth Five-Year Plan, then our economy has to be strong and vibrant and the fruits of development equitably shared. For this vision to be fulfilled, we must press ahead to complete our reform programme in the shortest possible time. The fruits of economic reforms would be realized only if suitable changes in institutional apparatus and organizations are implemented both at the central and state levels for attracting FDI inflows. There is also the need to suggest policy reforms in EPZs and NRI investments for higher FDI.

FDI is one of the key variables for achieving an 8 per cent growth during the Tenth Plan. A sharp step up in FDI is necessary for achieving the growth targets of the Tenth Plan. Thus, the momentum of economic reforms is necessary for achieving a higher growth coupled with positive political outlook.

As stated earlier, infrastructure and export sectors face serious investment constraints. These two sectors can be the key drivers of productivity change and economic growth. More open and liberal policies for investment in these sectors can attract the foreign investors who have easier access to capital resources and global expertise. Moreover, the knowledge, experience and connectivity of foreign companies to global markets give them an advantage in export market for manufactured goods.

Among the institutional changes, there is a need to strengthen FIPB and Foreign Investment Implementation Authority (FIIA), the nodal agencies for regulating and implementing foreign investments so as to increase their effectiveness in removing procedural bottlenecks and reducing bureaucratic red tape.

More and more areas of investment should be put on the automatic route. The real problem in India lies in the low levels of realization of FDI vis-à-vis the proposals cleared. The precise reason for the low levels of FDI realization is the post-approval procedures which have played havoc to project implementation.

Sector-wise FDI targets should be outlined and the respective ministries be made responsible for achieving this. All the wings of the government have to be made responsible and accountable for private investment in general and FDI in particular. These efforts need to be complemented by the sector-specific marketing strategy.

Apart from the above policy changes, there is a need to change the perception of foreign investors regarding their investments in India. The success stories of MNCs operating in India needs to be documented and made known to potential investors. The high degree of political and administrative uncertainty in the country, legal delays and bureaucratic delays have been perceived as major hurdles by foreign investors coming to invest. The government will have to revamp its whole publicity campaign and take steps to provide better and transparent information about policy, regulations and procedures governing the different sectors.

The need to develop SEZs has been highlighted a lot while demonstrating the experience of various countries including the success story of China. The efforts would involve improvement in the infrastructure facilities at these SEZs and investor-friendly legal and bureaucratic controls in these zones.

India's Investment Environment: Global Perspective

A recent report of the World Bank, indicates that India has made the highest progress among the South Asian nations in improving its investment climate and was rated among the top ten reformers in the world. It has established a private credit registry and made improvements in enforcing debt contracts and bankruptcy laws. But India still has a heavy regulatory burden on business and, also ranks in the bottom quartile on the ease of doing business. The World Bank's report shows that in China the average time taken to secure the necessary clearances for a start up, or to complete a bankruptcy procedure, is much shorter than in India. Also, Indian labour laws allow firms less latitude with their employees than the labour court does in China, Brazil or Mexico (see Table 3.2). The following points make the position further clear:

Table 3.2 *Indicators of Doing Business, 2004–2005*

Procedure	*Brazil*	*China*	*India*	*Sweden*
Time required for starting a business (days)	152	41	89	16
Time required for registering a property (days)	42	32	67	2
Time required for enforcing contracts (days)	566	241	425	208
Time required to complete insolvency proceedings (years)	10	2.4	10	2

Source: Government of India, *Economic Survey*, 2004–05

- India's investment climate is also affected by indirect taxes and import duties. Since a major share of tax revenue of the central and state governments comes from indirect taxes on the manufactured goods fiscal policy can be a major determinant of the investment climate in the country. At the central level, an excise duty and at the state level, sales and other local taxes influence an investor's attitude.
- Although, there has been a substantial reduction in duty on industrial products during 1991 and 2004, the peak rate of 20 per cent, which is also the minimum rate in most cases and the high total duties, acts as a drag on the efficiency of the Indian manufacturing industry. Excise duty is levied mostly at a comparatively high rate of 16 per cent. In addition, the states apply tax on the sales of goods with rates varying from 1 to over 30 per cent. Furthermore, sales

tax is applied at every point of sale, with no credit set off for the sales tax paid at the earlier stages. High taxes raise unduly the price paid by the consumer.

- Entry-exit barriers also adversely affect the investment climate. One of the determinants of the investment climate for industry is the ease with which firms are able to enter into and exit from business activities. Various studies have underlined the excessive regulation of entry and exit conditions. It is stated that a large number of clearances have to be taken, particularly in power and mining projects, both at the central and state levels. Such a system not only introduces delays but also creates avenues for corruption.

Doing business became easier in India in 2005–06. The reforms reduced the time, cost and hassle for businesses in India to comply with legal and administrative requirements, placing the country in the top 20 reformers worldwide. However, the World Bank 2008 database shows that among the South Asian economies in case of 'ease of doing business' India belongs to the lowest position, i.e., 120, whereas the rank of Bangladesh is 107. On the other hand, in India, the average time for getting credit and registering property is much shorter than in Bangladesh. However, investors are getting more protection in Bangladesh than in India, China and all other countries in South Asia (Table 3.2).

Determinants of FDI in India

To understand the scale and direction of FDI flows, it is necessary to identify their major determinants. Factors influencing the destination of investment, i.e., the host-country determinants, are explained below. The relative importance of FDI determinants varies not only between countries but also between different types of FDI. Furthermore, the relative importance of FDI determinants may change over time in a country.

Size of the Market

Large developing countries provide substantial markets where the consumers demand for certain goods far exceed the available supplies. This demand potential is a big draw for many foreign-owned enterprises. This explains the massive FDI flows into China since early 1980s. In many cases, the establishment of a low-cost marketing operation represents the first step by a multinational into the market of the country. This establishes a presence in the market and provides important insights into the ways of doing business and possible opportunities in the country.

Legal and Regulatory Framework

The transition to a market economy entails the establishment of a legal and regulatory framework that is compatible with private sector activities and the operation of foreign-owned companies. The relevant areas in this field include protection of property. The relevant rules and regulations of the host country governing foreign investment decide the quantum of the latter. These rules and regulations pertain to protection of property rights, ability to repatriate profits and free market for currency exchange. The rules, regulations and administrative procedures of the host country regarding foreign investment must be transparent.

Political Stability

In many countries the political situation is very unstable. Governments change frequently and so also the government policies and decisions. Foreign investors are generally reluctant to invest in countries where political situations are unstable. For example, due to the unstable political situation, not much foreign investment has been attracted in Bangladesh as compared to India and China.

Prices and Exchange Rate

Instability in the level of prices and exchange rate enhance the level of uncertainty, making business planning difficult. Price level in and exchange rates of the host country determine the foreign investment in the country. Instability in prices and exchange rates affect the inflow of foreign investment.

Access to Basic Inputs

FDI can be attracted by a country through the easy availability of factors of production. Many developing countries have large reserves of skilled and semi-skilled workers that are available for employment at wages significantly lower than in developed countries. This provides an opportunity for foreign firms to make investments in these countries to cater to the export market. The availability of and access to basic inputs such as oil and gas, minerals, forestry products, skilled and unskilled labour force, and so on determines the extent of FDI in a country.

Table 3.3 *Indicators of Doing Business*

Economy	*Ease of Doing Business Rank*	*Starting a Business*	*Dealing with Licenses*	*Employing Workers*	*Registering Property*	*Getting Credit*	*Protecting Investors*	*Paying Taxes*	*Trading Across Borders*	*Enforcing Contracts*	*Closing a Business*
Singapore	1	9	5	1	13	7	2	2	1	4	2
Hong Kong, China	4	13	60	23	58	2	3	3	3	1	15
Japan	12	44	32	17	48	13	12	105	18	21	1
Thailand	15	36	12	49	20	36	33	89	50	26	44
Malaysia	24	74	105	43	67	3	4	56	21	63	54
Mauritius	27	8	33	61	153	97	11	11	17	78	66
South Africa	35	53	45	91	76	26	9	61	134	85	68
Mexico	44	75	21	134	71	48	33	135	76	83	23
Maldives	60	34	8	7	178	135	64	1	110	94	120
Pakistan	76	59	93	132	88	68	19	146	94	154	51
China	83	135	175	86	29	84	83	168	42	20	57
Sri Lanka	101	29	160	111	134	97	64	158	60	133	39
Bangladesh	107	92	116	129	171	48	15	81	112	175	102
Nepal	111	60	125	155	25	97	64	92	151	123	95
Bhutan	119	52	119	14	33	158	122	68	149	38	178
India	120	111	134	85	112	36	33	165	79	177	137
Indonesia	123	168	99	153	121	68	51	110	41	141	136
Philippines	133	144	77	122	86	97	141	126	57	113	147

Note: The rankings are from the World Bank: *Doing Business 2008* report, covering the period April 2006 to June 2007.

Source: Doing Business in 2008; World Bank, IFC (available at www.doingbusiness.org/economyrankings)

Table 3.4 *Rankings Recalculated South Asian Region*

Economy	*Ease of Doing Business Rank*	*Starting a Business*	*Dealing with Licenses*	*Employing Workers*	*Registering Property*	*Getting Credit*	*Protecting Investors*	*Paying Taxes*	*Trading Across Borders*	*Enforcing Contracts*	*Closing a Business*
Maldives	1	3	1	1	8	6	4	1	4	2	5
Pakistan	2	5	2	7	3	3	2	6	3	5	2
Sri Lanka	3	2	8	5	5	4	4	7	1	4	1
Bangladesh	4	7	3	6	7	2	1	4	5	7	4
Nepal	5	6	5	8	1	4	4	5	7	3	3
Bhutan	6	4	4	2	2	7	7	3	6	1	7
India	7	8	6	4	4	1	3	8	2	8	6
Afghanistan	8	1	7	3	6	8	8	2	8	6	7

Source: Doing Business in 2008; World Bank, IFC (available at www.doingbusiness.org/economyrankings/)

Table 3.5 *Rankings Recalculated for Low Income Level*

Economy	*Ease of Doing Business Rank*	*Starting a Business*	*Dealing with Licenses*	*Employing Workers*	*Registering Property*	*Getting Credit*	*Protecting Investors*	*Paying Taxes*	*Trading Across Borders*	*Enforcing Contracts*	*Closing a Business*
Mongolia	1	8	4	11	2	5	2	19	45	2	22
Kenya	2	25	1	12	22	1	16	42	28	20	6
Pakistan	3	5	12	33	16	5	2	37	10	40	2
Vietnam	7	20	7	17	7	3	45	31	2	6	25
Bangladesh	10	16	18	32	48	3	1	16	15	49	17
Bhutan	16	3	21	2	6	38	23	11	29	5	37
India	17	24	28	18	21	2	4	48	6	50	30
Zimbabwe	30	35	49	30	13	10	20	35	46	13	36
Afghanistan	36	1	32	3	46	50	51	5	49	42	37
Burundi	48	27	48	23	24	45	37	25	44	35	37
Congo, Dem. Rep.	51	37	29	49	31	38	37	38	34	48	35

Source: Doing Business in 2008; World Bank, IFC (available at www.doingbusiness.org/economyrankings/)

Table 3.6

Country-wise Major Policy Reforms Issues in South Asia

	Country	Bangladesh	India	Nepal	Pakistan	Sri Lanka
1.	FD1 Policy Reforms	In the late 1980s and the 1990s, FDI is encouraged in industrial activities except arms and ammunitions; production of nuclear energy; security printing and minting; forestry in reserved forest areas. Investments may be undertaken either independently or through joint venture, either with the local, private or public sector. Foreign investors are provided with some incentives like tax exemptions for power generation and tax holidays for different industries. No import duty is charged in the case of capital machinery and spares for 100 per cent export oriented industries.	FDI is permitted in every sector except retail trading, atomic energy, gambling and betting; and lottery business. Tax holidays are offered in SEZs set up to make industry globally competitive. Special tax treatment and holidays are enjoyed by Infrastructure sector projects. Foreign nations are generally taxed only on their Indian income. Incentives for R&D measures are also provided to foreign investors by central government. All foreign investors are freely repatriable except for cases where NRIs choose to invest specifically under non-repatriable schemes. For certain sectors, foreign equity is allowed up to 100 percent.	A clear-cut policy towards FDI was introduced in the 1980s. FDI is allowed in most of the sectors except cottage industries, personal business services, arms and ammunitions and consultative services. Incentives are given to industries that are set up for export purposes. These include income tax exemption on export income, exemption on foreign investor's interest income earned abroad, and a relaxation of taxes on specific industries. Foreign equity was allowed up to 100 per cent for large industries exporting more than 90 per cent of total production.	Liberalization of FDI in Pakistan began in the end of 1980s. At present, FDI is opened up to sectors like services and agriculture, which constitute three fourth of GNP. The restricted sectors for FDI are arms and ammunitions, high explosives, radioactive substances, security printing currency and mint, and new units of alcohol manufacturing except industrial alcohol. Foreign investors are allowed to hold up to 100 per cent equity of industrial projects without any permission from the government except the restricted sectors. Attractive tariff and tax incentives have been given to foreign investors since 1997.	The notable feature of FDI policy measure in Sri Lanka was the establishment of the Board of Investment with wide powers of tax relief and administrative discretion in all maters related to FDI. FDI is permitted in most sectors but it is barred completely in non-bank money lending, pawn broking, retail trade with a capital investment of less than US$ 1 million. A range of tax incentives including breaks on taxes on corporate profits and dividends, value added tax and import and exercise duties. Except few sectors, automatic approval is given for equity participation up to 100 percent.

Cont'd...

...Cont'd

2. Trade Policy Reforms	In the early 1990s, the facility of duty-free import of machinery was introduced for 100 per cent export-oriented industries. An incentive to exporters is also provided in terms of duty drawbacks equal to custom duties and VAT paid on imported materials used in the manufacture of exports.	In 1991, the tariff rates were lowered on imports and the maximum tariff rate has set at 50 per cent from 250 percent. Tax exemption on export earnings and provision of concessional finance for exports and advance license scheme to allow duty-free import of intermediate goods for exports were introduced. The negative list for exports has been significantly pruned.	Significant tariff reforms, such as expanding the import license auction system, increasing the number of items under OGL system and bonded warehouse facilities for garments exports were introduced. In the mid-1980s, gradual relaxation of quantitative restrictions was observed. In 1989, government introduced a 25 per cent cash subsidy to jute exporters. In the same year, cash incentives ranging 10 per cent to 35 per cent of the value were offered to a range of export items.	In 1977, most of QRs were removed and replaced by import duties and import duties were raised. At the same time, export taxes were increased and export subsidies have reduced largely. In 1993, a reduction on the maximum nominal tariff on imports to 40 percent, introduction of a four bandtariff and the progressive elimination of export duty on traditional exports were observed.

Cont'd...

...Cont'd

3.	Foreign Exchange Rate Policy Reforms	On a daily basis the buying and selling rates of the US dollar on the basis of the real effective exchange rate were introduced in 1991. Banks are free to determine their own rates of US dollar and the cross-rates for all other currencies. Capital account is convertible for foreigners as well as expatriate Bangladeshis.	Rupee was made convertible for current account transactions in 1993. Realizing that Foreign Exchange Regulation Act (FERA) was not in tune with the economic reforms, the government replaced it with a new legislation, viz., Foreign Exchange Management Act (FEMA), 1999 which came into effect from 1 June 2000.	Rupee was experienced a large devaluation in 1985 and 1991 by 14.5 per cent and by 40 per cent respectively. A dual exchange rate system was introduced in 1992 and the DER system was abolished in 1993. In 1993, the government announced full convertibility of the Nepalese rupee for all current account transactions at the market determined exchange rates.	The exchange rate changed to 'managed float' against a trade weighted basket of currencies in 1982.	Unification of exchange rate and relaxation of exchange rate controls were observed in 1977. Large devaluation of the rupee occurred in 1989. In 1993, liberalization of exchange controls on the current account of the BoP and abolition of compulsory surrender requirements for exporters were introduced.

Cont'd...

...Cont'd

4.	Fiscal Policy Reforms	Domestic resources mobilization strengthened through improvement in tax policies, better tax collection and introducing of Value Added Tax (VAT) in 199 1. Every year government usually modifies the income tax rates, corporate tax rates, and tax holiday regulations.	The government reduced the income tax by 40 percent, abolished the estate duty, raised the wealth tax exemption limit and the effective rates of tax, and lowered taxes on corporation in 1985. Modified Value Added Tax (MODAT) was introduced in 1986. Tax reforms since June 1991 have helped in correcting structural imbalances in the tax system.	Measures, such as freezing salary increments, eliminating vacant positions and reducing financial commitments to public enterprises, had undertook to reduce budget deficit during 1985–86. Measures have been taken to increase tax collection such as improved tax administration, broadened the tax base and found alternative sources of revenue in the early 1990s. At the same period, measures, such as controlling salary increments, decreasing transfer payments to public enterprises and reducing subsidies on food and fertilizers, have been taken to control budget deficit and inflation.	Public expenditure was rationalized in 1977. Reform measures have been taken in the tax system, such as lowering income and corporate taxes (by 40% and 35% respectively), abolishing wealth and capital gain taxes with a view to stimulating the capital market, improving tax compliance and increasing administrative efficiency during 1989–93.

Cont'd...

...Cont'd

5.	Industrial Policy Reforms	Export-oriented, private sector-led growth strategy was adopted. No limitation pertaining to equity participation except five reserve sectors. Industries need only to be registered with the Board of Investment (BOI) to obtain institutional facilities. Foreign investors are allowed all the facilities available to domestic investors, and repatriation of profits.	Industrial licensing, permission from the Government of India for new investments and capacity expansions, has been abolished. Monopolies and Restrictive Trade Practices Act have also been eliminated. Majority foreign investment (up to 51%) is freely allowed in most industries.	Liberal industrial policy was declared. In 1987, provision of pre-export loans to exporters, provision of duty drawback to export-oriented industries, bonded warehouse facilities to EO industries, establishment of EPZs and industrial village and in 1992, reduction of sales tax and excise duties on locally produced goods were		
6.	Reforms in Public Sector Enterp-rises and Privati-zation	No government permission is necessary to set up new industries except in a few reserved sectors. Identify and remove legal, policy and regulatory constraints on private investment.	The government drastically reduced the significance of the Monopolies and Restrictive Trade Practices Act, by raising the minimum limit of assets of a company to come under the purview of the Act from ₹ 200 million to ₹ 1,000 million in 1985.	In 1991, a privatization cell was created and in 1993, two corporations were liquidated and eight enterprises were privatized.	Rationalization of public investment programme was initiated.	In 1977, expenditure on social welfare had reduced.

Cont'd...

...Cont'd

7.	Financial and Banking Sector Reforms	The policies of disinvesting a few nationalized banks were adopted and the permission had given for setting up of all kinds of financial institutions in private sector since the early 80s. The commercial banks were allowed to set their own bank rates freely. Reforms measures of NCBs have taken in terms accounting and auditing system and technical improvement of management. In 1990, an act to expedite NCB loan recovery was enacted.	In tune with the liberalization and privatization wave sweeping across the world, the Government of India reviewed banking policy in early 1990s. The highly regulated and directed banking system is now transforming itself into one characterized by openness, competition and prudence.	In 1986, foreign banks were permitted to operate. In the same year, interest rates were partially liberalized for commercial banks. However, in 1989, commercial banks were granted full freedom to set deposit rates. In 1993, a large reduction in the SLR took place with a view to increasing commercial banks liquidity and to enable them to reduce interest rates for lending. Nepal Stock Exchange was created in 1994.	De-control of prices and interest rate was introduced in 1977.

4

Foreign Direct Investment

Policy and Incentives Packages

One of the remarkable features of globalization in the 1990s was the flow of private capital in the form of foreign direct investment (FDI). FDI is an important source of development financing, and contributes to productivity gains by providing new investment, better technology, management expertise and export markets. Given resource constraints and lack of investment in developing countries, there has been increasing reliance on the market forces and private sector as the engine of economic growth. In the neo-classical growth model, FDI promotes economic growth by increasing the volume of investment and its efficiency. Therefore, all countries, particularly developing and least developed countries, seek to attract FDI for the benefits it brings along with it into the host country's economy. Foreign investment, especially FDI, not only supplements domestic investment resources but also acts as a source of foreign exchange and can relax balance of payment (BoP) constraints on growth. Considering the economic benefits and importance of FDI for promoting economic growth, most of the countries have formulated wide-reaching changes in their policies to attract FDI.

FDI Policy and Incentives in India

The policy of the Government of India with regard to FDI varied from decade to decade. The industrial policy resolution issued in 1948, soon after India's independence, spoke of regulating foreign capital in the national interest; however, practically no separate regulation specifically for foreign companies had been introduced. As a matter of principle, the existing foreign companies in India were not discriminated against similar Indian companies. During 1957–58, when India faced foreign exchange crisis, the government announced various incentives and concessions to MNCs for attracting more inflows of FDI in India. This liberal attitude continued till mid-sixties.

However, the Government of India realized that this attitude resulted in significant outflows of foreign exchange in the form of remittances of dividends, royalties, technical fees, etc., and created another foreign exchange crisis. Keeping in mind the continued foreign exchange crisis, the government changed its policy and started introducing restrictive policy, though in a gradual manner. In 1968, the Indian government established Foreign Investment Board (FIB) and introduced cumbersome FDI licensing procedure. In 1973, the Foreign Exchange Regulation Act (FERA) was introduced which imposed numerous restrictions on foreign equity participation and on the growth and expansion of foreign-owned companies. Under this Act, foreign companies were not allowed to remit dividend without prior approval of RBI. As a result of the restrictive FDI policies, India was not considered an attractive place for investment by MNCs. Consequently, the approved FDI inflows decreased to ₹ 31.77 million in 1975 from ₹ 58.40 million and ₹ 62.77 million in 1971 and 1972 respectively. These tightening restrictions also led to some withdrawals of FDI projects from India in the late 1970s, for example, IBM, Coca-Cola, etc.

In the early 1980s India's FDI policy took a new direction when the then government came out with a policy of liberalization. Under the liberalization programme, licensing procedure was abolished in a number of industries and foreign companies were permitted to diversify their product-mix and to increase their capacities without prior official approval. Various exemptions, rebates and incentives were provided to promote the export orientation of firms. However, in 1980s, the government showed more interest in import of foreign technology than in import of foreign capital.

In June 1991, the Government of India introduced a new radical reform programme, entitled the New Economic Policy (NEP), aimed at opening up the economy for foreign investment. In the NEP, the most important step is that RBI was empowered to grant automatic approval for FDI up to 51 per cent foreign equity in the high priority industries and trading companies primarily engaged in export activities. In 1992, a series of proposal was made to mismantle the barriers to FDI. In January 1993, FERA was amended to remove restrictions on foreign owned enterprises and accord them national treatment. As a result, foreign affiliates can freely transfer dividends and other profits abroad. They are also allowed to borrow or raise deposits in India to acquire or hold immovable property in India for business purposes and to take over any Indian business.

The Present FDI Policies of India

Since the mid-1990s, India has slowly implemented a programme of economic reforms, and relaxed many of its constraints gradually; nonetheless, FDI is still prohibited in some sectors or sub-sectors. India permits FDI or collaborations in almost all sectors except (1) atomic energy, (2) lottery business, (3) gambling and betting, and (4) retail trading (except single brand product retailing). A prior government approval is required for every foreign investment or collaboration/joint venture in India. The approval may be automatic or special. Automatic approvals are granted by the Reserve Bank of India (RBI) and special approvals are granted by Foreign Investment Promotion Board (FIPB). India has allowed automatic FDI approval in many sectors, gradually expanding the list over time. Where applicable, foreign investors do not need government licenses or approvals and simply notify the RBI of their investments. Other sectors require approval by either the FIPB or the Cabinet Committee on Foreign Investment. The rules vary from industry to industry and are frequently changed. Automatic approval up to 100 per cent FDI is allowed in advertising and films, seed industry, tea plantations, automobiles, coal processing plants, construction and maintenance of roads, highways, vehicular bridges, tunnels, ports and harbors, drugs, pharmaceuticals, e-commerce, building materials, the manufacture of textiles, paper, basic chemicals, rubber, plastic, non-metallic mineral products, metal products, ship building, information technology, software, electronics, except in the aerospace and defence sectors. FDI is allowed up to 100 per cent with automatic approval in non-banking financial companies such as merchant banking, underwriting, portfolio management, financial consulting, stock brokerage, asset management, venture capital, credit rating, housing finance, leasing of finance, credit card business, foreign exchange brokerage, factoring and custodial services and investment advisory services. Similarly, petroleum product pipeline, exploration, pollution control equipment manufacture, ports and harbors postal, courier services, printing science and technology magazines, journals, power projects relating to electricity generation, transmission and distribution, other than atomic reactor power plants are also allowed with 100 per cent FDI.

One of the biggest concerns for foreign investors is to repatriate funds from a host country to home country; however, the Government of India has liberalized its remittance policy recently. Now dividends, capital gains, royalties and fees can be repatriated easily with the permission of the RBI. Foreign partners may sell their shares to resident Indian investors without approval of RBI, provided shares were held on a repatriation basis. Rupee, the Indian currency, is convertible for the current account. Consequently, foreign exchange requirements for private travel, debt servicing, dividend or royalty payments and other remittances can be obtained from banks or exchange dealers at the current market rate.

There are no restrictions on remittances for debt service or payments for imported inputs. Foreign institutional investors (FIIs) may transfer funds from rupee to foreign currency accounts and vice versa at the market exchange rate. Government may also repatriate capital, capital gains, dividends, interest income, and any compensation from the sale of rights offerings, net of all taxes without approval. The RBI accords automatic approval to Indian industries for foreign collaboration agreements but limits lump sum payments at 2 million US$. For technology transfer agreements with foreign companies, Indian firms may remit royalties up to 5 per cent for domestic sales and 8 per cent for exports without approval. Where technology transfer is not involved, royalty payments for the use of trade marks and brand names are limited to 2 per cent on exports and 1 per cent on domestic sales.

Foreign banks may remit profits and surpluses to their headquarters, in compliance with the Banking Regulation Act, 1949. They may also issue credit cards without RBI approval. They are also permitted to offer foreign currency—rupee may be swapped without any limits to enable customers to hedge their foreign currency liabilities.

The new Foreign Trade Policy introduced in 2004 (replacing the Export-Import Policy) continued tax relief incentives for export-oriented industries and other targeted sectors. The policy allows exporting firms duty-free import of inputs and capital goods, exemption from excise taxes on capital goods, textile machinery, components and raw materials, as well as exemption from sales tax both at the federal and state levels. India provides a 10-year tax holiday for knowledge-based start ups. Import of consumables, professional equipment and spare parts in the service sector is allowed without any duty up to 10 per cent of the average foreign exchange export earnings.

The government has eliminated the restrictions on employing foreign technicians and managers, though employment of foreigners in excess of 12 months requires approval from the Ministry of Home Affairs. There is no such requirement to employ Indian nationals. India has established the International Centre for Alternative Dispute Resolution (ICADR) as an autonomous organization under the Ministry of Law and Justice and Company Affairs to promote settlement of domestic and international disputes through different modes of alternate dispute resolution. The country is not a member of the International Centre for the Settlement of Investment Disputes, but supports the New York Convention of 1958.

To encourage export-oriented production, India has established several foreign trade zones, in the form of the Special Economic Zone (SEZ), the Export Processing Zone (EPZ) and the Software Technology Park (STP)/Industrial Park. In addition, it also allows an individual firm to be designated as an export-oriented unit (EOU). All of these schemes are governed by separate rules and granted different benefits. Seeking to promote the SEZ model, the Government of India, in 2005, has announced plans to introduce legislation that would give additional fiscal incentives to SEZ developers and member-companies. In March 2012, the number of operational SEZs located in different parts of the country was 153. These zones are designed to provide internationally competitive infrastructure facilities and duty-free and low-cost environment.

The new Foreign Trade Policy provides substantial incentives for investments in EOUs. are industrial companies which can be established anywhere in India to export their entire production. As in 2008 were approximately 3,600 fully operational EOUs in India.

Automatic approvals are given by the Secretariat for Industrial Approval for setting up 100 per cent EOUs. Incentives and facilities available under the EOU scheme include concessional rent for lease of industrial plots, preferential power allocation and supply, duty-free import of intermediate goods, a ten-year income tax holiday, exemption from excise tax on capital goods, components and raw materials, and waiver of sales taxes.

EPZs are industrial parks with incentives for foreign investors in export-oriented business. STPs are special zones with similar incentives for software exports. EPZ/STP units may import intermediate goods duty-free. The minimum net foreign exchange earning as a percentage of exports by EPZ/STP units is required to be at least 3 per cent. EPZ/STP units may sell up to 50 per cent of their level of exports in the domestic market after payment of taxes, with the exception of motor cars, alcoholic beverages, tea, books and refrigeration units. India has entered into tax treaties with a number of countries, including Australia, Belgium, Canada, Denmark, France, Germany, Indonesia, Japan, Korea, Mauritius, Singapore, the United Kingdom and the United States. These treaties endeavour to avoid double taxation and attract know-how and technology. In many treaties, the withholding tax on royalties and fees for technical services emanating from India is lower than the general tax rate. In addition to incentives stated earlier, foreign investors are also entitled to the following:

- Foreign investors are free to select the location of a project for electronics, computer, printing and other non-polluting industries. In case of other industries, the proposed location should be at least 25 kilometres away from the urban area.
- Subject to certain sector-specific restrictions foreign entities may establish and own businesses in trading companies, subsidiaries, joint ventures, branch offices, project offices and liaison offices. NRIs and overseas corporate bodies (OCBs) are permitted 100 per cent equity investment in real estate.
- FIIs are allowed to invest in all securities traded on India's primary and secondary markets. The FIIs can also bypass brokers and deal directly with companies in open offers; however, they must register with the Securities and Exchange Board of India (SEBI).
- Subject to separate investment limitations, NRIs are allowed to repatriate dividends, rents and interest earned in India and their specially designated bank deposits are fully convertible.
- Companies incorporated outside India can raise resources in India's capital market through the issuance of Indian Depository Receipts (IDRs), subject to certain conditions established and monitored by SEBI.
- Local banks are bound to extend 40 per cent of their loans to 'priority' borrowers (agriculturists, exporters and small businesses). A similar requirement for foreign banks is 32 per cent of loans to exporters and small businesses.
- India allows external commercial borrowing (ECB) under the automatic route up to US$ 50 million when the average maturity exceeds five years, and up to US$ 20 million for three-five years average maturity.

FDI Policy in India

Evolution of the FDI Policy in India

There has been a gradual change in the government's attitude towards FDI since 1948. Being a resource-poor country, especially in capital resources, India has always been receptive to foreign investment. The foreign exchange crisis of 1957–58 led to a further liberalization of the government's attitude towards FDI. However, the government adopted a more restrictive attitude towards FDI in the late 1960s as local industries developed. In 1973, the new Foreign Exchange Regulation Act (FERA) came into force, requiring all foreign companies operating in India to register under Indian corporate legislation with up to 40 per cent equity. In the 1980s, as a part of the industrial policy resolutions, the attitude towards FDI was liberalized. However, through the new economic policy and the new industrial policy of 1991, a series of policy measures were announced to liberalize the FDI environment in the country. As a result, India today has one of the most attractive FDI policies in the South Asian region.

FDI Policy Framework and Incentives for FDI in India

The first and second generation reforms created a conducive environment for foreign investment in India. The FDI policy is reviewed on a regular basis and changes in sectoral policy/sectoral equity caps are notified through press notes by the Secretariat for Industrial Assistance (SIA), Department of Industrial Policy & Promotion. The FDI policy is also notified by the RBI under the Foreign Exchange Management Act (FEMA, 1999). Most of the sectors/activities are under the automatic approval route, except for a few sectors, where there are additional restrictions on FDI such as equity caps, divestment conditions, lock-in periods on investment, etc. These restrictions have been imposed in view of sectoral requirements, security and strategic concerns and in the interest of the domestic investments. There are only four sectors where FDI is not permitted.

Industrial Licensing

Industrial licensing policies and procedures have also been liberalized from time to time. All industrial undertakings are exempt from obtaining an industrial licence to manufacture, except for: (i) industries retained under compulsory licensing; (ii) items of manufacture reserved for the small-scale sector; and (iii) when the proposed location attracts locational restriction.

FDI-related Institutions

Foreign Investment Promotion Board

The Foreign Investment Promotion Board (FIPB), Ministry of Finance, is the nodal, single-window agency for all matters relating to FDI, which is aimed to promote FDI in India (i) by undertaking investment promotion activities, (ii) facilitating foreign investment, (iii) purposeful negotiation/discussion with potential investors, (iv) early clearance of proposals, and (v) reviewing policy and putting in place appropriate institutional arrangements, transparent rules and procedures and guidelines for investment promotion and approvals.

Secretariat for Industrial Assistance

The Secretariat for Industrial Assistance (SIA), Ministry of Commerce & Industry, provides a single-window service for entrepreneurial assistance, investor facilitation, receiving and processing all applications, assisting entrepreneurs and investors in setting up projects (including liaison with other organizations and state governments) and in monitoring the implementation of projects.

Foreign Investment Implementation Authority (FIIA)

FIIA provides a proactive one stop-after-service care to foreign investors by helping them obtain necessary approvals, sort out operational problems and meet with various government agencies to find solution to their problems.

Foreign Investment Policy

Foreign investment is permitted in virtually every sector, except those of strategic concern such as defence and transport. Foreign companies are permitted to set up 100 per cent subsidiaries in India. No prior approval from exchange control authorities (RBI) is required, except for certain specified activities. Under current policy, FDI can come into India in two ways as under:

(i) Automatic route

FDI in various sectors/activities to the extent permitted under the automatic route does not require any prior approval either by the government or RBI. The investors are only required to inform the proper regional office of the RBI within 30 days of the receipt of inward remittances and file the required documents within 30 days of the issue of shares to foreign investors.

Prior government approval route (for both foreign investment and foreign technical collaboration)

In the limited category of sectors requiring prior government approval, proposals are considered in a time-bound and transparent manner by the FIPB. For all activities that are not covered under the automatic route, government's approval through the FIPB is necessary. The FDIs under both the routes automatic approval and government approval—are regulated by the FEMA. There are also provisions for automatic approval for new and existing companies.

FDI in SEZs/EOUs/Industrial Parks/EHTP/STP

SEZs are specifically delineated duty-free enclaves and are deemed to be foreign territory for the purposes of trade operations and duties and tariffs. FDI up to 100 per cent is permitted under the automatic route for the establishment of SEZs. However, proposals not covered under the automatic route require approval by FIPB. FDI up to 100 per cent is permitted under the automatic route for setting up 100 per cent EOUs, subject to sectoral policies. Similarly, FDI up to 100 per cent is permitted under the automatic route for the establishment of industrial parks. Proposals for FDI/NRI investment in EHTP units are eligible for approval under the automatic route, subject to certain parameters listed by the government. Likewise, proposals for FDI/NRI investment in Software Technology Park (STP) units are eligible for approval under the automatic route, subject to parameters listed by the government.

Repatriation of Investment Capital and Profits

All foreign investments are freely repatriable except for cases where NRIs choose to invest specifically under non-repatriable schemes. Non-residents can sell shares on the stock exchange and repatriate sale proceeds if they hold a tax clearance certificate issued by authorities in charge of income tax. Profits, dividends, etc. (which are remittances classified as current account transactions) can be freely repatriated.

Important Labour Rules/Regulations Applicable in India

Under the Constitution of India, labour is a subject in the 'concurrent list,' under which both the central and state governments are competent to enact legislation subject to certain matters being reserved for the centre. There are several important Labour Acts enacted since 1952, which are highly protective of labour.

Policy Regarding Intellectual Property Rights

India is a signatory to the agreement concluding the Uruguay Round of GATT negotiations and establishing the World Trade Organization

(WTO). This agreement contains an agreement on Trade Related Aspects of Intellectual Property Rights (TRIPS), which lays down minimum standards for the protection and enforcement of intellectual property rights.

Taxation Policy in India and Tax Incentives

India is moving towards a reform of its tax policies and systems to facilitate the globalization of economic activities. The corporate tax rate for foreign companies at present is over 42 per cent. The net tax rate is far lower than this, however, on account of various deductions and exemptions available under the tax laws. Tax holidays are available in SEZs set up to make industry globally competitive. Infrastructure projects enjoy special tax treatment and holidays. Since March 2004, a user-friendly tax administration has been introduced with round-the-clock electronic filing of customs documents. Foreign nationals working in India are generally taxed only on their Indian income. Income received from sources outside India is not taxable unless it is received in India. Further, foreign nationals have the option of being taxed under the tax treaties that India may have signed with their country of residence. India has entered into Double Taxation Avoidance Agreements (DTAA) with 65 countries, including the US, UK, Japan, Germany and Mauritius. Though the Indian government gives different kinds of investment incentives, major incentives are given in the form of tax exemptions on profit from the development and operation of infrastructure projects including power.

Thus, we can conclude that there has been a positive change in policies with regard to FDI in countries. The low-income economies have now realized that FDI is not only a good debt, but also has a major role in enhancing economic development. Stepping up the economic reform process and making their economies politically stable and free from internal conflict would go a long way towards making them an attractive destination for FDI. Ongoing initiatives such as the further simplification of rules and regulations and improvements in infrastructure are expected to provide the necessary impetus to increase FDI inflows in the future. However, the image of South Asian countries, specifically Bangladesh and India, as corrupt nations with overprotective labour laws and internal law and order problems, will have to be mitigated to facilitate the entrance of much needed foreign investment.

Trends of FDI Inflows

The world economy witnessed a period of significant surge in the flows of FDI in 1980s when it grew at a rate of around 25 per cent per

Table 4.1 *Summary of Comparative Policy Analysis*

Countries	*Policies*			
	Openness and Permissible Sector	*Ownership and Control*	*Regulatory Procedure*	*Investment Incentives/Facilities*
Nepal	Foreign investment (FI) welcomed in every sector of medium and large industries except defence-related industries. Priority given to the industries prescribed by the government.	Encourages investment as joint ventures but up to 100 per cent foreign equity permitted in large and medium industries. Permission may be granted to use foreign tech. in the form of investment in cottage and small industries.	Application for investment should be submitted to FIPD under the ministry of industry. According to new act (1991),the Department of Industry will be organized as one-window service unit and the applicant and will be notified of permission within 30 days of the receipt of application.	No difference in incentives and concessions between domestic and foreign investors. A 30 per cent effective rate of protection. Income tax exemption of five years for tourist standard enterprises and 10 years for industries of national priority and long gestation period. Double taxation agreement with only India though agreements with other countries are underway.
India	Foreign investment (FI) welcomed only if accompanied by technology transfer. Priority for export-oriented industry.	Upper limit of foreign equity increased to 51 per cent recently but If the product is entirely for export, 100 per cent ownership could be given after negotiation with a special board.	FDI up to 100 per cent is allowed under the automatic route from foreign/NRI investor without prior approval in most of the sectors including services sector. Industrial licenses are regulated under the ndustries (Development and Regulation) Act, 1951. The requirements of industrial licence has been progressively reduced. Industrial licence is granted by the Government of India in the Secretariat for Industrial Assistance (SIA) on the recommendation of the licensing Committee.	No difference in incentives and concessions between domestic and foreign investors.

Cont'd...

...Cont'd

Pakistan	Every industry, business or service enterprise is open to private foreign investment.	Can now own 100 per cent of equity in any venture.	Barring industries like arms and ammunition, security printing, currency and mint, high explosives or radio active substances, government permission is not needed for setting up industry. Multinationals no more require work permit for their managerial and technical staff Bangladesh.	No discrimination between domestic and foreign investors in respect of tax concessions. Foreign investors free to choose plant sites within environmental considerations. Tax holiday of 3–8 years depending upon the location of industry. Industrial machinery required for rural or less developed area and the units like biotechnology, electronics, fertilizers, fibre optics and solar energy are allowed to import free of customs, sales tax and import surcharge.
Bangladesh	Foreign investment allowed in all sectors except seven sectors which constitute the reserved list.	Limit of foreign equity participation increased from 51 to 100 per cent. Technology collaboration allowed almost in all types of industries.	Can establish industries without any prior approval of the government.	Tax holiday of 5–9 years depending upon location (12 years for firms established in EPZs). Relief from double taxation.

Cont'd...

...*Cont'd*

Sri Lanka	Welcomes with open arms investment in FTZ but access to rest of the economy.	No limit on equity holdings who initially entered into agreement with GCEC.	Foreign investment promotion and approvals are handled by GCEC which also operates as a 'One Stop Centre'. The general policy is to grant approvals within one month of the receipt of an application.	Enterprises entering into agreement with GCEC to set up plant can qualify for 100 per cent tax exemption for corporate and personal income, royalties and dividends up to 10 years depending on net foreign exchange earned on exports, employment created and the magnitude of capital investment.
Singapore	Apart from public utilities and telecommunication, most economic activities are open to foreigners. Prefers investment in the areas which develop technological, management and labour skills.	No restriction on the amount of foreign equity participation. Wholly foreign-owned companies are very common in this country.	No special procedure for approving foreign investment unless the firm is seeking incentives. However, special licences required from the Monetary Authority of Singapore for the establishment of financial institutions and from registrar of Manufactures for the manufacture of certain goods.	The government offers a wide range of incentives to investment with pioneer status (the eligibility of status being decided by Minister of Finance on the recommendation of Economic Development Board). The pioneer companies also receive 5 to 10 years exemptions from 40 per cent corporate income tax. More exemption to industries which export at least 1/5 of production. Has double taxation agreement with number of countries.

Cont'd...

...Cont'd

Malaysia	Welcomes foreign investment only in manufacturing sector.	Encourages investment on joint-venture and allows up to 100 per cent foreign ownership depending upon export as percentage of production. For companies catering for domestic market, 100 per cent foreign ownership is allowed only if they are unable to find suitable local partner.		Does not discriminate between foreign and domestic investors in terms of incentives.
Indonesia	Restrictive involving greater specification by sector and location, increased local ownership and requirements for more rapid promotion of Indonesians to managerial position.			Provides various types of incentives to foreign investment established in priority areas. Also given certain rights for foreign exchange transfers.

Cont'd...

...Cont'd

	Policies			
Countries	*Repatriation*	*Investment Protection*	*Infrastructural facilities*	*Foreign Labour*
Nepal	Repatriation of capital on sale or liquidation at the rate of 20 to 25 per cent per year depending upon whether the shares were initially sold by the company or SEC.	Investments are assured of security of investment. Has Investment Protection agreement with France and Germany which guarantees the transfer of capital, profits and loans. Also ratified the convention for the settlement of disputes.	Has some industrial estates with necessary infrastructural facilities. Is in the process of establishing an EPZ.	Foreign management and technical experts can be employed with the prior approval of the government of Nepal. Such personnel coming from the countries with convertible currency are permitted to repatriate up to 75 per cent of the amount received as salaries and allowances.
India	All foreign investments are freely repatriable except for cases where NRIs choose to invest specifically under non-repatriable schemes. Profits, dividends, etc., which are remittances classified as current account transactions can be freely repatriated.	India has signed multilateral investment guarantee agency protocol (MIGA) for the protection of foreign investment on 13 April 1992. India is also a signatory to the agreement concluding the Uruguay round of GATT negotiations.	Various facilities including establishment of an EPZs/SEZs/Industrial parks.	There are several important Labor Acts since 1952, which are highly protective of labour. Allows particularly in the field where there is a shortage of skill locally.

Cont'd...

...Cont'd

Pakistan	Dividend and original investment can now be remitted abroad at any time.	Investment protected by an act of Parliament.		
Bangladesh	Guaranteed after settlement of local liabilities.	Guarantees against nationalization without proper compensation, fair and equitable treatment. Treaty with various countries.	Various facilities including establishment of an EPZ.	Allows particularly in the field where there is a shortage of skill locally.
Sri Lanka	GCEC provides free transfer of shares within and outside Sri Lanka without any tax or exchange control.	All investment made in free trade zones protected under the constitution the country is also a member of the World Bank's MICA.		
	Dividends of non-resident shareholders are exempt from taxes and remittances exempt from exchange control.			

Cont'd...

...Cont'd

Singapore	There are no restrictions on the transfer of profits, dividends, royalties or the repatriation of capital.			
Malaysia	There is no restriction on the repatriation of capital and profit.		As of 1988, the country had 10 FM (EPZs).	Allowed to have a maximum of 5 expatriate posts in 'Key positions' and the persons holding such post can work in Malaysia indefinitely. Additional posts for expatriates can also be applied.
Indonesia		Has investment guarantees with a number of developed countries and has Ratified the convention on the settlement of disputes between states and nationals of other states.		

Source: Chitrakar (1994) revised and rearranged by the author.

annum. This upward trend was continued in the late 1990s. At the beginning of the 21st century, the total inward stock of FDI has stood at approximate 7.1 trillion and at the end of the 2006, global FDI inflows have reached a new high at US$ 13.05 trillion (Tables 4.2, 4.3 and UNCTAD WIR, 2007).

Global Trends of FDI Flows

Since the early 1980s world FDI flows have grown rapidly. Developing countries received two-thirds of the increase in FDI worldwide between the late 1980s and 1990s—a sharp change from the previous decade, when flows to industrial countries dominated (World Bank, 1999). Global FDI flows have grown at an average annual rate of 20 per cent over the periods 1986–1990 and 1991–1995 respectively and at 40.1 per cent during 1996–2000. Flows increased from US$ 59 billion in 1982 to US$ 209 billion in 1990 and further to US$ 1,271 billion in 2000—a massive jump in a decade (Table 4.3). But these have declined sharply by 41 per cent in 2001, 13 per cent in 2002 and 12 per cent in 2003—around half of the peak in 2000. The year 2004 saw a slight rebound in global FDI after three years of declining flows. The upward trend in FDI that began in 2004 accelerated further in 2005 and 2006 at US$ 946 billion and at US$ 1,306 billion, respectively.

Likewise, FDI outflows increased in 2004 by 56.6 per cent to US$ 730 billion and down by 4.6 per cent in 2005. It was again increased in 2006 by 45.2 per cent. The stock of FDI in 2005 and 2006 has stood US$ 10 trillion and US$ 11.99 trillion, respectively (Table 4.2).

Distribution of World FDI Inflows

Overall Trends

Global FDI inflows grew in 2006 for the third consecutive year to reach US$ 1,306 billion, which is the second highest level ever recorded. All three major country groups—developed, developing and the transition economies of South-East Europe and the CIS—saw continued growth. FDI inflows in 2006 were 38 percent higher than in 2005, approaching the peak of US$ 1,411 billion reached in 2000 (Table 4.3). Although FDI flows to all three major country groups rose, they varied greatly among regions and countries (Table 4.3).

Regions receiving the bulk of FDI inflows are developed economies, Latin America and the Caribbean, Asia and the Pacific, and the transition economies of Central and Eastern Europe (UNCTAD WIR, 2007). Africa has suffered serious setback in the share of FDI

Table 4.2 *Selected Indicators of World FDI Flows, 1982–2011*

Item	*Value at Current Prices (US$ in billion)*													
	1982	*1990*	*2000*	*2001*	*2002*	*2003*	*2004*	*2005*	*2006*	*2007*	*2008*	*2009*	*2010*	*2011*
FDI inflows	59	209	1,271	735	651	633	648	946	1,306	1,982	1,761	1,137	1,350	1,632
FDI outflows	28	242	1,150	621	647	617	730	838	1,216	2,167	1,911	1,134	1,417	1,591
FDI inward stock	802	1,954	6,314	6,846	7,123	7,987	8,902	10,048	11,999	16,490	15,455	17,939	19,439	19,720
FDI outward stock	595	1,763	5,976	6,582	6,866	8,731	9,732	10,579	12,474	16,808	16,629	18,887	20,294	21,063
GDP (at current price)	11,758	22,610	30,875	31,900	32,227	36,327	40,617	44,486	48,293	52,356	56,322	60,768	64,987	68,457
GFCF	2,398	4,905	4,865	6,680	6,422	7,853	8,869	9,115	10,307	11,200	12,765	13,456	14,523	15,689
Item	*Annual Growth Rate (%)*													
	1986–90	*1991–95*	*1996–2000*	*2001*	*2002*	*2003*	*2004*	*2005*	*2006*	*2007*	*2008*	*2009*	*2010*	*2011*
FDI inflows	23.1	21.1	40.2	–40.9	–13.3	–11.7	2.5	27.4	38.1	39.4	50.32	59.63	70.11	80.45
FDI outflows	25.7	16.5	35.7	–40.8	–9.0	–5.4	18.4	–4.6	45.2	47.34	52.45	55.39	50.21	56.55
FDI inward stock	14.7	9.3	17.2	7.5	7.8	19.1	16.9	5.0	19.4	22.12	28.45	25.44	28.33	30.42
FDI outward stock	18.0	10.6	16.8	5.5	8.7	19.8	15.6	4.2	17.9	18.90	21.34	25.43	25.65	26.34
GDP (at current price)	10.8	5.6	1.3	–0.8	3.9	12.1	12.0	7.7	8.9	9.8	8.2	8.7	9.11	9.6
GFCF	13.4	4.2	1.0	–3.0	0.5	12.9	12.9	4.8	13.1	15.6	12.8	9.6	9.6	9.2

Source: World Investment Report, 1997–2011, UNCTAD.

Table 4.3 *Global Trends of Total Foreign Direct Investment Inflows, 1985–2011 (in million US$)*

Host Region/Economy	*1985–90*	*1991*	*1992*	*1993*	*1994*	*1995*	*1990–95*	*1996*	*1997*
World	1,41,930	1,58,936	1,73,761	2,18,094	2,38,738	3,16,524	2,25,321	3,86,140	4,78,082
Developed Economies	1,16,744	1,14,792	1,19,692	1,38,762	1,42,395	2,05,876	1,45,019	2,19,908	2,67,947
Developing Economies	24,736	41,696	49,625	73,054	90,462	96,330	74,288	1,52,685	1,91,022
Asia	13,492	23,129	29,632	50,924	57,507	65,249	47,321	93,331	1,05,828
East and South-East Asia	12,368	21,228	27,669	47,279	55,718	65,176	44,564	87,843	96,338
East Asia	5,930	7,358	14,859	30,704	37,985	41,299	26,440	54,853	61,031
China	2,654	4,366	11,156	27,515	33,787	35,849	19,360	40,180	44,237
Hong Kong, China	1,597	538	2,051	1,667	2,000	2,100	4,859	10,460	11,368
Korea, DPR	95	0	42	6	7	3	14	2	307
Korea, Republic	705	1,180	727	588	809	1,776	978	2,325	2,844
Macao, China	0	3	2	3	0	2	–1	6	2
Mongolia	0	0	2	8	7	10	8	16	25
Taiwan P China	879	1,271	879	917	1,375	1,559	1,222	1,864	2,248
South Asia	391	470	703	1,141	1,922	2,643	1,221	3,620	4,936
Afghanistan	0	0	0	0	0	0	0	1	–1
Bangladesh	2	1	4	14	11	2	6	14	139
Bhutan	0	0	0	0	0	0	0	1	–1
India	179	155	233	574	1,314	1,929	703	2,525	3,619

Cont'd...

...Cont'd

Maldives	4	7	7	7	6	5	7	9	11
Nepal	2	2	1	4	6	5	6	19	23
Pakistan	167	257	335	347	419	639	389	918	713
Sri Lanka	37	48	123	195	166	63	110	133	433
South-East Asia	6,047	13,400	12,107	15,434	15,811	21,234	16,932	29,370	30,369
Brunei Darussalam	0	1	4	14	6	7	102	654	702
Cambodia	0	0	33	54	69	151	80	586	–15
Indonesia	551	1,482	1,777	2,004	2,109	4,348	2,135	6,194	4,677
Lao People's DR	2	7	8	30	59	88	33	128	86
Malaysia	1,054	3,998	5,183	5,006	4,342	4,132	4,655	7,296	6,324
Myanmar	28	238	171	149	91	115	180	310	387
Philippines	413	544	228	1,238	1,591	1,478	1,028	1,520	1,249
Singapore	2,952	4,887	2,204	4,686	5,480	6,912	5,782	8,608	10,746
Thailand	1,017	2,014	2,114	1,730	1,322	2,003	1,990	2,271	3,626
Timor-Leste	0	0	0	0	0	0	0	0	0
Vietnam	30	229	385	523	742	2,000	947	1,803	2,587
Host Region/Economy	1998	1999	2000	2001	2002	2003	2004	2005	2006
World	6,94,457	10,88,263	14,91,934	8,17,578	7,16,128	6,32,599	7,42,143	9,45,795	13,05,852
Developed Economies	4,84,239	8,37,761	12,27,476	5,71,483	5,47,778	4,42,157	4,18,855	5,90,311	8,57,499

Cont'd...

...Cont'd

Developing Economies	1,87,611	2,25,140	2,37,894	2,19,721	1,55,528	1,66,337	2,83,030	3,14,316	3,79,070
Asia	96,109	1,02,779	1,33,707	1,11,854	92,009	1,01,278	1,69,999	2,08,744	2,59,434
East and South-East Asia	86,252	99,990	1,31,123	1,02,228	86,318	94,755	1,49,160	1,67,190	1,99,531
East Asia	64,187	77,188	1,16,973	78,644	67,282	72,060	1,06,314	1,16,253	1,25,774
China	43,751	40,319	40,772	46,878	52,743	53,505	60,630	72,406	69,468
Hong Kong, China	14,770	24,596	61,938	23,775	9,682	13,624	34,032	33,618	42,892
Korea, DPR	31	–15	5	–4	–15	158	197	50	135
Korea, Republic	5,412	9,333	9,283	3,683	2,975	[illegible],785	8,980	7,050	4,950
Macao, China	–18	9	–7	160	375	403	484	1,322	739
Mongolia	19	20	54	43	78	132	93	182	167
Taiwan P China	222	2,926	4,928	4,109	1,445	453	1,898	1,625	7,424
South Asia	3,560	3,099	3,095	3,983	4,528	5,331	7,601	9,866	22,274
Afghanistan	0	6	0	1	1	2	1	4	2
Bangladesh	190	178	280	79	52	268	460	692	625
Bhutan	0	0	0	0	0	1	3	9	6
India	2,633	2,168	2,319	3,403	3,449	4,269	5,771	6,676	16,881
Maldives	12	12	13	12	12	14	15	9	14
Nepal	12	4	0	21	–6	15	0	2	–7
Pakistan	507	530	305	385	823	534	1,118	2,201	4,273

Cont'd...

...Cont'd

Sri Lanka	206	201	178	82	197	229	233	272	480
South-East Asia	18,504	19,691	11,056	19,601	14,507	17,364	35,245	41,071	51,583
Brunei Darussalam	573	596	600	526	1,035	2,009	334	289	434
Cambodia	230	214	179	149	145	84	131	381	483
Indonesia	–356	–2,745	–4,550	–2,977	145	–597	1,896	8,337	5,556
Lao People's DR	45	52	34	24	25	19	17	28	187
Malaysia	2,714	3,895	3,788	554	3,203	2;473	4,624	3,965	6,060
Myanmar	314	253	255	192	191	291	251	236	143
Philippines	1,752	578	1,241	982	1,792	347	688	1,854	2,345
Singapore	6,389	11,803	5,407	15,038	5,822	9,331	19,828	15,004	24,207
Thailand	5,143	3,561	2,813	3,813	947	1,952	5,862	8,957	9,751
Timor-Leste					1	5	3	0	3
Vietnam	1,700	1,484	1,289	1,300	1,200	1,450	1,610	2,021	2,315

Host region/Economy	*2007*	*2008*	*2009*	*2010*	*2011*
World	19,75,537	17,90,706	11,97,824	13,09,001	15,24,422
Developed Economies	13,10,425	10,19,648	6,06,212	6,18,586	7,47,860
Developing Economies	5,74,311	6,50,017	5,19,225	6,16,661	6,84,399
Asia	3,49,412	3,80,360	3,15,238	3,84,063	4,23,157
East and South-East Asia	2,36,606	2,35,508	2,06,591	2,94,124	3,35,533

Cont'd...

...*Cont'd*

East Asia	1,51,004	1,85,253	1,59,183	2,01,364	2,18,974
China	83,521	1,08,312	95,000	1,14,734	1,23,958
Hong Kong China	54,341	59,621	52,394	71,069	83,156
Korea, DPR	67	44	2	38	55
Korea Republic	2,628	8,409	7,501	8,511	4,661
Macao China	2,305	2,591	858	2,828	4,365
Mongolia	373	845	624	1,691	4,715
Taiwan P China	7,769	5,432	2,805	2,492	–1,962
South Asia	34,695	52,869	42,370	31,746	38,942
Afghanistan	189	94	76	211	83
Bangladesh	666	1,066	700	913	1,136
Bhutan	3	7	18	16	14
India	25,506	43,406	35,596	24,159	31,554
Maldives	126	174	152	212	282
Nepal	6	1	39	87	95
Pakistan	5,590	5,438	2,338	2,022	1,327
Sri Lanka	603	752	404	478	300
South-East Asia	85,603	50,254	47,408	92,760	1,16,559
Brunei Darussalam	260	330	371	626	1,208

Cont'd...

...Cont'd					
Cambodia	867	815	539	783	892
Indonesia	6,928	9,318	4,877	13,771	18,906
Lao People's DR	324	228	319	333	450
Malaysia	8,595	7,172	1,453	9,103	11,966
Myanmar	715	978	963	450	850
Philippines	2,916	1,544	1,963	1,298	1,262
Singapore	46,930	11,798	24,418	48,637	64,003
Thailand	11,359	8,455	4,854	9,733	9,572
Timor-Leste	9	40	50	27	20
Vietnam	6,700	9,579	7,600	8,000	7,430

Source: World Investment Reports, various issues.

inflows, while the share for least developed countries (LDCS) stagnated at about 0.5 per cent of world FDI over the period. Within the developing world, FDI inflows are concentrated in about 10 developing countries, mainly in Asian newly industrializing countries (NICs) and Latin America. In 2001, for instance, the five largest host countries in the developing world received 62 per cent of total inflows into the region, while the 10 largest received three-quarters.

After record high levels of FDI in 2000, global flows declined sharply in 2001 for the first time in a decade and this declining trend remained continued for three consecutive years. The decline in FDI was mainly concentrated in developed economies, where the FDI inflows shrank by 59 per cent, compared to 14 per cent in developing economies. World inflows of FDI amounted to US$ 817 billion (2001), of which US$ 571 billion went to developed economies, US$ 219 billion to developing economies and the remaining US$ 27 billion to the transition economies of CEE. The shares of developing countries and those of CEE in global FDI inflows reached 28 per cent and 4 per cent respectively in 2001, compared to an average of 18 per cent and 2 per cent in the preceding two years. The 49 LDCs remain marginal recipients, with only 2 per cent of all FDI to developing countries or 0.5 per cent of the global total (UNCTAD WIR, 2002).

It is evident that the share of developing countries to FDI is much lower than developed countries during the whole period. FDI inflows to developing countries also fell from US$ 240 billion in 2000 to US$ 225 billion in 2001. However, the bulk of this decline was limited to a relatively small number of host countries. Africa remains a marginal recipient of FDI, even though FDI inflows rose from US$ 9 billion in 2000 to more than US$ 17 billion in 2004. The raising trend has observed in the next two consecutive years 2005 ($ 29 billion), and in 2006 ($ 35 billion). At first sight this increase looks impressive, but it masks fact that for most of African countries FDI flows remained at more or less the same level as in 2000 (ibid.).

However, during 2000–01, most of the Asian Tiger economies continued to attract more investment. India, Singapore, Korea and Vietnam were significant recipients in their respective sub-region. FDI in Singapore rose for the first time in four years by 59 per cent to US$ 9 billion, in Thailand it grew by US$ 1 billion to US$ 3.8 billion, and in Philippines from US$ 1.23 billion in 2000 to US$ 1.8 billion in 2001. Vietnam has entered a new era as a host to FDI. In Vietnam, FDI increased from US$ 1.2 billion in 2000 to US$ 1.3 billion in 2001 (ibid.).

Global FDI Inflows and South Asia

FDI flows to developed countries have typically been much higher than flows to developing countries. As a result, until very recently, the global trend largely mirrored trends in the developed world. A major break from this pattern took place in 2004, when FDI flows to developed countries declined, whereas global flows increased, spurred by the surge in FDI to developing countries (see Table 4.4). It can be seen from Table 4.4 that FDI flows to developed countries gradually declined from US$ 547 billion in 2002 to US$ 442 billion in 2003 and further to US$ 418 billion in 2004. After the years from 2005–06 developed economies witnessed sharp increases in FDI flows, which reached US$ 590 billion and US$ 857 billion, respectively. In fact, this is in line with the overall ups and downs in FDI flows to the world. On the contrary, along with the shift in trade to developing economies, there has been a consistent increase in FDI inflows to the developing world, with most of the growth being concentrated in Asia and Latin and Central America.

Table 4.4 *Global Trends of Total Foreign Direct Investment Inflows in South Asia, 1985–2011 (in million US$)*

	Host Region/Economy						
Year	*World*	*Developed Economies*	*Developing Economies*	*Asia*	*East and South-East Asia*	*South Asia*	*South-East Asia*
1985–90	1,41,930	1,16,744	24,736	13,492	12,368	391	6,047
1991	1,58,936	1,14,792	41,696	23,129	21,228	470	13,400
1992	1,73,761	1,19,692	49,625	29,632	27,669	703	12,107
1993	2,18,094	1,38,762	73,054	50,924	47,279	1,141	15,434
1994	2,38,738	1,42,395	90,462	57,507	55,718	1,922	15,811
1995	3,16,524	2,05,876	96,330	65,249	65,176	2,643	21,234
1990–95	2,25,321	1,45,019	74,288	47,321	44,564	1,221	16,932
1996	3,86,140	2,19,908	1,52,685	93,331	87,843	3,620	29,370
1997	4,78,082	2,67,947	1,91,022	1,05,828	96,338	4,936	30,369
1998	6,94,457	4,84,239	1,87,611	96,109	86,252	3,560	18,504
1999	10,88,263	8,37,761	2,25,140	1,02,779	99,990	3,099	19,691
2000	14,91,934	12,27,476	2,37,894	1,33,707	1,31,123	3,095	11,056
2001	8,17,578	5,71,483	2,19,721	1,11,854	1,02,228	3,983	19,601

Cont'd...

...Cont'd

2002	7,16,128	5,47,778	1,55,528	92,009	86,318	4,528	14,507
2003	6,32,599	4,42,157	1,66,337	1,01,278	94,755	5,331	17,364
2004	7,42,143	4,18,855	2,83,030	1,69,999	1,49,160	7,601	35,245
2005	9,45,795	5,90,311	31,416	2,08,744	1,67,190	9,866	41,071
2006	13,05,852	8,57,499	3,79,070	2,59,434	1,99,531	22,274	51,583
2007	19,75,537	13,10,425	5,74,311	3,49,412	2,36,606	34,695	85,603
2008	17,90,706	10,19,648	6,50,017	3,80,360	2,35,508	52,869	50,254
2009	11,97,824	6,06,212	5,19,225	3,15,328	2,06,591	42,370	47,408
2010	13,09,001	6,18,586	6,16,661	3,84,063	2,94,124	31,746	92,760
2011	15,24,422	7,47,860	6,84,399	4,23,157	3,35,533	38,942	1,16,559

Year	*Bangladesh*	*India*	*Pakistan*	*Sri Lanka*	*Nepal*	*Bhutan*	*Maldives*
1985–90	2	179	167	37	2	0	4
1991	1	155	257	48	2	0	7
1992	4	233	335	123	1	0	7
1993	14	574	347	195	4	0	7
1994	11	1,314	419	166	6	0	6
1995	2	1,929	639	63	5	0	5
1990–95	6	703	389	110	6	0	7
1996	14	2,525	918	133	19	1	9
1997	139	3,619	713	433	23	–1	11
1998	190	2,633	507	206	12	0	12
1999	178	2,168	530	201	4	0	12
2000	280	2,319	305	178	0	0	13
2001	79	3,403	385	82	21	0	12
2002	52	3,449	823	197	–6	0	12
2003	268	4,269	534	229	15	1	14
2004	460	5,771	1,118	233	0	3	15
2005	692	6,676	2,201	272	2	9	9
2006	625	16,881	4,273	480	–7	6	14
2007	666	25,506	5,590	603	6	3	126
2008	10,66	1,909	5,438	752	1	7	174
2009	700	3,048	2,338	404	39	18	152
2010	913	3,648	2,022	478	87	16	212
2011	1,136	4,150	1,327	300	95	14	282

Cont'd...

...Cont'd

Year	*China*	*Korea, Rep*	*Malaysia*	*Indonesia*	*Singapore*	*Thailand*	*Vietnam*	*Philippines*
1985–90	2,654	705	1,054	2,952	2,952	1,017	30	413
1991	4,366	1,180	3,998	4,887	4,887	2,014	229	544
1992	11,156	727	5,183	2,204	2,204	2,114	385	228
1993	27,515	588	5,006	4,686	4,686	1,730	523	1,238
1994	33,787	809	4,342	5,480	5,480	1,322	742	1,591
1995	35,849	1,776	4,132	6,912	6,912	2,003	2,000	1,478
1990–95	19,360	978	4,655	5,782	5,782	1,990	947	1,028
1996	40,180	2,325	7,296	8,608	8,608	2,271	1,803	1,520
1997	44,237	2,844	6,324	10,746	10,746	3,626	2,587	1,249
1998	43,751	5,412	2,714	6,389	6,389	5,143	1,700	1,752
1999	40,319	9,333	3,895	11,803	11,803	3,561	1,484	578
2000	40,772	9,283	3,788	5,407	5,407	2,813	1,289	1,241
2001	46,878	3,683	554	15,038	15,038	3,813	1,300	982
2002	52,743	2,975	3,203	5,822	5,822	947	1,200	1,792
2003	53,505	3,785	2,473	9,331	9,331	1,952	1,450	347
2004	60,630	8,980	4,624	19,828	19,828	5,862	1,610	688
2005	72,406	7,050	3,965	15,004	15,004	8,957	2,021	1,854
2006	69,468	4,950	6,060	24,207	24,207	9,751	2,315	2,345
2007	83,521	2,628	8,595	6,928	46,930	11,359	6,700	2,916
2008	1,08,312	8,409	7,172	9,318	11,798	8,455	9,579	1,544
2009	95,000	7,501	1,453	4,877	24,418	4,854	7,600	1,963
2010	1,14,734	8,511	9,103	13,771	48,637	9,733	8,000	1,298
2011	1,23,958	4,661	11,966	18,906	64,003	9,572	7,430	1,262

Source: World Investment Reports, various issues.

Figure 4.1 *Global Trends in FDI to Developing Countries*

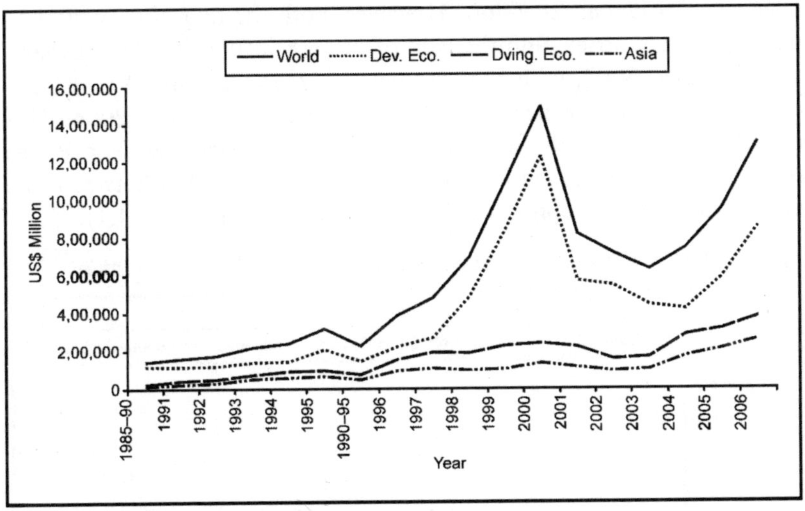

Figure 4.1 above looks at trends in global FDI flows to developing countries since the 1980s. World FDI flows were fairly stable in the first half of that decade, but started to rise steadily in the second half. This trend continued through the early 1990s, with the growth rate rising sharply in 1997. The years from 1997–2000 witnessed dramatic increases in FDI flows, which peaked in 2000 and declined sharply in the following three years, reflecting the global recession sparked by the dotcom crash in 2000, and the economic effects of 9/11 in the US. They recovered marginally in 2004 (by 2.46%), settling at close to their 1998 level. After 2004 global FDI inflows grew in 2005 and in 2006 for the second and third consecutive years to reach US$ 946 billion and US$ 1,306 billion—the second highest level ever recorded (UNCTAD WIR, 2007).

FDI flows to developing countries were fairly stable in the 1980s. The 1990s witnessed a gradual rise in FDI, largely brought about by the dramatic changes in the policy structures of the 'Asian Tigers', which had begun to embark on programmes of structural liberalization and open market reform, aimed at ushering in a phase of export-led growth. Another contributing factor may have been the recovery of the Latin American economies, which had begun to emerge from the debt crisis of the 1980s (Sahoo, 2006). Inflows stagnated in 1998, departing from the trend growth rate—a result of the East Asian financial crisis—but then bounced back by the following year. There was negative growth in FDI inflows in 2001 and 2002, partially because of a global recession. However, both the quantum of FDI to developing countries, and the rate of growth in FDI have been rising steadily since 2002, with FDI growing by 7 per cent in 2003, 41 per cent in 2004 and 9.8 per cent in 2005 and 17 per cent in 2006. This trend, combined with falling inflows to the developed world, has resulted in a new trend in the distribution of FDI between the developed and developing world (see Table 4.4 and Figure 4.1).

Figure 4.2 *Trends of FDI inflows to Developing and Asian Countries*

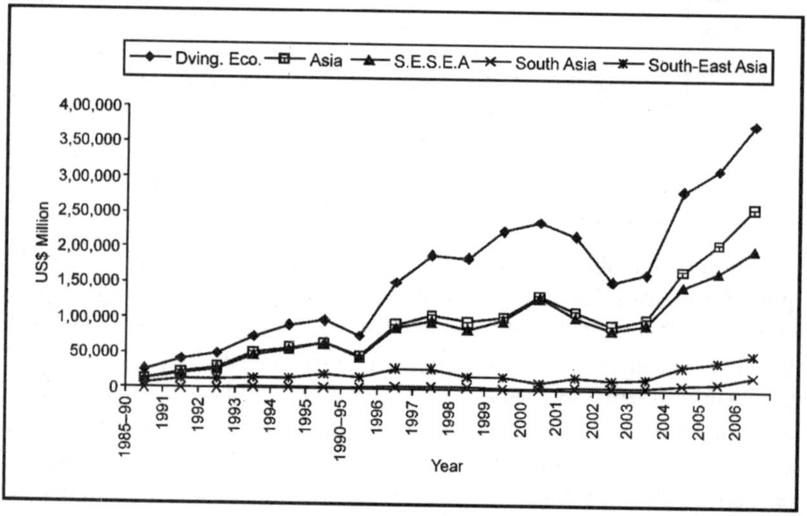

Trends of FDI Inflows to Developing Countries and South Asia

South Asia had not been traditionally a large recipient of FDI. The FDI flows to South Asia started picking up only in the mid-1990s. FDI inflows in absolute value to South Asia have continuously increased over the years and particularly since 2000. As compared to the 1990 the 2001 inflows of FDI increased almost 10-fold from US$ 391 million to US$ 3,983 million. They climbed for the sixth consecutive year from 2001 to 2006 (see Table 4.3). As a result, the share of South Asia in the global FDI flows gradually reached over 0.48 per cent from a mere 0.29 per cent within a decade. After 2002 its share in the world FDI flows has increased dramatically, reached over 1 per cent and in 2006 to 1.7 per cent. Similarly, its share in the total FDI flows to developing economies and Asian economies also recorded a remarkable increase from 1.5 per cent to almost 6 per cent and from 2.8 per cent to over 8.5 per cent respectively during the period from 1991 to 2006. An

Table 4.5 *Percentage Share of SAARC Region in the World FDI Inflows, 1985–2011*

Year	*World Total*	*SAARC (%) of World*	*Developing Economies*	*SAARC (%) of Developing Economies*	*China (%) of DC*	*Asia*	*SAARC % of Asia*	*South-East and South-East Asia*	*SAARC (%) of South-East and South-East Asia*
1985–90*	1,41,930	0.2755	24,736	1.5807	10.729	13,492	2.90	12,368	3.16
1991	1,58,936	0.2957	41,696	1.1272	10.471	23,129	2.03	21,228	2.21
1992	1,73,761	0.4046	49,625	1.4166	22.481	29,632	2.37	27,669	2.54
1993	2,18,094	0.5232	73,054	1.5619	37.664	50,924	2.24	47,279	2.41
1994	2,38,738	0.8051	90,462	2.1246	37.349	57,507	3.34	55,718	3.45
1995	3,16,524	0.8350	96,330	2.7437	37.215	65,249	4.05	65,176	4.06
1990–95*	2,25,321	0.5419	74,288	1.6436	26.061	47,321	2.58	44,564	2.74
1996	3,86,140	0.9375	1,52,685	2.3709	26.316	93,331	3.88	87,843	4.12
1997	4,78,082	1.0325	1,91,022	2.5840	23.158	1,05,828	4.66	96,338	5.12
1998	6,94,457	0.5126	1,87,611	1.8975	23.320	96,109	3.70	86,252	4.13
1999	10,88,263	0.2848	2,25,140	1.3765	17.908	1,02,779	3.02	99,990	3.10
2000	14,91,934	0.2074	2,37,894	1.3010	17.139	1,33,707	2.31	1,31,123	2.36
2001	8,17,578	0.4872	2,19,721	1.8128	21.335	1,11,854	3.56	1,02,228	3.90
2002	7,16,128	0.6323	1,55,528	2.9114	33.912	92,009	4.92	86,318	5.25
2003	6,32,599	0.8427	1,66,337	3.2049	32.167	1,01,278	5.26	94,755	5.63

Cont'd...

...Cont'd

2004	7,42,143	1.0242	2,83,030	2.6856	21.422	1,69,999	4.47	1,49,160	5.10
2005	9,45,795	1.0431	3,14,316	3.1389	23.036	2,08,744	4.73	1,67,190	5.90
2006	13,05,852	1.7057	3,79,070	5.8760	18.326	2,59,434	8.59	1,99,531	11.16
2007	19,75,537	1.6546	5,74,311	5.69	14.542	3,49,412	9.35	2,36,606	13.81
2008	17,90,706	2.5408	6,50,017	1.45	16.662	3,80,360·	11.96	2,35,506	19.32
2009	11,97,824	3.2828	5,19,225	1.26	18.296	3,15,238	12.47	2,06,591	19.03
2010	13,09,001	1.9920	6,16,661	1.23	18.605	3,84,063	6.78	2,94,124	8.86
2011	15,24,422	2.2822	6,84,399	1.07	18.115	4,23,157	8.22	3,35,533	10.36

Columns Cont'd...

Year	South Asia	South-East Asia	(%) of S-E Asia	Bangladesh	India	Pakistan	Sri Lanka	Nepal	Bhutan	Maldives	SESEA	China
1985–90*	391	6,047	6.47	2	179	167	37	2	0	4	21.46	2,654
1991	470	13,400	3.51	1	155	257	48	2	0	7	20.57	4,366
1992	703	12,107	5.81	4	233	335	123	1	0	7	40.32	11,156
1993	1,141	15,434	7.39	14	574	347	195	4	0	7	58.20	27,515
1994	1,922	15,811	12.16	11	1,314	419	166	6	0	6	60.64	33,787
1995	2,643	21,234	12.45	2	1,929	639	63	5	0	5	55.00	35,849
1990–95*	1,221	16,932	7.21	6	703	389	110	6	0	7	43.44	19,360
1996	3,620	29,370	12.33	14	2,525	918	133	19	1	9	45.74	40,180

Cont'd...

...Cont'd

1997	4,936	30,369	16.25	139	3,619	713	433	23	–1	11	45.92	44,237
1998	3,560	18,504	19.24	190	2,633	507	206	12	0	12	50.72	43,751
1999	3,099	19,691	15.74	178	2,168	530	201	4	0	12	40.32	40,319
2000	3,095	11,056	27.99	280	2,319	305	178	0	0	13	31.09	40,772
2001	3,983	19,601	20.32	79	3,403	385	82	21	0	12	45.86	46,878
2002	4,528	14,507	31.21	52	3,449	823	197	–6	0	12	61.10	52,743
2003	5,331	17,364	30.70	268	4,269	534	229	15	1	14	56.47	53,505
2004	7,601	35,245	21.57	460	5,771	1,118	233	0	3	15	40.65	60,630
2005	9,866	41,071	24.02	692	6,676	2,201	272	2	9	9	43.31	72,406
2006	22,274	51,583	43.18	625	16,881	4,273	480	–7	6	14	34.82	69,468
2007	34,695	85,603	40.53	666	25,506	5,590	603	6	3	126		83,521
2008	52,869	50,254	105.20	1,086	43,406	5,438	752	1	7	174		1,08,312
2009	42,307	47,408	89.24	700	35,596	2,338	404	39	18	152		95,000
2010	31,746	92,760	34.22	913	24,159	2,022	478	87	16	212		1,14,734
2011	38,942	1,16,559	33.40	1,136	31,554	1,327	300	95	14	282		1,23,958

Columns Cont'd...

Year	Republic of Korea	Malaysia	Indonesia	Singapore	Thailand	Vietnam	Philippines
1985–90*	705	1,054	2,952	2,952	1,017	30	413
1991	1,180	3,998	4,887	4,887	2,014	229	544

Cont'd...

...Cont'd

1992	727	5,183	2,204	2,204	2,114	385	228
1993	588	5,006	4,686	4,686	1,730	523	1,238
1994	809	4,342	5,480	5,480	1,322	742	1,591
1995	1,776	4,132	6,912	6,912	2,003	2,000	1,478
1990–95*	978	4,655	5,782	5,782	1,990	947	1,028
1996	2,325	7,296	8,608	8,608	2,271	1,803	1,520
1997	2,844	6,324	10,746	10,746	3,626	2,587	1,249
1998	5,412	2,714	6,389	6,389	5,143	1,700	1,752
1999	9,333	3,895	11,803	11,803	3,561	1,484	578
2000	9,283	3,788	5,407	5,407	2,813	1,289	1,241
2001	3,683	554	15,038	15,038	3,813	1,300	982
2002	2,975	3,203	5,822	5,822	947	1,200	1,792
2003	3,785	2,473	9,331	9,331	1,952	1,450	347
2004	8,980	4,624	19,828	19,828	5,862	1,610	688
2005	7,050	3,965	15,004	15,004	8,957	2,021	1,854
2006	4,950	6,060	24,207	24,207	9,751	2,315	2,345
2007	2,628	8,595	6,928	46,930	11,359	6,700	2,916
2008	8,409	7,172	9,318	11,798	8,455	9,579	1,544
2009	7,501	1,453	4,877	24,418	4,854	7,600	1,963
2010	8,511	9,103	13,771	48,637	9,733	8,000	1,298
2011	4,661	11,966	18,906	64,003	9,572	7,430	1,262

Source: Computed from UNCTAD, *World Investment Reports*, various years.

Table 4.6 *Percentage Share of SAARC Member countries in the Total FDI Inflows in South Asia, 1985–2011 (in million US$)*

Year	Developing Economies	SAARC (%) of Developing Economies	South Asian Economies	Bangladesh	% of SAARC	India	% of SAARC	Pakistan	% of SAARC
1985–90	24,736	1.58	391	2	0.51	179	45.78	167	42.71
1991	41,696	1.13	470	1	0.21	155	32.98	257	54.68
1992	49,625	1.42	703	4	0.57	233	33.14	335	47.65
1993	73,054	1.56	1,141	14	1.23	574	50.31	347	30.41
1994	90,462	2.12	1,922	11	0.57	1,314	68.37	419	21.80
1995	96,330	2.74	2,643	2	0.08	1,929	72.99	639	24.18
1990–95	74,288	1.64	1,221	6	0.49	703	57.58	389	31.86
1996	1,52,685	2.37	3,620	14	0.39	2,525	69.75	918	25.36
1997	1,91,022	2.58	4,936	139	2.82	3,619	73.32	713	14.44
1998	1,87,611	1.90	3,560	190	5.34	2,633	73.96	507	14.24
1999	2,25,140	1.38	3,099	178	5.74	2,168	69.96	530	17.10
2000	2,37,894	1.30	3,095	280	9.05	2,319	74.93	305	9.85
2001	2,19,721	1.81	3,983	79	1.98	3,403	85.44	385	9.67
2002	1,55,528	2.91	4,528	52	1.15	3,449	76.17	823	18.18
2003	1,66,337	3.20	5,331	268	5.03	4,269	80.08	534	10.02
2004	2,83,030	2.69	7,601	460	6.05	5,771	75.92	1,118	14.71

Cont'd...

...Cont'd

2005	3,14,316	3.14	9,866	692	7.01	6,676	67.67	2,201	22.31
2006	3,79,070	5.88	22,274	625	2.81	16,881	75.79	4,273	19.18
2007	5,74,311	5.69	34,695	666	2.03	25,506	78.02	5,590	17.10
2008	6,50,017	1.45	52,869	1,086	2.38	43,406	95.39	5,438	11.95
2009	5,19,225	1.26	42,370	700	1.78	35,596	90.52	2,338	5.94
2010	6,16,661	1.23	31,746	913	3.50	24,159	92.64	2,022	7.75
2011	6,84,399	1.07	38,942	1,136	3.26	31,554	90.69	1,327	3.81

Columns Cont'd...

Year	Sri Lanka	(%) of SAARC	Nepal	(%) of SAARC	Bhutan	Maldives	(%) of SAARC
1985–90	37	9.46	2	0.51	0	4	1.02
1991	48	10.21	2	0.43	0	7	1.49
1992	123	17.50	1	0.14	0	7	1.00
1993	195	17.09	4	0.35	0	7	0.61
1994	166	8.64	6	0.31	0	6	0.31
1995	63	2.38	5	0.19	0	5	0.19
1990–95	110	9.01	6	0.49	0	7	0.57
1996	133	3.67	19	0.52	1	9	0.25
1997	433	8.77	23	0.47	–1	11	0.22

Cont'd...

...Cont'd

1998	206	5.79	12	0.34	0	12	0.34
1999	201	6.49	4	0.13	0	12	0.39
2000	178	5.75	0	0.00	0	13	0.42
2001	82	2.06	21	0.53	0	12	0.30
2002	197	4.35	–6	–0.13	0	12	0.27
2003	229	4.30	15	0.28	1	14	0.26
2004	233	3.07	0	0.00	3	15	0.20
2005	272	2.76	2	0.02	9	9	0.09
2006	480	2.15	–7	–0.03	6	14	0.06
2007	603	1.84	6	0.01	3	126	0.38
2008	752	1.65	1	0.002	7	174	0.38
2009	404	1.02	39	0.09	18	152	0.38
2010	478	1.83	87	0.33	16	212	0.81
2011	300	0.86	95	0.27	14	282	0.81

Source: Computed from UNCTAD, *World Investment Reports,* various years.

improving economic situation and a more open FDI climate encouraged inflows to India, at record levels of US$ 16.8 billion in 2006. Cross-border M&As in India rose in 2006 as the telecommunications, business process outsourcing and pharmaceutical industries saw an increase in large deals. The improved investment environment and the privatization of assets in Pakistan and Bangladesh contributed to increased FDI inflows to those countries (Sahoo, 2006). Overall, business confidence in South Asia improved.

While the share of South Asia in the FDI inflows to developing countries was about 1.12 per cent in 1991 and 5.8 per cent in 2006, its share in the global FDI inflows was almost negligible at 0.29 per cent and 1.70 per cent in 1991 and in 2006 respectively. This figure was too much lower than that of China's share in the developing countries FDI flows. Around one quarter of all FDI inflows of developing countries and 45 per cent of FDI flows of South, East and South Asian economies are going to China and the other countries in South Asia are getting less than 1 per cent of the total FDI inflows to the developing countries. Even FDI inflows as a percentage of gross domestic capital formation (GDFC) in South Asian countries are quite low though they have increased gradually since 2000. The same trend is also seen in FDI stocks as a percentage of GDP.

Trends among the South Asian Countries

An examination of the FDI inflows to the individual South Asian countries reveals that most of the receiving countries have shown increasing but erratic trends (Table 4.6). This is more so in the case of Bangladesh and Sri Lanka. At the same time, it is found that India has been consistently taking an overwhelming part of the FDI flows into South Asia. In fact, this has more or less steadily gone up from around 45 per cent in 1985–90 to 76 per cent in 2006.

On the other hand, the share of Bangladesh had never crossed one per cent in 1985–1995. In the mid-1990s the trend was upward and percentage was increased, but it had fallen again due to the changing policy of the new government.

India has attracted the maximum FDI in South Asia. While India's share of FDI to developing countries has been, and still is, significantly lower than that of the major East and South Asian economies like China and Malaysia, it receives the most FDI in South Asia.

However, after economic reforms, India did better than Bangladesh and other nations in the region. Table 4.4 and 4.5 depict FDI inflows in South Asia, focusing on India, in comparison with those

Table 4.7 *Percentage Share of SAARC Region in the World FDI Inflows, 1985–2011*

Year	World	(%) of World	Developing Economies	(%) of Developing Economies	Asia	(%) of Asia	S, E and S-E Asia	% of S, E and S-E Asia	South Asia	South-East Asia	(%) of S-E Asia
1985–90	1,41,930	0.28	24,736	1.58	13,492	2.90	12,368	3.16	391	6,047	6.47
1991	1,58,936	0.30	41,696	1.13	23,129	2.03	21,228	2.21	470	13,400	3.51
1992	1,73,761	0.40	49,625	1.42	29,632	2.37	27,669	2.54	703	12,107	5.81
1993	2,18,094	0.52	73,054	1.56	50,924	2.24	47,279	2.41	1,141	15,434	7.39
1994	2,38,738	0.81	90,462	2.12	57,507	3.34	55,718	3.45	1,922	15,811	12.16
1995	3,16,524	0.84	96,330	2.74	65,249	4.05	65,176	4.06	2,643	21,234	12.45
1990–95	2,25,321	0.54	74,288	1.64	47,321	2.58	44,564	2.74	1,221	16,932	7.21
1996	3,86,140	0.94	1,52,685	2.37	93,331	3.88	87,843	4.12	3,620	29,370	12.33
1997	4,78,082	1.03	1,91,022	2.58	1,05,828	4.66	96,338	5.12	4,936	30,369	16.25
1998	6,94,457	0.51	1,87,611	1.90	96,109	3.70	86,252	4.13	3,560	18,504	19.24
1999	10,88,263	0.28	2,25,140	1.38	1,02,779	3.02	99,990	3.10	3,099	19,691	15.74
2000	14,91,934	0.21	2,37,894	1.30	1,33,707	2.31	1,31,123	2.36	3,095	11,056	27.99
2001	8,17,578	0.49	2,19,721	1.81	1,11,854	3.56	1,02,228	3.90	3,983	19,601	20.32
2002	7,16,128	0.63	1,55,528	2.91	92,009	4.92	86,318	5.25	4,528	14,507	31.21
2003	6,32,599	0.84	1,66,337	3.20	1,01,278	5.26	94,755	5.63	5,331	17,364	30.70
2004	7,42,143	1.02	2,83,030	2.69	1,69,999	4.47	1,49,160	5.10	7,601	35,245	21.57

Cont'd...

...Cont'd

2005	9,45,795	1.04	3,14,316	3.14	2,08,744	4.73	1,67,190	5.90	9,866	41,071	24.02
2006	13,05,852	1.71	3,79,070	5.88	2,59,434	8.59	1,99,531	11.16	22,274	51,583	43.18
2007	19,75,537	1.65	5,74,311	5.69	3,49,412	9.35	2,36,606	13.81	34,695	85,603	38.18
2008	17,90,706	2.54	6,50,017	6.99	3,80,360	11.96	2,35,506	19.32	52,869	50,254	90.54
2009	11,97,824	3.28	5,19,225	7.57	3,15,238	12.47	2,06,591	19.03	42,307	47,408	82.94
2010	13,09,001	1.99	6,16,661	4.22	3,84,063	6.79	2,94,124	8.86	31,746	92,760	28.11
2011	15,24,422	2.28	6,84,399	5.08	4,23,157	8.22	3,35,533	10.36	38,942	1,16,559	29.84

Columns Cont'd...

Year	Bangladesh	Bangladesh (%) of Developing countries	India	India (%) of Developing countries	Pakistan	Sri Lanka	Nepal	Bhutan	Maldives
1985–90	2	0.0081	179	0.72364	167	37	2	0	4
1991	1	0.0024	155	0.37174	257	48	2	0	7
1992	4	0.0081	233	0.46952	335	123	1	0	7
1993	14	0.0192	574	0.78572	347	195	4	0	7
1994	11	0.0122	1,314	1.45254	419	166	6	0	6
1995	2	0.0021	1,929	2.00249	639	63	5	0	5
1990–95	6	0.0081	703	0.94632	389	110	6	0	7
1996	14	0.0092	2,525	1.65373	918	133	19	1	9

Cont'd...

...Cont'd

1997	139	0.0728	3,619	1.89455	713	433	23	–1	11
1998	190	0.1013	2,633	1.40344	507	206	12	0	12
1999	178	0.0791	2,168	0.96296	530	201	4	0	12
2000	280	0.1177	2,319	0.97480	305	178	0	0	13
2001	79	0.0360	3,403	1.54878	385	82	21	0	12
2002	52	0.0334	3,449	2.21761	823	197	–6	0	12
2003	268	0.1611	4,269	2.56648	534	229	15	1	14
2004	460	0.1625	5,771	2.03901	1,118	233	0	3	15
2005	692	0.2202	6,676	2.12398	2,201	272	2	9	9
2006	625	0.1649	16,881	4.45327	4,273	480	–7	6	14
2007	666	0.1159	25,506	4.44114	5,590	603	6	3	126
2008	1,086	0.1670	43,406	6.67767	5,438	752	1	7	174
2009	700	0.1348	35,596	6.8556	2,338	404	39	18	152
2010	913	0.1480	24,159	3.9177	2,022	478	87	16	212
2011	1,136	0.1659	31,554	4.6104	1,327	300	95	14	282

Source: UNCTAD, World Investment Report, Various Issues.

of its counterparts. India's share in FDI inflows to developing countries rose to 1.9 per cent in 1997, but declined sharply to 1 per cent in 1999 and 2000. However, 2001 saw an increase in FDI inflows. This trend continued until 2003 when it reached a peak of 2.6 per cent. In 2004, there was a slight fall to 2.03 per cent. In 2005 it was recovered by 2.12 per cent and climbed to 4.45 per cent in 2006. The sum total of FDI inflows into India in 2003 and 2004 was US$ 4.2 billion and US$ 5.3 billion respectively. However, India saw a dramatic raised its inflows from US$ 6.6 billion in 2005 to US$ 16.88 billion in 2006. Thus, in absolute amounts, 2006 saw a sudden rise in FDI inflows to India (see Table 4.7).

Bangladesh has been competing to attract FDI with a large number of developing countries. In recent years, there has been a marked upward trend of FDI to developing countries (see Table 4.3). At present, if we look the position of FDI in Bangladesh along with that of some selected Asian countries (see Table 4.8) of somewhat similar economic and demographic characteristics on the basis of the figures revealed by the *World Investment Reports*, it will be evident that Bangladesh received the FDI amounting to US$ 2 million and US$ 8 million (the lowest amount) per year on an average during the period 1985–1990 and 1991–1996 respectively, which does not have any match with the FDI figures of India, Pakistan Sri Lanka, Thailand, Indonesia and Malaysia. We see that Vietnam had received the second lowest amount of FDI (US$ 30 million) during the period 1985–1990 whereas Sri Lanka received US$ 125 million in the period 1991–1996 which was much higher than the amount received by Bangladesh. Within the next few years the scenario of FDI inflows in this region has changed dramatically. FDI flows to all countries increased rapidly. From the both tables it is evident that Bangladesh received average US$ 152 million in 1997–2002, and US$ 511.2 million in 2002–2006, which was much lower than any other Asian countries shown in the Table 4.8.

Table 4.8 *Trends of FDI Inflows in Selected Asian Countries, 1980–2006, in annual average (in million US$)*

Country	*Average annual FDI (1980–85)*	*Average annual FDI (1985–90)*	*Average annual FDI (1991–96)*	*Average annual FDI (1997–2002)*	*Average annual FDI (2002–06)*
Bangladesh	0.1	2.0	8.0	152	511.25
India	62	169	1,085	2,932	8399.25
Indonesia	NA	551	2,985	–7,776	3,798

Cont'd...

...Cont'd

Pakistan	75	167	501	544	2031.5
Sri Lanka	42	37	125	214	303.5
Malaysia	NA	1,054	5,436	3,413	4280.5
Thailand	NA	1,017	1,964	4,283	6630.5
Vietnam	NA	30	1,217	1,593	1849
China	NA	2,654	25,476	44,771	64002.3

Sources: UNCTAD, *World Investment Reports*, various years.
Asian Development Bank, 2007.
Key Indicators of Developing Asia and Pacific Countries, ADB, 2007.

A similar picture can be observed from the Table 4.5 with regard to FDI inflows into Bangladesh. Bangladesh has received a very negligible amount of FDI compared to India during the same period, thus occupying the bottom position within the South and South-East Asian region except Bhutan.

FDI flows to SAARC countries, especially India, were outstanding. India received bulk share of the total, which was 75.79 per cent in 2006, whereas Bangladesh received only 2.8 per cent of the total. Year-wise analysis of FDI flows depicts that in 1997 Bangladesh received 2.81 per cent of the total, which increased to 5.42 per cent in 1998 and further to 7.01 per cent in 2005. It increased a bit during 1997–2003 due to the opening of the gas sector for the foreign investors. However, this change was not comparable with the neighbour country like India (see Tables 4.6 and 4.7).

Table 4.9 *FDI Inflows in SAARC countries, Bangladesh and India, 1980–2011 (in million US$)*

Year	*SAARC countries*	*Yearly growth (%)*	*Bangladesh*	*Yearly growth (%)*	*India*	*Yearly growth (%)*
1980–85*	178.8		0.1		62	
1986	255	42.62	2.4	2300.00	118	90.32
1987	405	58.82	3.2	33.33	212	79.66
1988	326	–19.51	1.8	–43.75	91	–57.08
1989	481	47.55	0.3	–83.33	252	176.92
1990	458	–4.78	3.2	966.67	162	–35.71
1991	470	2.62	1.4	–56.25	155	–4.32
1992	703	49.57	4	185.71	233	50.32

Cont'd...

...Cont'd

1993	1,141	62.30	14	250.00	574	146.35
1994	1,922	68.45	11	–21.43	1,314	128.92
1995	2,643	37.51	2	–81.82	1,929	46.80
1996	3,620	36.97	14	600.00	2,525	30.90
1997	4,936	36.35	139	892.86	3,619	43.33
1998	3,560	–27.88	190	36.69	2,633	–27.25
1999	3,099	–12.95	178	–6.32	2,168	–17.66
2000	3,095	–0.13	280	57.30	2,319	6.96
2001	3,983	28.69	79	–71.79	3,403	46.74
2002	4,528	13.68	52	–34.18	3,449	1.35
2003	5,331	17.73	268	415.38	4,269	23.78
2004	7,601	42.58	460	71.64	5,771	35.18
2005	9,866	29.80	692	50.43	6,676	15.68
2006	22,274	125.77	625	–9.68	16,881	152.86
2007	32,689	46.76	666	6.56	25,506	51.09
2008	45,500	39.19	1,086	63.06	43,406	70.17
2009	39,323	–13.57	700	–35.54	35,596	–17.99
2010	26,076	–33.68	913	30.42	24,159	–32.13
2011	34,791	33.42	1,136	24.42	31,554	30.60

Source: UNCTAD, *World Investment Reports*, various years.

Figure 4.3 *FDI Inflows in India, 1972–2006*

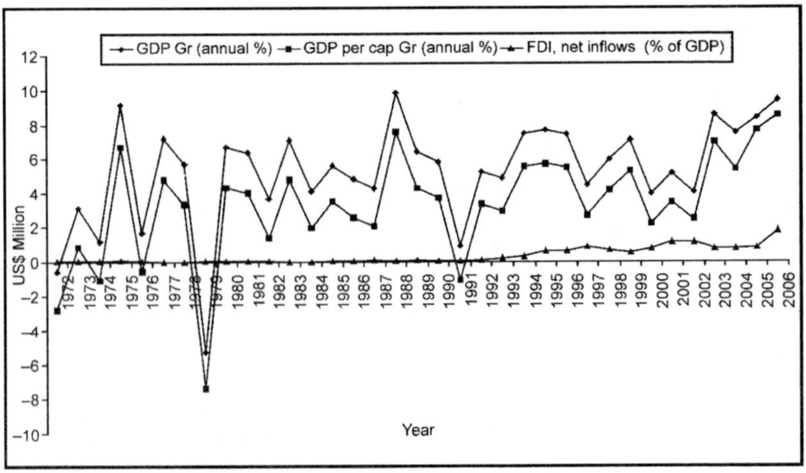

Table 4.10 *FDI Flows as a percentage of GFCF of some Selected Countries, 1981–2011*

Economy	*1981–90*	*1991*	*1995*	*2000*	*2001*	*2002*	*2003*	*2004*	*2005*	*2006*	*2007*	*2008*	*2009*	*2010*	*2011*
China	14.5	3.3	25.7	10.3	10.5	10.4	8.6	8.2	9.2	8	6.0	5.8	4.3	4.4	3.7
South Korea	1.9	1	1.1	7.1	3.1	1.9	2.1	3.8	3.1	1.9	0.9	3.1	3.1	2.9	1.5
Bangladesh	0.3	0.1	na	2.7	0.8	0.5	2.2	3.5	4.9	3.9	4.0	5.6	3.2	3.7	4.0
India	1.2	0.3	3.6	2.3	3.2	3	3.2	3.4	3.5	8.7	6.3	9.9	8.2	4.4	6.4
Pakistan	5.1	3.3	6.7	3.7	4.9	7.2	4.3	6.2	13	24.1	18.7	18.3	8.1	7.5	5.3
Sri Lanka	6.9	2.4	2	3.8	2.4	5.6	5.6	5.1	5.5	6.2	7.5	7.3	4.3	4.0	2.1
Indonesia	7.6	3.6	6.5	–14.3	–10.8	0.4	–1.3	1.9	8.5	6.4	6.4	6.6	2.9	6.1	7.0
Malaysia	43.7	23.8	17.9	16.5	2.5	14.5	10.8	19.1	15.2	20.1	21.3	16.5	3.7	18.9	21.4
Singapore	59.3	33.6	24.6	45.6	43.8	25.6	41.7	77.5	78.9	79.5	117.2	22.5	47.7	89.7	105.2
Thailand	10.2	4.9	2.9	12.4	14.4	3.3	5.7	2.5	7.2	16.5	17.4	11.3	7.5	12.2	10.6
Vietnam	Na	na	na	15	13.7	11	11.6	11.3	11.3	12.5	24.7	30.4	23.4	22.4	22.1

Source: UNCTAD, *World Investment Reports*, compiled from various years.

Table 4.9 shows a fluctuating trend of the FDI inflows over the last 21 years. Data in the table reveals that in 1999 there was a sudden fall in the FDI, and again in 2001 and 2002 the falling trend continued for many reasons. Among others serious political unrest during the period was a major factor that discouraged foreign investment in these years and it took quite some time to regain the confidence of foreign investors. It stabilized afterwards but remained below the average achieved during 1997–2000. Later on, during next four years, it became alive again. The following graphical presentation gives us clearer picture of the FDI inflows into India over the years:

Figure 4.4 *FDI as percentage of GFCF, 1980–2002*

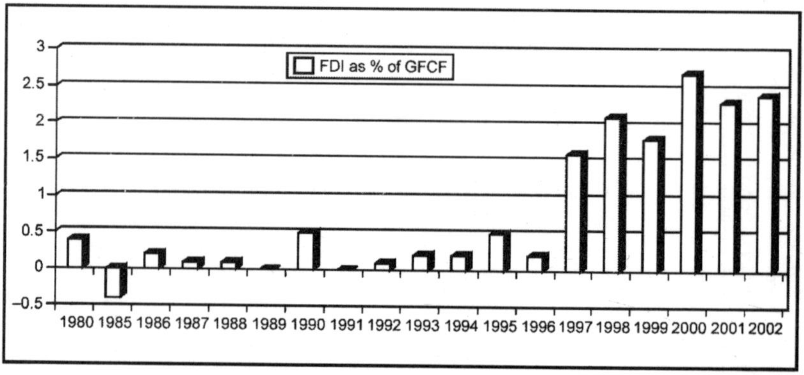

There was a rising trend from 1996 to onward until the year 2000. It reached peak at US$ 280 million in 2000, and a tapering off thereafter in the trend. FDI inflows have dramatically decreased from 2000 and it reached to only US$ 45 million in 2002. In recent years the trend has increased gradually and the figure reached at US$ 625 million in 2006 which was US$ 692 in 2005.

On the other hand, there was a rising trend from 1999 onward until the year 2006. It reached at peak at 1997 followed by a declining trend for three consecutive years. After that the FDI inflows have been raising rapidly and in 2006 it reached at US$ 16,881 million in comparison to US$ 6,676 in 2005.

In order to properly capture a country's performance, it is necessary to supplement the analysis of trends in absolute volume of FDI inflows by the analysis on relative role played by FDI in gross fixed capital formation (GFCF). The contribution of FDI in GFCF was not so significant in Bangladesh during eighties and nineties. It was below 0.1 per cent. However, after 1997, the ratio has increased gradually,

Table 4.11 *FDI Stocks as a Percentage of GDP of Some Selected Countries, 1980–2011*

Economy	*1980–90*	*1991*	*1995*	*2000*	*2001*	*2002*	*2003*	*2004*	*2005*	*2006*	*2007*	*2008*	*2009*	*2010*	*2011*
Bangladesh	0.6	0.7	0.9	2.2	2.3	5.2	5	6.1	5.7	6.3					
China	2.4	3.6	19.3	32.3	33.2	35.4	35.6	14.9	14.3	11.1	20.1	20.3	26.3	24.9	24.7
India	0.5	0.5	1.9	4.1	4.6	5.2	5.4	5.9	5.8	5.7	8.8	9.8	12.7	12.8	12.0
Indonesia	26.5	36.5	25.2	39.6	39.5	33.3	27.5	4.4	7.7	5.2	18.5	14.2	20.2	22.7	22.0
S. Korea	2	2.2	2.3	13.7	9.5	8	7.8	8.1	8	8	11.6	10.2	14.5	13.2	12.2
Malaysia	28.3	36.8	52.1	58.8	60.5	59.5	57.2	39.3	36.5	36	na	na	na	na	na
Pakistan	3.5	5.4	62.7	11.2	9.2	10	10.7	9.2	8.8	11.4	na	na	na	na	na
Singapore	67.6	75.6	67.4	103.8	132.2	153.9	161.3	150.2	158.6	159	na	na	na	Na	na
Sri Lanka	7.6	8.4	9.9	15	15.5	16.1	15.6	10.8	10.4	10.9	na	na	na	na	na
Thailand	5.8	9.5	10.3	20	25.3	27.7	25.8	29.7	33.5	33	na	na	na	na	na
Vietnam	1.95	7.4	30.8	46.7	48.4	50.5	50.6	66.3	61.2	54.8	na	na	na	na	na

Source: UNCTAD, *World Investment Reports*, compiled from various years.

which is sign of good performance. Figure 4.4 provides that between 1980 and 1995, FDI inflows were less than 1 per cent of GFCF in India, whereas it increased to more than 3 per cent of GFCF during 2000–2006.

Probably, the most systematic investment regime in South Asia exists in Bangladesh, mainly due to the active role of its Board of Investment in promoting and facilitating investment climate in the country. A noteworthy development of Bangladesh in receiving FDI is that it entered the first three FDI recipients of South Asia list for the first time during 2000–2006 and became one of the most attractive destinations for foreign investment in the region. Among the FDI recipient sectors, the services sector has attracted the highest investment, especially the telecommunication industry, followed by IT and manufacturing sectors. However, in recent times, textiles and agro-based industries are receiving comparatively larger amount of FDI in Bangladesh.

Among the South Asian countries, India can claim to have a favourable environment for FDI. However, FDI in India has been consistently below than that of most other South, East and South-East Asian countries, particularly China. But if India's position is compared with that of Bangladesh, it looks very impressive.

Table 4.4 reveals that FDI inflows in India are very low compared to other developing countries such as China, Malaysia, Thailand or Singapore. On the other hand, Bangladesh has received a very insignificant amount of FDI compared to India and other countries in the South Asia.

Sources of FDI and Sectors Attracting Maximum FDI in South Asian Countries

Though the South Asian countries have lagged behind in attracting FDI compared to their counterparts in East Asia and South-East Asia, in recent years, they have managed to consistently step up their FDI inflows mostly from the developed countries. The following section briefly presents the sources of FDI and sectors attracting the maximum FDI in India.

Country-wise FDI Inflows to India

The analysis of country-wise break-up of FDI inflows in India presented in Table 4.12 indicates that the top ten countries are the major sources of FDI (about 86% of total investment) in India.

Table 4.12 *Country-wise FDI Inflows in India in 1991–2011 (in million US$)*

Country	1991–2002 (Aug–Dec)	2003 (Jan–Dec)	2004 (Jan–Dec)	2005 (Jan–Dec)	2006 (Jan–Dec)	2007 (Jan–Dec)	2008 (Jan–Dec)	20\09 (Jan–Dec)	2010 (Jan–Dec)	2011 (Jan–Dec)	Cumulative FDI Inflows (in ₹)	Cumulative FDI Inflows (in US$)	Share in (%)
Mauritius	308226.14	25859.33	46162.14	94078.28	222207.52	319437.05	598586.46	560128.88	329399.98	737791.67	2817218.47	62658.31	38.49
USA	131648.83	19040	29791.68	20700.41	33203.78	36383.72	75419.79	98730.55	64824.03	47127.75	473329.18	10472.81	13.58
UK	54922.31	8628.97	6585.36	9578.08	78247.3	19670.99	70085.39	22594.22	34243.61	128557.27	410834.38	9228.65	8.81
Netherlands	45002.48	11618.83	22779.26	5277.35	22457.28	278940.49	42813.50	40056.00	52061.05	5889.06	307106.55	6792.23	5.97
Japan	69320.44	4343.86	5337.44	7449.55	5229.22	27751.60	16976.32	60943.17	58578.58	143486.13	567762.89	12109.86	5.23
Singapore	21277.3	1680.46	2855.01	14168.96	28532.04	58360.08	157758.64	148262.44	967575.80	195969.66	713175.23	15895.36	3.81
Germany	39842.1	3624.98	7274.88	3683.13	13972.47	14155.04	33288.58	28182.82	9034.62	67162.83	197340.66	4404.34	3.97
France	24307.05	1642.51	5289.3	1288.29	3876.56	5208.04	20444.93	14360.47	34062.66	22555.13	123396.51	2719.21	2.06
Korea (South)	23699.89	1128.62	1227.14	2943.09	2935.48	2805.80	6214.49	3207.16	9878.30	6182.96	39302.10	872.15	1.96
Switzerland	14120.56	4289.59	3137.05	3689.39	3151	9017.24	6268.80	6983.69	40527.23	9681.70	92915.03	2047.10	1.64
Italy	16872.19	616.83	1177.52	1434	2576.28	1171.16	14868.48	7249.58	8359.70	6207.66	51312.74	1165.66	1.30
Bermuda	2760.73	10.06	143.09	5.72	18554.13	3.62	1430.49	487.24	45.83	100.54	22512.98	502.07	1.16
Sweden	12880.95	2104.84	3439.22	1377.94	274.33	3427.04	3993.54	11862.72	1232.96	1468.95	37085.75	816.93	1.15
UAE	2033.38	827.02	1346.12	2104.72	10972.14	8842.18	12416.59	30148.01	16732.06	10418.11	95472.86	2091.46	0.92
Hong Kong	10860.08	124.15	1105.43	1231.8	2142.14	4083.23	5663.63	7017.87	8117.97	7428.44	38101.44	843.01	0.99

Cont'd...

...Cont'd

Belgium	4878.54	641.02	204.79	126.75	3834.28	828.18	4719.11	1476.96	1483.15	5065.14	20777.14	455.12	0.55
Australia	4489.32	915.23	848.66	260.63	1869.57	1821.98	3136.01	1941.60	7053.00	2448.79	22221.14	487.58	0.47
Cyprus	1729.01	149.42	166.32	3066.72	2570.04	22043.19	58250.15	77691.41	42099.00	61530.75	268321.71	5839.09	0.42
Denmark	2925.23	556.63	1019.8	1938.04	239.23	248.61	660.32	1114.44	2210.41	2363.82	11442.90	253.3	0.39
Russia	4938.84	1.7	12.32	3.64	1188.31	43.18	14870.84	290.79	4463.36	11.4	24075.76	508.11	0.34
Others	40435.63	7835.09	7911.2	18300.67	45539.42	na	na	na	na	na	na	na	7.16
Total	8,37,171	95639.14	147813.73	192707.16	503572.52	814242.4	11,47,866	11,22,731	16,91,983	11,61,448	63,33,705	140162.4	100

Source: SIA Newsletter, January 2011.

Mauritius, a new middle-income country, was not only the biggest investment country in India but was also a significant investor (about 39% as whole period and 46% during 2006) in the country. It is important to note that some Asian countries, such as Japan, Singapore and South Korea, not only made a significant investment in India, but were also placed among the top 10 investing countries in India.

Among the countries with high FDI inflows into India is Mauritius. This may be attributed to the double taxation treaty that India has signed with Mauritius and also to the fact that most investment into India from the United States is being routed through that country. However, the US is the second largest investor in India, followed by Netherlands and Japan and the other developed countries such as United Kingdom, Germany, Singapore, France, etc., which are India's major trading partners.

The sectors that received the highest cumulative inflows of FDI over the period August 1991 to September 2006 (see Table 4.13) are electrical equipment (16.65%), services (16.62%), telecommunication (9.28%), transport (8.59%) and fuels (6.67%).

Table 4.13 *Sector-wise/Year-wise FDI Inflows in India*

	Cumulative FDI Inflows		
Sectors	*(in ₹)*	*(in US$)*	*Share in (%)*
Electrical Equipments (including S/W and Electrical)	302558.2	6922.69	16.65179
Services Sector	301327.91	6911.43	16.6247
Telecommunications	165535.08	3861.13	9.287535
Transportation Industry	149924.62	3545.5	8.52832
Fuels (Power and Oil Refinery)	118485.53	2773.32	6.670924
Chemicals (Other Than Fertilizers)	92518.11	2289.66	5.507532
Drugs and Pharmaceuticals	50262.84	1164.67	2.801489
Food Processing Industries	49240.88	1227.19	2.951874
Cement and Gypsum Products	41832.59	956.41	2.300542
Metallurgical Industries	34943.75	802.88	1.931242
Consultancy Services	25859.93	565.76	1.360875
Textiles (include Dyed, Printed)	22131.9	547.6	

Cont'd...

...Cont'd

Miscellaneous Mechanical and Engineering	21624.01	542.48	1.304878
Hotel &Tourism	21372.81	488.63	1.175347
Trading	18614.8	459.01	1.104099
Paper and Pulp including Paper Product	14272.83	368.43	0.886219
Rubber Goods	10686.23	251.73	0.60551
Glass	10368.94	257.08	0.618378
Industrial Machinery	9423.26	230.79	0.555141
Commercial, Office and Household Equipment	8671.97	237.89	0.572219
Machine Tools	8210.54	189.97	0.456952
Agricultural Machinery	8042.86	191.96	0.461739
Ceramics	5481.1	134.18	0.322756
Timber Products	4668.78	107.12	0.257666
Medical and Surgical Appliances	4561.27	103.58	0.249151
Others		6442.16	15.49593
Total	1776903.55	41573.25	100

Source: SIA Newsletter, January 2007.

Table 4.14 *Share of Top Five Investing Countries in FDI Inflows during 2006*

(in millions)

Ranks	*Country*	*Amount of FDI received during 2006 (during 2005)*	*(%) age share to total during 2006 (April–December)*	*(%) age growth during 2006 over previous year of 2005*
1	Mauritius	4,215 (1,900)	46%	(+)122%
2	UK	1,682 (198)	18%	(+)749%
3	USA	607(377)	7%	(+) 61
4	Singapore	533 (187)	6%	(+) 185 %
5	Netherlands	488	5%	(+)597%

Source: SIA Newsletter, January 2011.

Similarly, during 2006, the sectors that received the most FDI included electrical equipment (18.3%), services (35.46%), telecommunications (8.65%), fuels (2.26%), miscellaneous industries (2.40%) and transport (3.63%). Investment rose in industries such as cement, sugar, plastics and rubber, and hotels (*SIA Newsletter*, January 2007).

Table 4.15 *Share of Top Five Sectors Attracting Highest FDI inflows in India during 2006*

(in million)

Ranks	*Sectors*	*Amount of FDI received during 2006 (during 2005)*	*(%) age share to total during 2006 (April–December)*	*(%) age growth during 2006 over previous year of 2005*
1	Services Sector	3,820 (462)	41%	(+)727%
2	Electrical Equipments (including computer software & electronics)	1,429 (841)	16%	(+)70%
3	Construction Activities	764 (102)	8%	(+) 649%
4	Telecommunications	490 (198)	5%	(+)147%
5	Real Estates	448	5%	—

Source: SIA Newsletter, January 2007.

The sectors in which FDI grew most dramatically between 2003 and 2006 were cement and gypsum products, metallurgical industry, ceramics, textiles, and paper and paper products. The sectors in which FDI fell during the same period were glass, fuel, power and oil, food processing, transport (including auto industry) and consultancy services. Table 4.13 shows the details of sector-wise FDI and the top five sectors receiving the maximum FDI, respectively. However, the only striking feature about the sectors receiving the most FDI in India is that most FDI is coming into transport, electrical equipment, infrastructure, etc., but very little is flowing into India's export sector. Therefore, there appear to be problems with the synchronization of policies. India should make an effort to attract FDI in its export sector such as gems and jewellery, pharmaceuticals, textiles, marine products and light engineering goods and this would be one way of stepping up FDI on the whole. Though further empirical investigation is required to arrive at any concrete conclusion, it can be inferred that FDI inflows to India are domestic market-oriented.

Engineering, services, electronics and electrical equipment and computers are the main sectors receiving FDI in recent years (Table 4.13). Domestic appliances, finance, food and dairy products which were important sectors attracting FDI in the early nineties have now seen a downward trend. Services and computers have seen an increasing trend in the latter half of the nineties. On the whole, there have been significant changes in the pattern and composition of FDI inflows during the last decade.

The state-wise trends in FDI, as shown in Table 4.16, make clear that the advanced states such as Mumbai (Maharashtra), Delhi, Tamil Nadu, Karnataka, Andhra Pradesh and Gujarat have been the largest recipients of FDI during the last five years. This may be attributed to their better resources, infrastructure such as roads and power, and investor-friendly policies like single window clearances and investment promotion schemes including special economic zones, etc. However, competition among the states in attracting FDI has led to increasing trends in states like Gujarat and Andhra Pradesh (see Table 4.16).

Table 4.16 *Statement on RBI's Region-wise (with state covered) FDI Inflows in India*

(in millio US$)

Regional Offices of RBI	*States Covered*	*Amount of FDI Inflows*		*(%) age of total FDI Inflows*
		(in ₹)	*(in US$)*	
Mumbai	Maharashtra, Dadra and Nagar Haveli, Daman and Diu	338,860.80	7,486.63	24.91
New Delhi	Delhi, Part of Up and Haryana	318,608.93	7,045.03	23.42
Chennai	Tamil Nadu, Pondicherry	103,956.24	2,295.13	7.64
Bangalore	Karnataka	92,753.34	2,052.38	6.82
Hyderabad	Andhra Pradesh	52,547.98	1,157.19	3.86
Ahmedabad	Gujarat	44,319.90	970.28	3.26
Chandigarh	Chandigarh, Punjab, Haryana, Himachal Pradesh	15,624.53	338.08	1.15
Kolkata	West Bengal, Sikkim, Andaman and Nicobar Islands	15,321.70	336.78	1.13
Panaji	Goa	8,352.54	181.35	0.61
Kochi	Kerala, Lakshadweep	3,934.43	87.07	0.29
Bhubaneswar	Orissa	3,652.58	81.21	0.27
Jaipur	Rajasthan	2,486.45	54.01	0.18
Bhopal	Madhya Pradesh, Chhattisgarh	2,383.10	52.36	0.18

Cont'd...

...*Cont'd*

Kanpur	Uttar Pradesh, Uttaranchal	556.45	12.36	0.04
Guwahati	Assam, Arunachal Pradesh, Manipur, Meghalaya, Mizoram, Nagaland, Tripura	417.43	9.03	0.03
Patna	Bihar, Jharkhand	33.35	0.75	0.00
State not indicated		356,499.48	7,834.03	26.21
	Total	1,360,309.23	29,993.67	—

Source: SIA Newsletter, January 2007.

Why has India Succeeded?

From the above detailed discussion one thing is certain that India has succeeded in attracting largest share of FDI. But some interesting comparisons are here. First, in India the saving ratio to GDP is around 32.4 per cent and the investment rate is nearly 33.8 per cent resulting into a difference of 1.4 per cent (Economic Survey, 2006–07). This means India has not succeeded in maintaining higher investment rate than saving rate resulting in low rate of capital formation.

The reasons for the success of India are as under:

(a) India has been attracting FDI mainly both into export-oriented sector and domestic market.
(b) A large amount of FDI in India comes from its wealthy overseas Indians.
(c) The Indians are more committed to their motherland.
(d) Infrastructure handicaps are solved better and faster in India.
(e) India has succeeded in cutting red tapism to a larger extent.

It is almost clear that in respect of FDI inflows in India. India has played a successful role in attracting FDI for the benefit of its economy. There are various factors responsible for such a trend as mentioned below:

- Factors such as procedural disputes regarding land availability, environmental clearance, delays at authority level in getting power and other infrastructural back up, etc., result in delays in the commencement of many projects.
- Non-implementation of approved projects for establishing industrial activities results in slow industrial growth rate in both domestic and export industries. It is also observed that the exports

from developing countries are associated with international firms choosing to use a country as target for FDI and for production destined for global markets.

- Sizeable investment flows are concentrated in the infrastructure industries like power, refineries, telecom, etc., where gestation period is long and projects take time to materialize.
- India is an attractive FDI destination because of its infrastructural facilities and less bureaucratic structure.

Competitive Advantages of India

India is a strategic location with access to a vast domestic and South Asian market both. Its share in world's total flow of direct investment to developing countries was 4.45 per cent in 2006. India also has large natural resource endowments. In addition, India's physical infrastructure is more competitive, particularly in the coastal areas. It also has an advantage in technical manpower, particularly in information technology. It also has better English language skills.

Some of the differences in competitive advantages of the two countries are illustrated by the composition of their inward FDI flows. In information and communication technology, India has become a key centre for hardware designing and manufacturing by such companies as Acer, Ericsson, General Electric, Hitachi Semiconductors, Hyundai Electronics, Intel, LG Electronics, Microsoft, Mitac International Corporation, Motorola, NEC, Nokia, Philips, Samsung Electronics, Sony, Toshiba and other major electronics MNCs. However, India specializes in IT services, call centres, business back-office operations and R&D. Bangladesh also gaining expertise in IT services, business back office operations and R&D.

Rapid growth in India has increased the local demand for consumer durables and non-durables such as home appliances, electronics equipment, automobiles, housing and leisure. This rapid growth in local demand as well as competitive business environment and infrastructure has attracted many market-seeking investors. It has also encouraged the growth of many local indigenous firms that support manufacturing.

In India, there are FDI restrictions only in the small-scale sector and 22 sensitive industries. Unlike in China, almost the entire manufacturing sector and infrastructure sector have been opened up to FDI. In telecommunications, foreign equity of 74 per cent is permitted.

Table 4.17 *Component-wise FDI Inflows in India upto 2006–2007*

(in million US$)

Financial Year (April–March)	*Equity*		*Re-invested earnings*	*Other capital*	*Total FDI Inflows*	*(%) age growth over previous year*
	FIPB Route/RBI's Automatic Route/Acquisition Route	*Equity capital of unincorporated bodies#*				
August 1991–March 2000	15,483	—	—	—	15,483	—
2000–01	2,339	61	1,350	279	4,029	
2001–02	3,904	191	1,645	390	6,130	(+) 52.15%
2002–03	2,574	190	1,833	438	5,035	(–) 17.86%
2003–04	2,197	32	1,460	633	4,322	(–)14.16%
2004–05 (P)	3,250	528	1,904	369	6,051	(+) 40.00%
2005–06 (P)	5,540	280	1,676	226	7,722	(+)27.62%
2006–07 (P) (upto November 2006)	7,233	240	944	135	8,552	—
Sub-total (from April 2000–November 2006)	27,037	1,522	10,812	2,470	41,841	—
Cumulative Total (from August 1991 To November 2006)	42,520	1,522	10,812	2,470	57,324	—

Source: SIA Newsletter, January 2007.

5

Motivating Factors, Determinants and Problems of FDI Inflows into India

Motives and Determinants of FDI

Attracting FDI is not, however, an easy job. An understanding of the foreign investors motives in going for foreign production can be expected to help in this effort. The motives of all foreign investors are not, however, the same. Besides, a foreign investment is rarely undertaken for a single motive.

Regarding the motives of FDI itself, a large literature looks at the host country's factors separately. The factors may also differ according to the types of industries like import substituting or export promoting and sectors of investment like production of raw materials (mining, petroleum and agriculture), manufacturing and services. Investors of the developed and developing countries may also have different motives.

According to Buckley and Brooke (1992), 'The motives, the process of direct investment and the entry strategy into a particular foreign market vary greatly according to the characteristics of the entrant firm, its past relationship to the market and the nature of foreign market'. Besides, the firm's objective has a bearing on the motives for an investment, which is the possible contribution of investment to the firm's profitability or growth or other objectives.

Pointing out the relevance of examining reasons for FDI, Lal (1975) says, 'First, it will determine the areas into which foreign investment is likely to flow, and secondly, it will determine the minimum acceptable terms under which the foreign investor will be likely to come to the host country.' An OECD publication (1987) has broadly divided the determinants of direct foreign investment into (a) macro-economic determinants, and (b) sectoral determinants.

The present section will first look at macroeconomic factors influencing FDI followed by firm-specific, industry-specific, country-specific and other factors. Here, the emphasis is on the host country's factors which it can itself manipulate to attract foreign investment.

Macroeconomic Factors

It is generally argued that the most important considerations are the host government's attitudes, political stability, the prospect of market growth and the threat to established markets. Cost considerations, tax incentives or short-term gains are often seen as less significant though this may not be true in all cases. About the factors that inhibit FDI, Lall and Streeten (1977) write, 'the dangers posed by threats of political action, expropriation or arbitrary changes in ownership or remittance policies, and lengthy bureaucratic procedures, are, on the other hand, significant deterrents in particular area.'

OECD studies (1983 and 1987) have found that the most important determinants of direct foreign investment are the macro-determinants of a long-term nature, i.e., the demand prospects of the markets aimed at whether local or worldwide, and cost considerations as long as host country's policies are not extreme and retain relatively stable.

Among the regulatory or policy aspects influencing investment, the above study identifies four factors, namely, authorizations for new investments and attached conditions, investment incentives, ownership, and transfer of funds. The most frequently encountered requirements are conformity with the objective of development policies and national economic planning of developing countries. They often involve local content, exports, imports, technology transfer and use of appropriate technologies, training and use of local manpower and management, and health and safety or the protection of environment.

Wallace (1990) made a survey of 500 major corporations investing in least developed countries (LDCs) where the corporations were asked to express their most pressing concerns relating to market entry, cost of FDI and return on FDI. The study which had received response from 295 corporations found guaranteed remittance of earnings and protection from expropriation as the two most critically positive factors and threat of war/hostilities and unfavourable investment laws as the two most critically negative factors for market entry. In case of factors which influence costs associated with FDI, host remittance policies and host tax law and policies were found to be critical factors followed by host ownership percentage requirements. Similarly, the critical factors expected to influence the return on FDI were found to be projected market growth, host tax policies and pricing controls.

Firm-specific Factors

Various theories of firm behaviour offer explanations of firm-specific factors in FDI. Dunning (2002) (also known as Dunning's Eclectic Theory) integrates the theories of international trade and foreign investment into a unified theory of international production and identifies three types of advantages as under:

1. Ownership-specific advantages (of property rights and intangible assets), which arise from the firm's size and access to markets and resources, the firm's ability to co-ordinate complementary activities, such as manufacturing and distribution, and the ability to exploit differences between countries. These are the advantages possessed by the enterprises concerned, and include proprietary technology, management skills, natural resources information and the advantages associated with size and established position and geographical spread.
2. Location-specific advantages, which include differences in country's natural endowments, transport costs, macro-economic stability, cultural factors and government regulations. These advantages help determine which countries are host to multinational enterprises' foreign production.

   The literature indicates that the key locational factors determining FDI are host country's market size, input costs—notably of natural resources and labour — and the riskiness of investment, both in terms of the economic and the political environment. Market size, typically measured by host country's gross domestic product (GDP), captures potential economies of large-scale production. In the transition context, survey evidence suggests most firms invested in search of new market opportunities, which can also be related to absolute market size.
3. Internalization incentive advantages, favour a decision to exploit an advantage within the firm, and include market control, reduction of transaction and negotiating costs, assurance of stability, protection of proprietary and technical skills and the

economies associated with vertical and horizontal integration. These advantages arise from exploiting imperfections in external markets, which include the reduction of uncertainty and transactions costs in order to generate knowledge more efficiently; and the reduction of state-generated imperfections such as tariffs, foreign exchange controls and subsidies (Dunning, 2002).

If only the first condition (i.e., ownership-specific advantage) is met, firms will rely on exports, licensing or the sale of patents to serve a foreign market. In the presence of internalization incentives (e.g., protection from supply disruptions and price hikes, lack of suitable licensee and economies of common governance) FDI becomes the preferred mode of servicing foreign markets, but only if location-specific advantages are present. Within the trinity of conditions for FDI to occur, *locational determinants* are the only ones that host governments can influence directly.

Whereas it has not been possible to arrange firms locational-specific decisions into a uniform theoretical pattern so far, the literature cites a large number of very different factors that impact on business potential and the risks associated with individual locations. They can be grouped into three broad categories: (i) national policy framework for FDI, (ii) business facilitation, and (iii) economic motives. The most important determinants for the location of FDI are economic considerations. They come into full play once an enabling FDI policy framework is in place. Following from the principal motivations for investing in foreign countries, economic determinants can be grouped into three clusters: (i) resource-seeking, (ii) market-seeking, and (iii) efficiency-seeking. Availability of natural resources, cheap (unskilled or semi-skilled) labour, creative assets and physical infrastructure promotes (*resource-seeking activities*).

Historically, the most important host country's determinant of FDI has been the availability of natural resources, for example, minerals, raw materials and agricultural products. Up to the Second World War, about 60 per cent of the world stock of FDI was in natural resources. However, by itself, the presence of natural resources was not sufficient for FDI to take place. Comparative advantage in natural resources usually gave rise to trade rather than to FDI. Investment took place when resource abundant countries either lacked the large amounts of capital typically required for resource extraction, or did not have the technical skills needed to extract or sell raw materials to the rest of the world (Dunning, 1981). In addition, infrastructural facilities for exporting the raw materials to their final destination had to be in place or needed to be created (*World Investment Report, 1998*).

Labour-seeking investment is usually undertaken by manufacturing and service multinational enterprises from countries with high real labour costs. These enterprises set up, or acquire, subsidiaries in countries with lower real labour costs to supply labour-intensive intermediate or final products. Frequently, to attract such production, host countries have set up free trade or export processing zones (Dunning, 1981). Other highly important determinants of FDI are known as *market factors,* which are market size, in absolute terms as well as in relation to the size and income of its population, and market growth. For firms, new markets provide a chance to stay competitive and grow within the industry as well as achieve scale and scope economies. The motivation of *efficiency-seeking* FDI is to rationalize the structure of established resource-based, or market-seeking, investment in such a way that the investing company can gain from the common governance of geographically dispersed activities. The intention of the efficiency-seeking firms is to take advantage of different factor endowments, cultures, institutional arrangements, economic systems and policies, and market structures by concentrating production in a limited number of locations to supply multiple markets. Moreover, in order to efficiency-seeking foreign production to take place, the macroeconomic and political situation has to be stable, cross-border markets must be both well developed and open (Dunning, 2002).

In addition to the above economic factors, Hodgson and Herander (1983) also list a number of non-economic factors which may motivate MNEs to start production abroad. These non-economic factors include the socio-political characteristics of the prospective host country like:

1. Attitude of the host government towards the presence of foreign-owned firms within its border. This includes the host government's attitudes towards repatriation of profit and capital and the requirements of local content.
2. Stability of the government: The changes in the leadership of a nation or in the basic form of government are likely to affect the environment in which MNE subsidiaries operate.

Lal (1975) argues that the theory of direct investment is an integral part of the theory of monopolistic competition. The foreign investors must possess some advantages which allow them to overcome socio-economic costs and earn higher rate of return than the local investor.

Sector-specific Factors

The growth rate and costs of production in the host country are again the most important motivating factors. To quote OECD (1987) again, 'Cost considerations are expected to play a more important role from now on and this has implications for host country policies as regards, notably, reducing inflation and maintaining realistic exchange rates are concerned'. The other motivating factors noted by the study were trade barriers, investment incentives/dis-incentives and the availability of skilled labour. The creation of export processing zones is also expected to remain an important factor for export-oriented investment. But, with the coming of new automated and computerized technologies, the developing countries are facing the problem of capital intensive investment which made developed countries competitive again.

With reference to the mining sector, the OECD study (1987) has pointed to an availability and cost of raw materials as the important determinants of investment. The other factors noted were the security of investment, the modalities and prospects for renegotiation of contracts, the possibility of recourse to international dispute settlement and arbitration, the recognition of the principles of international law and the relation between companies and host governments involved.

One dominant model explaining foreign investment in manufacturing is, however, the product cycle model evolved by Vernon, Huffbauer and Hirsch. According to this model, the advanced countries generate new technology-intensive products with the technological and skilled manpower they have and export them to the developing countries. With the increasing imitation of the product by the competitors, the investors in the last stage of product life cycle move to developing countries with cheap labour.

In the case of export promoting versus import substituting investment in manufacturing, the host government's tariff and non-tariff barriers may encourage investment intended to meet local demand but discourage export-oriented investment, by making necessary imports more costly.

Export-oriented manufacturing investment is less affected by the domestic economic situation of the host country compared to the international situation, for example, the maintenance of an open market in developed countries. Domestic costs, however, remains an important factor in order to maintain international competitiveness. Mentioning the recent increase in investment in service sectors like banking, insurance, advertising, both OECD (1987) and UNCTAD (2007) have found that service multinationals follow their manufacturing or primary-industry multinational clients. The advertising multinationals are also found to be attracted to developing countries by local production firms who are willing to hire their services in order to gain access to the marketing techniques required to compete. The above mentioned factors are also applicable to other service sectors like consultancy and accountancy.

Country-specific Factors

FDI is an important element of economic integration, because it opens possibilities for accelerated growth, technical innovation and enterprise restructuring, as well as capital account relief.

Now, let us look at the country-specific explanatory variables that have attracted and distracted foreign investment. In case of India and Malaysia, the country's natural resources formed the strongest attraction for foreign investment.

According to Oman (1993), 'Foreign investors find the country's abundant supply of petroleum, natural gas, rubber, oil palm and timber to be strategic factors in improving its comparative advantage in manufacturing'. The country's socio-political stability was found to be another strong variable for attracting foreign investment. The other factors attracting investment in the country were: openness of its financial system (almost unrestricted remittances of funds into and out of the country), unprotected domestic market in the sense that there is a presence of MNEs even in domestic consumption sectors like consumer durable, clothing, footwear, food and beverages, an abundant supply of young and skilled labour, a good infrastructure system (comprehensive network of roads, railways and utility facilities) and an environment conducive to new innovations and technologies.

A study by Wong and Khan (1991) in Singapore based on interviews of 10 wholly foreign-owned and highly export-oriented multinational managers revealed political stability as the main motivating factor. This was followed by the factors like strategic location, disciplined labour force, good and efficient government and adequate infrastructure.

The study done in Thailand by Patarasuk (1991) based on the surveys and interviews of 16 firms in eight industries found the most important motivating factors to be low wages, investment incentives and access to local relatively cheap raw materials.

Marino (2001), on the basis of the survey of 14 TNC subsidiaries representing various manufacturing enterprises in the Philippines, found the strategic location of the country, low wage costs and access to local markets as main motivating factors. The motivating factors identified by the firms in this study were basically the factors which minimize costs.

The developing countries, especially newly industrializing countries (NICs), have now created their own transnational corporations (TNCs). The motives of these multinationals going abroad have also been examined to find whether such motives differ from those of developed country's multinationals.

The OECD study (1987) revealed that the motivating factors of developed as well as developing country multinationals are often similar. Country case studies have, however, shown that such factors may be different.

According to Lall (1993), the major home country factors for investing abroad by multinationals from India were found to be the restrictive environment in the home country including infrastructural and bureaucratic problems, a firm's willingness to gain experience of international operations so as to benefit from a company image at home (prestige attached to being multinational), proprietary advantages and the wish to develop their own technologies or capture export markets. The most important host country factors found by the study were the protective policies in the host countries, skill and infrastructural base, political stability and a supporting investment climate.

The same study revealed two main home country factors motivating Hong Kong multinationals as the shortage of factor supply and factor cost (mainly labour) in the country and the possibility to facilitate exports in the face of trade restrictions, competition and demand saturation in certain markets.

In the case of host country factors, Hong Kong MNEs found political stability to be the main factor attracting their foreign investment. This was followed by the availability of cheap land and labour, good infrastructure, government efficiency, tax concessions and the absence of foreign exchange control. Hong Kong MNEs were also much more concerned about cost reduction than the opening up the host country market. Regarding the reasons for investing in the developed countries like Canada, USA, UK and Switzerland, the convenience of acquiring foreign technology was found to be the main motive.

Regarding the motivation for overseas production of multinationals from two Latin American countries, the home country factors for

Argentine multinationals were found to be the domestic market and the structural limits of the growth process (that is, the small-to-medium-size nature of the local economies), and the possibility of international vertical integration. In case of host country factors, Argentine foreign investment firms were found to be motivated by access to local raw materials, capturing a presently or potentially unsatisfied market and fiscal and other benefits extended by the host country. The other factors found by the study were taking advantage of regional agreements, reducing production cost, blocking third parties from duplicating proprietary technology and capturing economies of scale through specialization. The Brazilian multinationals were found to go for overseas production due to the government's motivation to go abroad and the provision of large number of fiscal and credit incentives for export promotion. In case of host country factors, host government policies to protect their domestic production were the main motivating factors.

Factors that Attracting Foreign Direct Investment

The major recipients of FDI possess great advantages. The developing countries that received the lion's share of the surge in FDI flows during the 1990s had more open policy regimes or hospitable regulatory framework, large markets, and favourable economic environment. For example, new laws on foreign investment have been formed to permit profit repatriation since the early 1990s, while accessions to international agreements and institutions as well as conclusions of bilateral investment treaties and double taxation treaties have accelerated (UNCTAD, 2001). According to a survey conducted by UNCTAD in 1997, 26 of the 32 least developed countries in Africa had a liberal or relatively liberal regime towards the repatriation of capital. The liberalization of the rules governing FDI in developing countries has also encouraged higher rates of foreign investment. The FDI to some of the larger recipients has been boosted by good policies. The largest FDI recipients have an average World Bank policy rating of 4.1, compared with 3.3 for other developing countries.

The favourable regulatory or policy framework may be implemented in a variety of ways, such as through privatization, rules regarding entry and operations, institutional environment for financial and corporate restructuring, liberal trade policy (tariffs and non-tariffs) and tax policy, etc.

The growth rate of FDI is high in countries with good policies and rapid expansion of trade. The adoption of sound economic policies encourages increased FDI flows. Also, the policy measures such as steps to reduce the risk of nationalization were found to have had positive effects on FDI. Given their improved policy and strong economic performance since the 1980s, many developing countries, such as Malaysia, Thailand and Chile, continued to attract significant FDI flows. Similarly, Latin American countries like Argentina, Brazil and Mexico, became major recipients of FDI in the late 1980s, after emerging from the debt crisis and beginning steps to improve their policy environments. The FDI has increased in countries with strong economic programmes that liberalize the rules governing FDI. For instance, FDI has responded to government decisions on privatization programmes. Seven of the ten largest FDI recipients received more than US$ 1 billion in foreign funds to finance privatization activities in 1999 (World Bank, 1999).

Privatization also appears to be an important source of FDI flows to many developing countries even during the recent financial crisis 1997–98. For instance, the largest privatization among developing countries in 1998 was Telebras, Brazil's state-owned telecommunications operator, which raised US$ 19 billion. Other privatization transactions also include telecommunications companies involving foreign investors, such as US$ 1.9 billion for Rom Telecom, the Romanian state-owned telephone operator; US$ 1.5 billion for Bulgarian Telecommunications Company (BTC); and a 60 per cent stake of Lietuvos Telekomas, the Lithuanian telecoms utility. In addition, one of the larger privatizations planned in Eastern Europe is the proposed sale of a 5 per cent stake of Gazprom, Russia's biggest natural gas producer, half of which was sold in 1998 (for US$ 660 million).

Similarly, Armenia pushed ahead with opening various sectors to foreign investors and promoting privatization, which led to an 80 per cent upsurge in FDI as ratio to GDP over the past decade. Privatization transactions accounted for a significant share of FDI inflows in some of these countries (15% in Uganda from 1992–97 and 25% in Bolivia from 1995–99).

Developing countries that made progress in improving the investment climate during the 1990s attracted large FDI. In the countries where policy and institutional performance improved most, FDI as a ratio to GDP increased by 25 per cent per year, while in the countries whose policies improved least, the FDI to GDP ratio increased by less than 6 per cent annually.

The relationship between improvements in the investment climate and increases in FDI flows is also seen in the experiences of individual developing countries. The surge in FDI reflects the improvements in the investment climate in the poor countries. Global FDI flows increased by 24 per cent per year during 1991–2000. Developing countries as a group saw rise in FDI flows by 20 per cent at constant prices.

An improved investment climate in many reforming countries contributed to an increase in FDI flows from US$ 5.4 billion in 1997 to US$ 5.9 billion in the Middle East and North African region in 1998. The largest inflows went to the Republic of Egypt, Morocco and Saudi Arabia. Countries that have undergone an improvement in the investment climate may see a large inflow of FDI until the stock reaches the levels desired by foreign investors. The huge surge in FDI to China with the introduction of market reforms is perhaps the most spectacular example of this phenomenon (ibid.).

Furthermore, changes in FDI flows in many developing countries in a liberalizing and globalizing world economy reflected changes in the overall economic environment, such as the market size, low-cost labour and raw materials, infrastructure (telecommunications, roads, power, etc).

Market size appears to be a major explanation of concentration of FDI flows in a few developing countries. Of the top ten developing countries' FDI recipients, six are also among the top ten countries in terms of GDP. For example, China has been able to attract substantial FDI flows (and the largest volumes of FDI) because of its large domestic markets, availability of low-priced Chinese labour, together with increased openness. The boom in FDI in China has also been attributed to the anticipation of accession and entrance to the World Trade Organization (WTO). Similarly, flows to Mexico were boosted by Mexico's entrance into the North American Free Trade Agreement (NAFTA).

The favourable economic environment in the FDI recipient countries can help attract and sustain its flows to developing countries. Several studies have found that exchange rate depreciation in the host country tends to attract FDI inflows. For example, during the Mexican peso crisis, the large currency depreciation and decline in domestic asset prices (in US dollars) helped sustain FDI flows. The depreciation of the peso increased the attractiveness of investments in sectors that can switch easily between producing for the domestic market and for export.

Also, the growth rate of GDP has been found to be associated with larger FDI inflows (World Bank, 1999), export orientation (by providing greater access to export markets), and better investment climate (in terms of sound macroeconomic policies, open regimes towards FDI, non-discriminatory frameworks for business facilitation). This is particularly true in the context of developing countries. For instance, the better prospects or an anticipated economic growth for Korea and Thailand are reflected in the increased FDI flows in 1998 (UNCTAD, 1999).

In addition, some examples of developing countries that have recently attracted increased FDI inflows, based on improved structural and macroeconomic performance, include Bangladesh, Bolivia and Uganda. In Bangladesh, the FDI inflows surged from minimal levels before 1995 to an annual average of US$ 170 million during 1996–99 (about 4% of domestic investment). This growth followed a programme of macroeconomic policy reforms undertaken since the early 1990s, and moves more recently to encourage private investment. In Bolivia, which was an early heavily indebted poor country (HIPC), the FDI flows rose after a successful programme to eliminate a hyper-inflation in 1985, followed by ongoing structural reform. From minimal levels in the late 1980s, FDI flows grew to an average of US$ 818 million a year during 1996–99. At the same time, (domestic gross fixed capital (DGFC) formation increased considerably. FDI inflows remained high in 1999 despite short-term macro-economic difficulties. Similarly, in Uganda, the FDI inflows began to grow in 1993, averaging US$ 182 million per year during 1997–99, or nearly 20 per cent of GFCF. Uganda was one of the first countries to benefit from the Initiative for the HIPC reflecting its commitment to sound macro-economic policy sector-led development and poverty reduction (World Bank, 1999).

Factors Discouraging FDI

Country experiences indicate that while favourable economic environment and regulatory or policy framework help induce FDI flows, there are also a number of forces that tend to discourage such flows.

Many developing countries have, during the past decade or so, begun liberalizing their national policies to establish a hospitable regulatory framework for FDI by relaxing rules regarding market entry and foreign ownership, improving the standards of treatment accorded to foreign firms, and improving the functioning of markets. These core policies are important because FDI will simply not take place where it is forbidden or strongly impeded. However, changes in policies have an asymmetric effect on the location of FDI: changes in the direction of greater openness allow firms to establish themselves in a particular location. In contrast, changes in the direction of less openness (for example, nationalization or closure to entry) will ensure a reduction in FDI (UNCTAD, 1999).

The regulatory restrictions, including tariffs and quotas, tend to discourage cross-border acquisitions by multinational enterprises. Countries that impose restrictions on foreign entry and ownership and foreign exchange transactions, as well as discriminatory tax provisions, tend to hamper FDI flows. For example, in Kenya, foreign investors face multiple licensing requirements and high withholding taxes on royalties, and FDI remained less than 0.2 per cent of GDP during 1991–99. Also, in Yemen, where sizeable outflows of FDI have been recorded since the mid-1990s, licensing requirements discouraged new investments, despite incentives such as tax holidays and customs exemptions.

Some of the developing countries have not achieved the improvements in the investment climate necessary to encourage higher FDI flows. While the poor prospect for growth and unfavourable economic environment have impeded the FDI flows to many countries, a number of other factors (such as the political and structural factors) have also been the important discouraging factors.

For instance, the economic uncertainty has restrained greenfield FDI in Brazil, and private sector merger and acquisition transactions have slowed down with the increasing economic difficulties in Argentina. In Indonesia, the severe recession, uncertainty over economic policies, and political disturbances that reduce future economic prospects have discouraged foreign investors in 1998. Similarly, Pakistan has seen a steady decline in FDI inflows since 1996 due to investor concerns over political developments.

In addition, recent analyses find that those developing countries with stronger policy environments attract a larger share of the total FDI flows to developing countries, whereas the higher levels of corruption act as a deterrent. Moreover, in Korea, the process of corporate and financial restructuring has slowed the FDI flows.

In a survey, it was found that the foreign investors' main motives in investing in India is the existence of market opportunities, make profits (though it can be assumed that all firms wish to make profit) and expand or diversify their activities (see Table 5.1). Some of the investors seem to have invested mainly because they are interested in cheap labour and raw materials.

The data further reveal that about 63 per cent of the respondents believe that the commercial objective like making profit is a significant motive to invest in India. Cheap labour, business expansion and host

Table 5.1 *Main Motives and Determinants of Investing in India*

Motives	*Strongly disagree*	*Partially disagree*	*Neither agree nor disagree*	*Agree*	*Strongly agree*	*Total*
Market opportunity/size (f)	2	1	1	29	53	86
%	2.33	1.16	1.16	33.72	61.63	100.00
To make profit (f)	1	4	3	23	54	85
%	1.16	4.65	3.49	26.74	62.79	98.84
Business expansion/diversification (f)	2	7	10	37	30	86
%	2.33	8.14	11.63	43.02	34.88	100.00
Low labour cost (f)	3	4	3	26	50	86
%	3.49	4.65	3.49	30.23	58.14	100.00
Help in the development of the country (f)	17	19	24	17	9	86
%	19.77	22.09	27.91	19.77	10.47	100.00
Availability of skilled labour (f)	3	4	3	20	56	86
%	3.49	4.65	3.49	23.26	65.12	100.00
Access to subsidized land (f)	1	3	14	26	42	86
%	1.16	3.49	16.28	30.23	48.84	100.00
To take advantage from govt. services (f)	6	12	14	35	18	85
%	6.98	13.95	16.28	40.70	20.93	98.84
Political stability (f)						
%						

Cont'd…

Cont'd...

Like the country and its people (f)	19	12	27	19	9	86
%	22.09	13.95	31.40	22.09	10.47	100.00
Source of raw materials (f)	1	4	26	37	18	86
	1.16	4.65	30.23	43.02	20.93	100.00
Natural beauty and culture of the country (f)	2	5	22	35	22	86
%	2.33	5.81	25.58	40.70	25.58	100.00
Security of investment (f)	2	7	10	37	30	86
%	2.33	8.14	11.63	43.02	34.88	100.00
Duty-free export-import (f)	3	13	14	32	24	86
%	3.49	15.12	16.28	37.21	27.91	100.00

Note: f = frequencies of respondents.
(%) = percentage of respondents.

Source: Field survey.

country's market size attract around 60 per cent of the respondents. Out of 8,654 respondents (62.79%) opined that the main motive to invest in the country is to make profit, whereas 40.70 per cent respondents think that FDI is coming due to government services and 37 respondents (43.02%) opined that the main objective of foreign inventors is to expand their business. Most of the investors are aware about their security of investment and the respondents' perception is 43.02 per cent regarding this factor. About 48.84 respondents think that FDI is coming due to the subsidies land.

The non-commercial motives like the interest of natural beauty, culture and people of the country are given by the respondents as low significant factors as the motive of investment.

Around 59 per cent of the respondents strongly agree that the low labour costs, market size/opportunity, business expansion/diversification are significant determinants of FDI inflows in India. Cheap labour reduces the cost of production and products can be sold at competitive prices. So, this factor is also quite significant in its positive impact on FDI inflows in India.

Of all the factors related to the characteristics of Indian economy, the huge size of its market is considered the most important factor attracting FDI in the country. Every international firm wants to produce on a large scale to reap the benefits of scale and to reduce the cost of production. India is an enormous untapped market for US, and a perfect site for its industry to gain a foothold in Asia. It is much more attractive than other countries in Asia and in a very advantageous position. According to the study by Pant (1995), Japanese and other FDIs are driven basically by the size of Indian market.

Availability of skilled labour is revealed as a significant determinant of FDI in India. Among the factors grouped under characteristics of Indian economy, it has occupied top place. According to John S. Clarkson, Boston consulting group president and CEO, there is terrific talent in India that needs to be unleashed. The skills available here in software, for example, is world class.

On the other hand, asked about the favourable and unfavourable factors for FDI in India, especially as compared to other countries in South Asia, the various favourable factors reported by the respondents are presented in Table 5.2.

The main favourable factors for investment operations in India as revealed by above table are domestic market size, and labour-related factors like obedient and disciplined employees, low labour costs and

Table 5.2 *Favourable Factors for FDI in India*

Favourable Factors	*Not at all favourable*	*Unfavourable*	*Little bit favourable*	*Favourable*	*Highly favourable*	*Total*
Attractive incentive packages/financial facilities (f)	7	15	31	23	8	84
%	8.14	17.44	36.05	26.74	11.63	100.00
Available raw materials (f)	2	11	28	31	14	86
%	2.33	12.79	32.56	36.05	16.28	100.00
Market size/opportunity (f)	3	4	12	25	42	86
%	3.49	4.65	13.95	29.07	48.84	100.00
Availability of cheap and skilled labour (f)	1	10	11	30	34	86
%	1.16	11.63	12.79	34.88	39.53	100.00
Adequate infrastructures facilities (f)	17	12	39	14	4	86
%	19.77	13.95	45.35	16.28	4.65	100.00
Personal security (f)	7	16	27	30	6	86
%	8.14	18.60	31.40	34.88	6.98	100.00
Access to subsidized land	4	12	13	40	17	86
%	4.65	13.95	15.12	46.51	19.77	100.00
Duty-free export and import (f)	10	15	39	18	4	86
%	11.63	17.44	45.35	20.93	4.65	100.00
Multiple entry visas (f)	11	11	26	27	10	85
%	12.79	12.79	30.23	31.40	11.63	98.84

Cont'd...

...Cont'd

Lower corporate tax rate (f)	4	13	24	36	9	86
%	4.65	15.12	27.91	41.86	10.47	100.00
Guarantee against nationalization of investment (f)	7	14	21	35	9	86
%	8.14	16.28	24.42	40.70	10.47	100.00
Natural resources (f)	3	14	25	35	9	86
%	3.49	16.28	29.07	40.70	10.47	100.00
Favourable government policy (f)	3	8	13	38	24	86
%	3.49	9.30	15.12	44.19	27.91	100.00

Note: f = frequencies of respondents.
(%) = percentage of respondents.

Sourc. Field survey, 2006.

Table 5.3 *Problems of FDI Inflows in India*

Unfavourable Factors	*Strongly Disagree*	*Partially Disagree*	*Indifference*	*Partially Agree*	*Strongly Agree*	*Total*
Lack of raw materials (f)	26	30	14	13	3	86
%	30.23	34.88	16.28	15.12	3.49	100.00
Unfavourable labour laws (f)	3	17	15	33	18	86
%	3.49	19.77	17.44	38.37	20.93	100.00
Lack of sufficient fiscal incentives (f)	8	20	23	31	4	86
%	9.30	23.26	26.74	36.05	4.65	100.00
Political unrest (f)	30	16	16	15	9	86
%	34.88	18.60	18.60	17.44	10.47	100.00
Political instability (f)	25	24	13	17	7	86
%	29.07	27.91	15.12	19.77	8.14	100.00
Macroeconomic instability (f)	17	30	22	15	2	86
%	19.77	34.88	25.58	17.44	2.33	100.00
Social unrest (f)	17	36	17	11	5	86
%	19.77	41.86	19.77	12.79	5.81	100.00
Complicated investment procedure (f)	5	10	22	37	11	85
%	5.81	11.63	25.58	43.02	12.79	98.84

Cont'd...

...Cont'd

Bureaucratic complexities (f)	1	7	15	41	22	86
%	1.16	8.14	17.44	47.67	25.58	100.00
Customs problems (f)	4	21	24	24	13	86
%	4.65	24.42	27.91	27.91	15.12	100.00
Unfavourable law and order situation (f)	13	23	26	17	6	1
%	15.12	26.74	30.23	19.77	6.98	1.16
Lack of good governance (f)	4	18	21	30	13	86
%	4.65	20.93	24.42	34.88	15.12	100.00
Lack of developed infrastructure (f)	4	7	8	43	24	86
%	4.65	8.14	9.30	50.00	27.91	100.00
Lack of cooperation of local partner (f)	8	29	26	16	7	86
%	9.30	33.72	30.23	18.60	8.14	100.00
Lack of earnestness of local investors (f)	14	22	27	17	6	86
%	16.28	25.58	31.40	19.77	6.98	100.00

Note: f = frequencies of respondents.
(%) = percentage of respondents.

Source: Field survey.

Table 5.4 *Problems Faced by Foreign Direct Investors doing Business in India*

	Strongly Disagree	*Partially disagree*	*Indifference*	*Partially Agree*	*Strongly Agree*	*Total*
Power and gas supply difficulties (f)	0	8	13	46	19	86
%	0.00	9.30	15.12	53.49	22.09	100.00
Political unrest in host economy (f)	19	25	15	17	10	86
%	22.09	29.07	17.44	19.77	11.63	100.00
Corruption and malpractices in all sectors (f)	4	4	15	43	20	86
%	4.65	4.65	17.44	50.00	23.26	100.00
Lack of efficient labour (f)	19	29	22	14	2	86
%	22.09	33.72	25.58	16.28	2.33	100.00
Regional bilateral trade agreement (f)	7	30	28	18	3	86
%	8.14	34.88	32.56	20.93	3.49	100.00
Frequent changes in government policies (f)	8	24	14	28	12	86
%	9.30	27.91	16.28	32.56	13.95	100.00
Lack of export incentives (f)	9	29	30	11	7	86
%	10.47	33.72	34.88	12.79	8.14	100.00

Cont'd...

...Cont'd

Shortage of working capital availability(f)	14	25	22	17	8	86
%	16.28	29.07	25.58	19.77	9.30	100.00
Future competition in the market (f)	9	29	18	20	9	85
%	10.47	33.72	20.93	23.26	10.47	98.84
High tax rates (f)	10	25	26	20	5	86
%	11.63	29.07	30.23	23.26	5.81	100.00
Labour unions (f)	7	13	23	36	7	86
%	8.14	15.12	26.74	41.86	8.14	100.00
Registration complexities (f)	7	9	23	37	10	86
%	8.14	10.47	26.74	43.02	11.63	100.00
Lengthy customs procedures (f)	7	10	25	37	7	86
%	8.14	11.63	29.07	43.02	8.14	100.00
Expensive port (f)	7	15	25	31	8	86
%	8.14	17.44	29.07	36.05	9.30	100.00
Corruption in all areas (f)	4	8	16	38	20	86
%	4.65	9.30	18.60	44.19	23.26	100.00
Lack of credit rating agencies (f)	11	24	.26	19	6	86

Cont'd...

...Cont'd

%	12.79	27.91	30.23	22.09	6.98	100.00
Poor law and order situation (f)	17	17	24	23	5	86
%	19.77	19.77	27.91	26.74	5.81	100.00
Cultural gap (f)	10	21	28	18	9	86
%	11.63	24.42	32.56	20.93	10.47	100.00
Amusement problems (f)	14	21	29	19	3	86
%	16.28	24.42	33.72	22.09	3.49	100.00
Banking problems (f)	19	29	18	17	3	86
%	22.09	33.72	20.93	19.77	3.49	100.00
Delay of air consignments (f)	11	31	23	19	2	86
%	12.79	36.05	26.74	22.09	2.33	100.00

Note: f = frequencies of respondents.
% = percentage of respondents.

Source: Field survey.

availability of required labour. On the other hand, except attractive incentive package and infrastructure facilities, all other factors are also considered as favourable factors for operations in India by foreign investors, especially as compared to other South Asian countries. These two factors are thought as little bit favourable factors for investing in India, according to the respondents.

The respondents are asked as many as unfavourable factors/problems relating to FDI for foreign investment in Bangladesh and India which are listed along with their responses in Tables 5.2 and 5.3.

Thus, the main unfavourable factors as revealed by the above table are bureaucratic complexities (the government's procedural delays), undeveloped infrastructure, complicated investment procedure, unfavourable labour laws, lack of gas and power, and lack of good governance.

The other unfavourable factors such as lack of raw materials, unfavourable law and order situation, customs problem, lack of earnestness of local investors and small size of the market for which respondents were indifference. Thus, the unfavourable factors for FDI inflows in India are also the combinations of policy, infrastructure and resource factors.

The present survey shows that bureaucratic complexities, lack of necessary infrastructure, transportation facilities, expensive port facilities and lack of good governance are main unfavourable factors and can be taken into account as the main problems relating to FDI in the country.

Though finding a local partner could be a problem in case of joint ventures, this was not so in India, as 33.72 per cent of the respondents partially disagree with this. The main reasons for not facing problems were the Indian partner finding the foreign partner, that is the other way round, and the investors knowing each other before entering into a joint venture operation. This implies that any further government effort to bring together Indian and foreign partners will help promote FDI.

From the Table 5.4, it is clear that almost 50 per cent of the respondents replied that they experienced corruption in all sectors and malpractices problems in India. The main problems faced by the investors in doing business in India are lack of power and gas supply, difficulty of labour unions, corruption and malpractices, followed by problems in the registration complexities, expensive port, poor law and order situation, and lengthy customs procedures.

Table 5.5 below presents opinions of the respondents regarding promoting FDI inflows in India:

Table 5.5 *Respondents' opinion regarding promoting the FDI in India*

	Strongly disagree	*Partially agree*	*Indifference*	*Partially agree*	*Strongly agree*	*Total*
Main political stability (f)	3	4	12	25	42	86
%	3.49	4.65	13.95	29.07	48.84	100.00
Positive attitude of political parties (f)	2	5	12	29	38	86
%	2.33	5.81	13.95	33.72	44.19	100.00
Necessary promotion activities (f)	1	4	10	38	32	85
%	1.16	4.65	11.63	44.19	37.21	98.84
New international market search (f)	0	4	23	33	26	86
%	0.00	4.65	26.74	38.37	30.23	100.00
Wide publicity (f)	1	6	17	40	22	86
%	1.16	6.98	19.77	46.51	25.58	100.00
Reducing corruption (f)	1	9	5	25	45	85
%	1.16	10.47	5.81	29.07	52.33	98.84
Positive bureaucratic attitude (f)	2	3	9	27	44	85
%	2.33	3.49	10.47	31.40	51.16	98.84
Enhance country image (f)	1	5	12	29	39	86
%	1.16	5.81	13.95	33.72	45.35	100.00

Note: f = frequencies of respondents. % = percentage of respondents.

Source: Field survey.

FDI has been welcomed in power, oil, telecommunications, infrastructure, etc. This step is highly applauded by the respondents. From their point of view, this has significantly positive influence on FDI inflow in India. Agro-processing and bio-technology sectors have emerged new areas for targeting more FDI in India.

So far as the priority measures to attract FDI are concerned, most of the respondents strongly agree that ensure political and economic stability, remove procedural barriers, improve macro-economic stability, develop infrastructural facilities, improve customs services, ensure good governance, improve port services and facilities, improve banking and financial institutional facilities, and improve the performance of government officials are very significant factors to be taken into consideration in this regard.

Table 5.6 *Sectors should be targeted for FDI in India*

Sectors	*Don't at all prefer*	*Don't prefer*	*Indifference*	*Somewhat prefer*	*Strongly prefer*	*Total*
Energy and power (f)	7	8	3	26	42	86
%	8.14	9.30	3.49	30.23	48.84	100.00
Infrastructure (roads and high-way) (f)	3	4	3	26	50	86
%	3.49	4.65	3.49	30.23	58.14	100.00
Real estate (f)	20	31	19	12	4	86
%	23.26	36.05	22.09	13.95	4.65	100.00
Telecom and IT (f)	1	14	12	33	26	86
%	1.16	16.28	13.95	38.37	30.23	100.00
Agro-processing (f)	6	9	10	35	26	86
%	6.98	10.47	11.63	40.70	30.23	100.00
Biotechnology (f)		5	10	32	38	85
%		5.81	11.63	37.21	44.19	98.84
Retail (f)	17	19	24	17	9	86
%	19.77	22.09	27.91	19.77	10.47	100.00
Textiles (f)	12	20	20	19	15	86
%	13.95	23.26	23.26	22.09	17.44	100.00
Heavy machines (f)	1	6	9	37	32	85
%	1.16	6.98	10.47	43.02	37.21	98.84
Tourism (f)	5	13	16	26	26	86
%	5.81	15.12	18.60	30.23	30.23	100.00
Car manufacturing and transport (f)	2	8	12	36	28	86
%	2.33	9.30	13.95	41.86	32.56	100.00
Others (f)	3	11	26	32	14	86
%	3.49	12.79	30.23	37.21	16.28	100.00

Note: f = frequencies of respondents.
% = percentage of respondents.

Source: Field survey.

Table 5.7 *Priority Measures to attract FDI in India*

	Strongly disagree	*Partially agree*	*Indifference*	*Partially agree*	*Strongly agree*	*Total*
Ensure political and economic stability (f)	2	3	9	26	46	86
%	2.33	3.49	10.47	30.23	53.49	100.00
Remove procedural barriers (f)	3	1	10	27	45	86
	3.49	1.16	11.63	31.40	52.33	100.00
Improve macro-stability (f)	2	3	15	29	37	86
%	2.33	3.49	17.44	33.72	43.02	100.00
Develop infrastructural facilities (f)	1	4	3	23	54	85
%	1.16	4.65	3.49	26.74	62.79	98.84
Strengthen the registered authorities (f)	2	1	12	32	39	86
%	2.33	1.16	13.95	37.21	45.35	100.00
Improvement of banking and financial institution facilities (f)	2	7	10	37	30	86
%	2.33	8.14	11.63	43.02	34.88	100.00
Improve customs services (f)	1	2	21	30	32	86
%	1.16	2.33	24.42	34.88	37.21	100.00
Improvement of law and order situation (f)	2	3	21	28	32	86
%	2.33	3.49	24.42	32.56	37.21	100.00
Ensure good governance (f)	1	3	14	26	42	86
%	1.16	3.49	16.28	30.23	48.84	100.00
Strengthen environment regulations (f)	2	9	16	21	38	86
%	2.33	10.47	18.60	24.42	44.19	100.00
Strengthen promotional activities (f)	1	11	17	34	23	86
%	1.16	12.79	19.77	39.53	26.74	100.00
Set up industrial parks,SEZs, EPZs (f)	6	9	17	26	28	86
%	6.98	10.47	19.77	30.23	32.56	100.00
Improve port services (f)	1	4	11	33	37	86
%	1.16	4.65	12.79	38.37	43.02	100.00
Regional and sub-registered cooperation (f)		5	13	40	28	86
%		5.81	15.12	46.51	32.56	100.00
Improve the perference of government office (f)	2	3	6	40	35	86
%	2.33	3.49	6.98	46.51	40.70	100.00

Notes: f = frequencies of respondents.
% = percentage of respondents.

Source: Field survey.

In general, around 45 per cent of the respondents in India strongly agree with the statements such as ensure political and economic stability, remove procedural barriers, improve macro-economic stability, develop infrastructural facilities, strengthen the regulatory authority and ensure good governance to attract more FDI in India. The same percentage of respondents (46.51%) have expressed their partial agreement for regional and sub-regional cooperation, and improve the performance of government officials in this regard. Only around 30 per cent of respondents have expressed the view that the establishment of EPZs or SEZs will help promote FDI in India.

Conclusion

The foreign investors who have invested in India are found to be motivated both by commercial and non-commercial objectives. The non-commercial motives included natural beauty of the place of the local people.

In the case of commercial objectives, cheap labour and profit-making are found to be the important factors for the investors to invest in the host country. Like other developing countries, access to subsidized land, low labour costs, market size, business diversification and security of the investment are found to be the main motives of FDI inflows in India. In spite of the big size of the Indian market, most of the investments are found to aim at both the export and the domestic markets.

However, in a subsequent question asked about the favourable and unfavourable factors of foreign investment, as compared with other South Asian countries, it is found that the main favourable factors for investment operations in India are domestic market size, and labour-related factors like low labour costs and availability of required labour.

The main unfavourable factors are found the government bureaucracy and procedural delays, customs problem, undeveloped infrastructure, inefficient capital market, lack of good governance and lack of raw materials of the country. It is found that foreign investor, on average, have to spend 134 days in obtaining a licence and 111 days to start a business in India. The lack of special incentives to the foreign investors and the non-implementation of the facilities already given by the Act are other two major complaints made by the respondents.

On the basis of the survey findings, it can be concluded that the first thing the government needs to do to promote foreign investment is to simplify bureaucratic procedures and avoid bureaucratic harassment. The Board of Investment (BOI) and Foreign Investment Promotion Board (FIPB), which are supposed to provide a one-stop service to the foreign investors, is not doing it. It, therefore, needs to be given the necessary powers and responsibilities to provide a real one-stop-service. It seems that the agencies need to be reorganized and strengthened with necessary equipment and qualified staff.

In order to attract foreign investment in India, the industrial development policy needs to be kept clear and stable. Besides, the foreign investors should be provided with incentives comparable to those provided by other South Asian countries. Also, the foreign investors should not find difficulty in getting whatever facilities are being provided legally. As the present promotional activities are not found to be sufficient, an increase in such activities also seems necessary.

In the case of the suggestions made by respondents, the interview survey emphasized the need to simplify the bureaucratic procedure, and strengthen the BOI or FIPB. The survey suggested the need for improving infrastructure, port facilities, more incentives, clear information and government departmental coordination. It also suggested the need, to improve labour's skills and abolish labour unions and more facilities to NRBs or NRIs.

6

Impact of FDI on Economic Growth in India

An Empirical Investigation

Many studies discuss the ways in which inward FDI can contribute to the growth of a host country's economy (see, for example, Wei, 2000; Balasubramanyam and Mahambare, 2003; De Mello, 1997). In general, these studies argue that the impact of FDI on growth is complex. First, through capital accumulation in a recipient economy, FDI is expected to be growth enhancing by encouraging the incorporation of new inputs and technologies into the production function of a host economy. Second, FDI improves the efficiency of locally-owned host country's firms via contact and demonstration effects, and their exposure to fierce competition. Last and most importantly, FDI is believed to be a leading source of technological change and human capital augmentation in developing countries. Technological progress takes place through a process of 'capital is deepening' in the form of the introduction of new varieties of knowledge-based capital goods. It also proceeds via specific productivity-increasing labour training and skills acquisition promoted by transnational corporations (TNCs). A recent embellishment in the growth literature is to highlight the dependence of the domestic growth rate on the state of technology relative to that in the rest of the world (De Mello, 1997).

The basic shortcoming of conventional neo-classical growth models, as far as FDI is concerned, is that long-run growth can only be achieved by technological progress, which is considered to be exogenous. FDI would only affect output growth in the short run and, in the long run, under the conventional assumption of diminishing returns to capital inputs with a given technology, FDI would have no permanent impact on output growth. Within the new growth framework, FDI is treated as one of the factor inputs along with labour and (domestic) capital and is expected to promote growth in the long run. Whether or not technological progress is best described as exogenous to the world as a system, the role of FDI in diffusing technology (both hard and soft) to developing countries appears clear. Under either interpretation, technology created in the developed world is exogenous to a developing country. Consequently, a positive relationship between FDI and long-run growth in a developing host country should be expected.

It should be pointed out that the direction of causation may run either way. FDI may be drawn to regions of faster growth or greater potential because their growth prospects have made it more attractive to foreign TNCs. De Mello (1997) envisions a case in which the size of the consumer market in a recipient economy is getting larger, as a result of faster growth leading to rapid increases in the potential purchasing power of consumers in a host country. Consequently, it is tenable that growth itself may be an important determinant of FDI in addition to those listed above.

Khawar (2005) conducted an empirical cross-country growth analysis to investigate the impact over two decades of foreign direct investment at the 'aggregate' level and found that it has significant and positive relationship with real income per capita, irrespective of any human capital requirements. The researcher tested the impact of contemporaneous FDI on growth during the period from 1970 to 1992 using the method of ordinary least squares (OLS). The study found that FDI was significant and positively correlated with growth as was domestic investment. The population growth rate, initial GDP and political instability variables were negatively correlated with growth, which was in keeping with the findings in the empirical growth literature. The human capital measure was not significant in the analysis

Hassan (2003), analysed the casual relationship between FDI and GDP in a sample of 31 developing countries concerning 31 years. Using estimators for heterogeneous panel data, they found a directional causality between FDI to GDP ratio implying that FDI causes growth.

Within an evaluation of the impact of FDI-induced technological change on growth in developing countries, Blomstrom and Kokko (1996); Lipsey (1999) find that (positive and statistically significant impact of FDI), there is higher level of development in a host country, pursuing the effects of preconditions in a developing host country, Borensztein et al. (1998) find that FDI is more productive than domestic investment only when the host country has a minimum threshold stock of human capital. De Mello (1997) also found a positive impact of FDI on output growth regardless of the technological status of a host country as a technological leader or follower.

Dritsaki, Dritsaki and Adamopoulos (2004) investigate the relationship between trade, FDI and economic growth for Greece over the period 1960–2002 and suggested that there is a long-run equilibrium relationship. They also used the Granger causality test and the results showed that there is a casual relationship between the examined variables. A similar type of study regarding the relationship between FDI and economic growth for Cyprus over the period 1976–2002, conducted by Fried Livshits (2005) using the methodology of Granger causality, also shows that the economic growth as measured by GDP in Cyprus is caused by the FDI, but not vice versa.

Flexner (2000) employs ordinary least squares (OLS) estimation to examine the effect of FDI on per capita GDP growth in Bolivia over the period 1990–1998 and found that FDI has a statistically significant impact on per capita GDP growth.

Chowdhury and Mavrotas (2003) examined the casual relationship between FDI and economic growth for Chile, Malaysia and Thailand using time series data covering the period 1969–2000 and their empirical findings clearly suggested that it is GDP that causes FDI in the case of Chile and not vice versa, while for both Malaysia and Thailand, there is a strong evidence of a bi-directional causality between the two variables.

Athukorala (2003) examined the relationship between FDI and GDP also using time series data from the Sri Lankan economy. Their econometric result also shows that FDI inflows do not exert an independent influence on economic growth. And also the direction of causation is not towards from FDI to GDP growth but GDP growth to FDI.

Lensink and Morrissey (2001) estimated the standard model using cross-section, panel data and instrumental variable techniques and found that FDI has a positive effect on growth whereas volatility of FDI has a negative impact. They also found that the evidence for a positive effect of FDI is not sensitive to which other explanatory variables are included, although the significance of the estimated coefficient does vary according to the specification.

Empirical findings have so far not offered clear-cut conclusion with respect to the causality between FDI and growth. The surge of FDI might be associated with domestic policy variables, and this was evidenced in the case of Latin America. De Mello (1997) finds that FDI plays an important role in increasing both output and TFP in Chile, while capital accumulation and TFP growth precede FDI in Brazil. In both cases, the direction of the relevant causalities cannot be determined. The direction of causality between FDI and growth may well depend on the determinants of FDI. If the determinants have strong links with growth in the host country, growth may be found to cause FDI, while output may grow faster when FDI takes place in other circumstances.

Data and Research Methodology

The following is a description on the variables we have used in this study, and how the data has been constructed for each variable:

- *FDI inflows are net inflows* of investment to acquire a lasting management interest (10% or more of voting stock) in an enterprise operating in an economy other than the home country of the investor. The measure is the sum of equity capital, reinvestment of earnings, other long-term capital and short-term capital as shown in the balance of payments. No private portfolio investment is considered in this study. Data of net inflows of FDI are collected from WIR and WDI-CD-Rom version as percentage of GDP.
- *GDP in current market price* and *per capita GDP data* are collected from various publications of World Bank, UNCTAD. and IMF.
- *Annual growth rate of GDP* has been collected from World Bank publications and Economic Survey of India.
- *Degree of openness (XM)* is calculated as the sum of exports and imports divided by GDP. This ratio of trade to GDP provides a measure of the degree of economic openness.
- *Human capital (HC)* proxied by percentage of relevant group participating in higher secondary education. Higher secondary education completes the provision of secondary education that

began after the completion of secondary level, and aims at laying the foundations for lifelong learning and human development, by offering more subject or skill-oriented instruction using more specialized teacher.

Human capital enhances the productivity of physical capital and labour. The accumulation of human capital has both internal effects (the effects of an individuals' human capital on his own productivity) and external effects (the contribution to the productivity of all factors of production by the average level of skill or human capital) (Lucas, 1988).

- *Gross domestic investment (GDI)* consists of outlays on additions to the fixed assets of the economy plus net changes in the level of inventories. It is coded as percentage of GDP.
- *Government's expenditure (GE)* denotes central government's development expenditure, also indicated by percentage of GDP.
- *Gross fixed capital formation (GFCF):* Investment has made the GFC. So, we want to observe the contribution of GFCF to economic growth with others variable (savings have not been considered, because, S =/= I, some portion has been invested and other portion has consumed).
- *Credit/GDP (DCR)* is domestic credit provided by the banking sector to GDP. It includes all credit to various sectors on a gross basis, with the exception of net credit to the central government. The banking sector includes monetary authorities and deposit money banks, as well as other banking institutions where data are available (including institutions that do not accept transferable deposits but do incur such liabilities as time and savings deposits). Examples of other banking institutions are savings and mortgage loan institutions and building and loan associations.
- *Dummy variable (Dm) (D=1 for democratic government, D = 0 for otherwise):* To capture the effect of good governance in affecting the FDI, a dummy variable is used. Good governance is proxied by democratic government.

Empirical Model Specification and Methodology

The conventional approach to investigating the relationship between growth and FDI involves running regressions for the rate of output growth on the rate of FDI growth. Often, additional explanatory variables (for example, the rate of growth of the domestic capital stock, domestic labour force growth) are included in order to control for other influences upon the rate of economic growth. Such models are often presented in terms of a production function-type of framework that treats FDI (foreign capital) as a factor input.

It is not the purpose of this study to offer either a new theory or specification of a new growth model. Rather, the main objective is to shed fresh light on the linkages between FDI and economic growth at the country level by extending a model that is already familiar from studies at the national and international level. However, our study does employ additional and theoretically pertinent variables, thereby enabling us to focus on a broader range of issues. Although our model cannot be considered to be perfect, it can claim to be well justified in the light of our discussion above. The purpose of our empirical investigation is to analyse the effects of FDI on economic growth in India.

The empirical growth literature has identified a number of variables that are typically correlated with economic growth. Borensztein et al. (1998); Makki and Somwaru (2004); Sahoo (2006); Khawar (2005); IMF Staff Country Report (1998). In the light of the discussion in the literature review and variables definition sections, the following equation is used as the basic model:

GDP per capita Growth = ∫ [(nFDI, ExpoImp, Govt.DevExp, DomsInv, GFCF, Hum Cap, DCR, good Governance (democratic government)]

... (1)

where,
nFDI = net foreign direct investment inflows,
ExpoImp = the sum of total export and import,
Govt.DevExp = Government development expenditure,
DomsInv = Gross domestic investment,
GFCF = gross fixed capital formation,
HumCap = human capital,
DCR = Domestic credit provided by banking sector, and
Good governance is proxied by a dummy variable.

Our econometric model is derived from a production function in which the level of country's productivity depends on FDI, trade (export and import), domestic investment, human capital, government development expenditure and GFCF. The model is based on endogenous growth theory, in the tradition of Balasubramanyam, Salisu, and Sapsford and Borensztein, Gregorio, Khawar, Flexner, and Lee, where FDI contributes to economic growth directly through new technologies and inputs as well as indirectly through improving human capital, infrastructure and institutions.

The following regression model is specified to measure the effects of FDI on economic growth. We estimate the effects of FDI on economic growth by ordinary least squares (OLS) method:

$$g = \alpha_0 + \beta_1 (FDI) + \beta_2 (XM) + \beta_3 (GE) + \beta_4 (HC) + \beta_5 (GFCE) + \beta_6 (DI) + \beta_7 (DCR) + D_{m+} \varepsilon \quad \ldots (2)$$

where,
g = GDP growth;
FDI = net foreign direct investment inflows as percentage of GDP;
XM = trade openness (the sum of total export and import as percentage of GDP);
GE = government development expenditure as ratio of GDP;
HC = human capital; GFCF = gross fixed capital formation to the share of GDP;
DI = gross domestic investment is coded as percentage of GDP;
DCR = ratio of domestic credit provided by banking sector to real GDP;
Dm = dummy variable; and
ε = error term.

Positive relationships are expected between the dependent variable and all explanatory variables. We expect the estimated coefficients for these variables to be positive. If the model specification is reasonable, the estimated coefficient of FDI will indicate the direction and magnitude of the impact of FDI on economic performance.

While equation (2) captures the impact of most of the important variables, it does not account for the possibility of bi-directional relationship between growth and FDI highlighted in the recent literature. To capture these possible temporal causality relationships, the techniques of Granger causality are employed (Granger and Engle, 1987, 1991). The test involves estimating the regressions has discussed in the section below.

First, we tested the impact of FDI on economic growth during the period 1974–2011, using the method of bi-variate regression. Secondly, we have discussed our methodology for estimating our empirical model and produced empirical analysis. The main results from the bi-variate regression are summarized below:

Bi-variate Regression Results

This section includes a series of regressions to underscore the many advantages and growth prospects that FDI inflows have brought to the Indian economy. The methodology of the empirics constitutes a series of regressions using the ordinary least squares (OLS) model to prove a significant correlation between FDI and economic growth. The tables express the coefficients and t-statistics of each independent x-variable to demonstrate its level of significance. The R-squared or coefficient of determination is included to represent how much variation in the dependent y-variable is captured by the regression. To find out the individual influence of FDI on GDP and other variables, firstly, we have considered several bi-variate regression analysis.

Table 6.1 *Bi-variate Regression Results*

	Independent Variable: Foreign Direct Investment (FDI)			
Case of India	*(1.1)*	*(1.2)*	*(1.3)*	*(1.4)*
Dependent Variables	GDP (mn$)	GDP gr	GDP pc (US$)	GDP pcGr
Constant coefficient	2,16,429	4.8506	278	2.60
Co-efficient	42.312 (9.64)***	1.881 (1.67)*	0.030437 (9.82)***	2.642 (2.34)**
R^2	73.8%	8.2%	75.7%	15.0%
Standard Error (Se)	4.389	1.128	0.003099	1.131
R^2 Adjusted	73.0%	5.3%	74.9%	12.2%
df	34	32	32	32

Notes: 1. Absolute value of t-statistics in parentheses.
2. * Significant at 10%; ** Significant at 5%; *** Significant at 1%.

The bi-variate regression results of the economic growth of India based on FDI are presented in Table 6.1. Firstly, dependence of the growth of GDP on FDI are found out, and secondly, dependence of other variables on FDI is found out individually.

Table 6.1 also reveals that if there is no change in the independent variable, the GDP growth in India would remain 4.85 per cent with standard error of 0.112. The R^2 shows at 0.082.

Other variables such as domestic savings, domestic investment, government expenditure, export, import, value added in various sectors show significant constants which present less influence of FDI inflows on their growth for the both countries.

In general way, without testing any statistical significance, the above discussion reveals that FDI inflows influence the growth of GDP and also per capita GDP growth. But we are getting apparently a good relationship between FDI and GDP growth by a two-variable regression. But, when we introduce more independent variables in the regression, the coefficient of FDI reduces significantly and the test does not give any statistically significant result.

However, we have used time series data for the study. All macroeconomic time series data show some trend. When working with the time series data, the first issue is whether the series are stationary or not. Without following the standard methods for test, the statistical significance of the variables or estimator, the outcome will be of no practical use. Here is our analysis of the estimation using econometric issues.

Table 6.2 *Regression Results*

Dependent Variable: GDP_GR

	Coefficient	*Std. Error*	*t-Statistic*	*Prob.*
C	7.871426	8.475552	0.928721	0.3619
FDI	0.519785	2.684937	0.193593	0.8481
GFCF	1.254110	0.611654	2.050358	0.0510
DI	–0.666125	0.405818	–1.641436	0.1132
DCR	–0.373347	0.150578	–2.479430	0.0203
GE	–0.450052	0.251890	–1.786701	0.0861
XM	–0.194434	0.305093	–0.637295	0.5297
HC	7.272236	4.045374	1.797667	0.0843
DM	–5.472754	2.040267	–2.682372	0.0128
R-squared	0.421506	Mean dependent var		5.451290
Adjusted R-squared	0.236387	S.D. dependent var		2.910013
S.E. of regression	2.542912	Akaike info criterion		4.926424
Sum squared resid	161.6601	Schwarz criterion		5.330461
Log likelihood	–74.74921	Hannan-Quinn criter.		5.064212
F-statistic	2.276954	Durbin-Watson stat		2.556735
Prob(F-statistic)	0.055343			

A glance at these results would suggest that we have the multicollinearity problems, as most of the variables are statistically insignificant, which is a classical symptom of multicollinearity. To shed more light on this, we present in Table 6.3 the intercorrelations among the all regressors.

Table 6.3 *Correlation Matrix*

	GDPPG	*GDPGR*	*FDI*	*XM*	*GE*	*HC*	*GFCF*	*DI*	*SR*	*DCR*
GDPPG	1	0.99	0.38	0.48	–0.31	0.50	0.44	0.42	0.31	0.43
GDPGR	0.99	1	0.29	0.38	–0.25	0.40	0.35	0.30	0.25	0.36
FDI	0.38	0.29	1	0.88	–0.50	0.82	0.66	0.73	0.45	0.51
XM	0.48	0.38	0.88	1	–0.54	0.91	0.78	0.77	0.5	0.63
GE	–0.31	–0.25	–0.50	–0.54	1	–0.67	0.75	–0.75	–0.62	–0.75
HC	0.50	0.40	0.82	0.91	–0.67	1	0.90	0.84	0.70	0.82
GFCF	0.44	0.35	0.66	0.78	–0.75	0.90	1	0.93	0.84	0.87
DI	0.42	0.35	0.73	0.77	–0.75	0.84	0.93	1	0.77	0.78
SR	0.31	0.25	0.45	0.52	–0.62	0.70	0.84	0.77	1	0.72
DCR	0.43	0.36	0.5	0.63	–0.70	0.82	0.87	0.78	0.72	1

The matrix of pairwise correlation coefficients is presented in the above table. We observe multicollinearity among the variables which will affect our regression results. The correlation matrix indicates that we can use only GDPG, FDI, GFCF, SR and DCR as our key variables because others share multicollinearity. As we wanted to see the rate of change of these variables, we used log linear function. We did not consider the savings ratio at our study and here we have found that the DCR is not stationary at any level. So, we have excluded the DCR from our analysis. Using Eviews software package, the results of the Augmented Dickey-Fuller test are presented in Table 6.4.

From the Table 6.4 it is found that all variables contain unit root. To make the variables stationary, the first difference of all variables was taken and it was found that variables were integrated of order one, i.e., I (1). The results show that LogGDPG, LogFDI and LogGFCF are non-stationary at 1 per cent, 5 per cent and 10 per cent levels, but first difference stationary. However, LogFDI is also trend stationary at its level.

Table 6.4 *ADF Unit Root Test Results*

Variables	Level		First difference	
	Constant[1]	Constant & trend[2]	Constant	Constant & trend
LnGDPG	1.994977	–1.499016	–6.255618*	–6.933209*
LnFDI	–1.063633	–3.846211**	–6.554034*	–6.516964*
LnGFGC	0.674260	–2.263001	–3.303879**	–3.418022**
Dm	–1.098996	–1.849582	–5.656854*	–5.574069*

Notes: 1. Critical values for 1%, 5% and 10% significance levels are –2.6369, –1.9513 and –1.6107 respectively.
2. Critical values for 1%, 5% and 10% significance levels are –3.7700, –3.1900 and –2.8900 respectively.
3. *, **, and *** indicate significance at 1%, 5% and 10% levels respectively.

Next, cointegration test is carried out among the variables that are first difference stationary, (i.e., LnGDPG, LnFDI, LnGFCF and Dm) and the results are reported in the Table 6.5:

Table 6.5 *Johansen Cointegration Test*

Hypothesized		Trace	0.05	
No. of CE(s)	Eigen value	Statistic	Critical Value	Prob.**
None *	0.711030	50.82098	47.85613	0.0256
At most 1	0.379291	17.30234	29.79707	0.6177
At most 2	0.135782	4.426228	15.49471	0.8663
At most 3	0.017843	0.486121	3.841466	0.4857

Trace test indicates 1 cointegrating eqn(s) at the 0.05 level

* denotes rejection of the hypothesis at the 0.05 level

**MacKinnon-Haug-Michelis (1999) p-values

Unrestricted Cointegration Rank Test (Maximum Eigen value)

Hypothesized		Max Eigen	0.05	
No. of CE(s)	Eigen value	Statistic	Critical Value	Prob.**
None *	0.711030	33.51864	27.58434	0.0077
At most 1	0.379291	12.87611	21.13162	0.4637
At most 2	0.135782	3.940107	14.26460	0.8656
At most 3	0.017843	0.486121	3.841466	0.4857

Max-eigen value test indicates 1 cointegrating eqn(s) at the 0.05 level

* denotes rejection of the hypothesis at the 0.05 level

**MacKinnon-Haug-Michelis (1999) p-values

According to the co-integration test, the variables share one co-integrating relation as per trace and maximum eigen value statistics.

Based on the co-integration analysis, the growth model is re-specified with the variables having the same order of integration, that is, LnGDPG, LnFDI, LnGFCF and Dm. The re-specified model is as follows:

LnGDPG= f(LnFDIt, LnGFCFt, Dm)

OLS estimation of the above model yields the following output:

Regression Result

Substituted Coefficients:

$LNGDPG_t$ = –3.252697 – 0.041359*LNFDI + 1.024521* LNGFCF + 0.02730560*DM

t-statistics (–2.914444) (–1.275099) (12.86845) (12.86845)

Variable	*Coefficient*	*Std. Error*	*t-Statistic*	*Prob.*
C	–3.252697	1.116061	–2.914444	0.0068
LOG(FDI)	–0.041359	0.032436	–1.275099	0.2124
LOG(GFCF)	1.024521	0.079615	12.86845	0.0000
DM	0.027306	0.096904	0.281781	0.7801
R-squared	0.961113	Mean dependent var		12.53026
Adjusted R-squared	0.957091	S.D. dependent var		0.611246
S.E. of regression	0.126617	Akaike info criterion		–1.182085
Sum squared resid	0.464925	Schwarz criterion		–1.000690
Log likelihood	23.50440	F-statistic		238.9187
Durbin-Watson stat	0.646429	Prob (F-statistic)		0.000000

From the above regression results, it is seen that, the highest impact comes from GFCF, which is quite obvious. The sign of LNFDI coefficient is negative and it is statistically insignificant also. The result indicates that FDI is negatively correlated to the economic growth of India and it has not yet been established as a significant determining factor for the economic growth of India till now.

The estimated coefficient for FDI is negative and statistically insignificant. When the coefficient is insignificant, no inference can be drawn from the result under the used data set and the model. Thus, it cannot be said that FDI has a positive or negative impact on economic growth for India. The result is ambiguous for India. The result of this analysis is consistent with the findings of Athukorala (2003), Carkovic and Levine (2002). Alam asserted that FDI inflows to India has lack of infrastructural facilities, resource constraints and lack of entrepreneurial knowhow so that the country has not been getting benefit from FDI which will create more conducive environment for enhancing the economic growth.

On the other hand, the estimated coefficient of GFCF is positive and highly statistically significant. The coefficient of capital formation (GFCF) is significant at the 1 per cent level and the sign is positive indicating that 1 per cent increase in gross fixed capital will increase the growth rate of GDP by 12.86%. This means that GFCF has highly significant positive impact on GDP growth as expected. The other variable—dummy variable—has very small positive influence on GDP growth but not statistically significant. This result reveals that all types of governments in India have been contributing to the economic growth.

R^2 and adjusted R^2 indicate that the behaviour of FDI in case of India is almost completely explained by the independent variables included in the model. F statistics shows that the independent variables are jointly highly significant. The coefficient of determination (R2 = 0.96) is quite high and reveals almost a perfect fit of the model. This indicates the proportion of total variation in GDP growth explained by the explanatory variables.

FDI inflows to India have been increasing dramatically during the recent times. India has opened up its economy for about two decades and reforms have been taken from that time. It has a very large number of locked land and also a big number of population—the world's second largest population. Since it has lack of infrastructural facilities, resources and entrepreneurial know-how, it has not been able to get benefit from FDI and create more conducive environment for enhancing the economic growth.

One of the significant observations that this study has derived is that the growth effect of GFCF is highly significant than FDI to the level of GDP growth in India. It is true that capital formation has a positive influence on economic growth. Government can give more attention to build more fixed capital formation as a level playing field for economic growth. The study also found that the government has significant role to promote the economy of a country.

Granger Causality Test between FDI and Economic Growth

The Granger-causality test is used to ascertain the direction of causality between GDPGR and FDI. This test assumes that the underlying time series data are stationary, i.e., I(0) processes. Therefore, it is imperative to examine whether GDPGR and FDI are stationary. Augmented Dickey-Fuller (ADF) test is employed to check the stationary property of these two variables. One of the implications of Granger causality test is that if two variables, say X and Y, are cointegrated and each is individually I(I), that is, integrated of order one, then either X must Granger cause Y, or Y must Granger cause X. Therefore, it is necessary to ascertain whether two variables X and Y are cointegrated, that is, whether there is any long-run relationship between these two. The Johansen cointegration test has also been performed in this study.

The casual relationship between GDPGR and FDI is examined by standard Granger-causality test. Following equations are estimated for this purpose:

$$GDPG_t = \sum_{i=1}^{n} a_i GDPG_{t-i} + \sum_{j=1}^{m} b_j FDI_{t-j} + u_{1t} \qquad ...(1)$$

$$FDI_t = \sum_{i=1}^{n} c_i GDPG_{t-i} + \sum_{j=1}^{m} d_j FDI_{t-j} + u_{2t} \qquad ...(2)$$

The rejection of null hypothesis that FDI does not Granger-cause GDPGR requires that (a) estimated coefficients on the lagged FDI in (1) are statistically different from zero, (i.e., $\Sigma b_j \neq 0$) and (b) the set of estimated coefficient on the lagged GDPGR in (2) is not statistically different from zero, (i.e., $\Sigma c_j \neq 0$). Similarly, rejection of null hypothesis that GDPGR does not Granger cause FDI requires that (a) the estimated coefficients on the lagged FDI in (1) are not statistically different from zero, (i.e., $\Sigma b_j \neq 0$) and the set of estimated coefficient on the lagged GDPGR in (2) is not statistically different from zero, (i.e., $\Sigma c_j \neq 0$).

As Granger causality test is very sensitive to the number of lags used in estimation procedure, optimum lag length is determined by applying Schwarz Criterion (SC). According to this criterion, optimum lag length m is obtained by minimizing the function:

SC = ln à^2 + $m$ln$n$

where, à^2 is the maximum likelihood estimate of a^2 (RSS/n).

The results of Granger causality tests are reported in Table 6.6. The Schwartz Information Criterion (SC) has been used to determine the optimal lag length in the test.

The results reported in Table 6.6 show that null hypothesis that FDI does not Granger cause GDPGR is not rejected because the F statistics yields a value of 0.33376 which is below the critical value of $F_{0.01}$ = 5.53. Thus, we cannot reject the null hypothesis (bj = 0). This signals that FDI does not Granger cause growth in Bangladesh. On the other hand, the next portion of the results in the table indicates that GDP growth Granger causes FDI in Bangladesh (F statistics 5.5776, which exceeds the critical value of $F_{0.01}$ = 5.53).

Table 6.6 *Granger Causality Test*

Null Hypothesis:	*Obs*	*F-Statistic*	*Probability*
FDI does not Granger Cause GDP	32	2.34934	0.11465
GDP does not Granger Cause FDI		4.52114	0.02025*

Causality test indicates that there is a unidirectional causality from GDP to FDI in case of India.

Similar result is observed also in case of India. The results reported in Table 6.6. show that null hypothesis that FDI does not Granger cause GDPGR is not rejected because the F statistics yields a value of 0.33376 which is below the critical value of $F_{0.01}$ = 5.53. Thus, we cannot reject the null hypothesis (bj = 0). This signals that FDI does not Granger cause growth in India. On the other hand, the next portion of the results in the table indicates that GDP growth Granger causes FDI in India. The result also confirms that there is no bi-directional causality (feedback) between GDPGR and FDI.

That is, causality test indicates that there is a unidirectional causality from GDP to FDI. So, the conclusion is that there is a long-run equilibrium relationship between economic growth and FDI and economic growth Granger-causes FDI for both the countries in Bangladesh and India.

Hypothesis Testing

H_1: GDP growth rate of India depends upon FDI inflows.

The estimated coefficient for FDI is negative and statistically insignificant. The result indicates that FDI is negatively correlated to the economic growth of India and it has not yet been established as a significant determining factor for the economic growth of India till now. When the coefficient is insignificant, no inference can be drawn from the result under the used data set and the model. It cannot be said that FDI has a positive or negative impact on economic growth for India. Accordingly, no inferences cannot be made on the remaining hypothesis under the present study.

Conclusions

This chapter examines the relationship and impact of FDI on economic growth in India. In order to know the relationship between FDI and GDP growth, we have used the OLS regression estimation process. By this way we have tested stationarity of time series data with ADF unit root test. Johansen cointegration test confirms that used variables are cointegrated. Granger causality test is employed to ascertain the direction of causality and it is found that there is unidirectional causality from GDP growth to FDI for the country.

On the other hand, the estimated coefficient for FDI is negative and statistically insignificant. The result indicates that FDI is negatively correlated to the economic growth of the country and it has not yet been established as a significant determining factor for the economic growth of the country till now. When the coefficient is insignificant, no inference can be drawn from the result under the used data set and the model. Thus, it cannot be said that FDI has a positive or negative impact on economic growth for India. The result is also ambiguous for India.

The findings of the study show that FDI has not yet been considered as a significant determining factor for the economic growth of India. FDI policy should be formulated in such a way that causes attraction of more foreign potential direct investors and NRIs (or NRBs) to invest in the country in those sectors which create employment and income in a larger scale. The country needs more FDI to the priority sectors, so that it could get immediate yields from the investment. Investment in infrastructures and export-led manufacturing sectors can contribute more and FDI is imperative in this case. In the era of globalization, advantages of internationalization and regional integration should be utilized properly to attract more FDI.

7

Summary, Concluding Observations and Policy Recommendations

Foreign direct investment (FDI) is often seen as an important catalyst for economic growth in developing countries. Development economists have long argued that countries pursuing externally-oriented development strategies are more likely to achieve higher rates of economic growth than those that are internally focused. A number of studies have examined the relationship between inward FDI and economic growth in the developing host countries (De Mello, 1997). A generally accepted conclusion is that FDI has played a significant role in promoting economic growth in host countries because FDI represents 'the transmission to the host country of a package of capital, managerial skills, and technical skills'. An interesting finding of previous studies is that the economic and technological conditions of a recipient economy influence the extent to which FDI contributes to growth.

Since the late 1980s the conception started to change in favour of FDI inflows into developing countries, due to a possibly positive contribution of FDI to growth through capital formation and technology transfer, enabling them to convert their comparative advantage into a global force. The lack of available capital for rapid industrialization in developing countries also recognized the role of FDI as a channel of capital mobility in the host economy. For these reasons, the inflow of FDI increased rapidly during the late 1980s and the 1990s in almost every region of the world, lending support to the view that FDI and economic growth are positively correlated.

The gains from FDI inflows are unquestionable as it contributes to economic growth through an increase in productivity by providing new investment, better technologies and managerial skills to the host countries. The ultimate impact of FDI on economic growth depends on the degree of capacity of the host country to use FDI as efficiently as possible. Similarly, trade liberalization may facilitate economic growth through efficiency in production by utilizing the abundant factors of production more effectively and absorbing better technologies from advanced countries on the one hand, it may harm the growth process through various forms of macroeconomic instability such as terms of trade deterioration and balance of payments crisis, on the other. Thus, it is a challenge for developing countries to find out the appropriate direction of the role of FDI and trade liberalization in economic growth.

As a developing world, India was also concerned with issues pertaining to foreign private capital inflow and trade liberalization initially. However, it later moved to liberalize its trade and investment policies to include various investment incentives, particularly for foreign investors. Along with these, India has maintained high and steady economic growth, single-digit inflation rate, a growing domestic market, a large number of low-paid workers with growing number of skilled personnel and a more favourable investment climate. As a consequence, India, as a host country, has been successful in attracting a significant amount of FDI and raising its volume of trade (export plus import) as percentage of GDP during the last two decades. The question which naturally arises here is whether the increase in growth was brought about by trade liberalization and FDI inflows. Therefore, it is important to explore the impact of FDI on the growth process, quantitatively India for a better understanding about the linkages among FDI and economic growth.

This study seeks to find answer to the questions: (i) what is the relationship of FDI and economic growth India, and (ii) what is the direction of causality among FDI, and GDP growth rate. To do so, the study first explains the historical trends of FDI, economic reforms, trade liberalization and economic growth using yearly data over a long time period of 1974–2008. Secondly, the empirical analysis is conducted by applying OLS regression analysis.

The period chosen for the study is 1974–2008 which is significant as a period characterized by substantial inflows of FDI to countries in South Asia as well as a period of extensive reforms, particularly in policies related to trade, industry, fiscal and public sector enterprises and privatization.

As the study is about FDI and economic growth India over a period, a number of developments have taken place during this period. To trace this, a detailed existing literature on FDI and economic growth with particular emphasis on developing countries has been reviewed. An ambiguous picture is observed regarding the FDI-growth relationship because the contribution of FDI to economic growth has been debated extensively in literature: some found positive relationship between FDI and economic growth, some found no effects and some even conclude that there are negative effects.

The study also presents a brief account of Indian economy and also background information of the FDI policies of the Indian government. It then discusses the structure and nature of industrial policies of Indian government. The study thus represents the theoretical background of the determinants of FDI in India.

India is the second largest country in the world, both in terms of population and area. It has 17 per cent of the world's population and roughly 2.4 per cent of the world's land mass. It is also the sixth largest economy in terms of gross domestic product (GDP). Some of the problems faced by the country like inadequate employment opportunities, inequalities in the socio-economic status and poverty can prove disastrous to any globalizing economy. Some of the other concerns regarding the Indian economy are poor infrastructure, fiscal deficit and a large amount of non-performing assets (NPAs).

India has changed from public sector domination in industries to an increasingly liberalized system, with both domestic and foreign players. It has also changed from a sellers' market with limited competition to a buyers' market with increased competition, from a country with quantitative restrictions and tariffs to quota-free and open economy and from a restricted financial market to a liberalized financial market with prudential norms. These changes are a testimony to the dynamic nature of the Indian economy.

In 1991, Indian economy faced a severe financial crisis. The Government of India then implemented some very effective stabilization measures in order to correct the imbalances in the Indian economy. It is clear that the new industrial policy of 1991 has effected some very fundamental policy changes such as near abolition of licensing system, easing of the rigours of Monopoly and Restrictive Trade Practices (MRTP) Act and Foreign Exchange Regulation Act (FERA), reduced list of industries for the public sector, automatic approvals of foreign technology agreements and for 51 per cent foreign equity participation, private investment in infrastructure, liberal location policy for industry, freer import of capital goods, deregulation in small-scale industrial units and liberal policy measures for attracting FDI and NRI investment. The main objective of the liberalized policy measures was to enhance the productivity and competitive efficiency in the industrial sector.

Economic reforms started in the early eighties, but a comprehensive liberalization and privatization process started in July 1991 in the backdrop of the balance of payment and foreign exchange liquidity crises faced by the economy. Economic reforms were indeed critical at the first phase of transforming the economy. The most important changes implemented in the new economic reform package have been in the sphere of industrial policy, removing several barriers to entry in the earlier economic system.

The Government of India initiated major structural changes in its economic policy since July 1991. The main aim of the policy is to make Indian industry more competitive, as these changes include some critical reforms in its industrial policy, trade policy, policy towards financial markets and institutions and towards FDI. The role of FDI has been clearly mentioned in the process of economic development of India.

India launched its second-generation reforms in 2002, with a focus on reducing the fiscal deficit, improving infrastructure, reforming labour laws and energizing the states to participate actively in stepping up the pace of reforms. India raised its FDI limits in many important sectors including infrastructure, telecommunications, banking and insurance and civil aviation. The ongoing economic reforms process should be reappraised and revitalized to give the entire national development effort a more humane face. Recently, the Government of India has not only raised its FDI limits in many sectors but also opened it for retail multi-brand sector.

After independence, the Government of India has formulated policies for industrial growth and development. Industrial policy statements have been announced from 1948 onwards. The study examines the following industrial policy resolutions and the important aspects involved in the industrial policies:

- Industrial Policy Resolution of 1948
- Industrial Policy Resolution of 1956
- Industrial Policy Statement of 1973
- Industrial Policy Statement of 1977
- Industrial Policy Statement of 1980
- The New Industrial Policy of 1991

At the time of independence, policy towards FDI was largely conditioned by two factors: the Industrial Policy Resolutions of 1948 and 1956 and the foreign exchange crisis, especially in the late fifties. In this phase the government policy was largely determined by the struggle between the state and monopoly foreign interests.

A more liberal attitude towards foreign investment emerged after 1980 or so. This phase begins with the Industrial Policy Statements of 1980 and 1982 and, more importantly, the technology policy statement of 1983. For one, the policy statements began the process of de-lincensing and, to some extent, reversing the negative effects on growth and competition of the Industrial Policy Revolutions of 1948 and 1956. At the same time, some of the restrictive features of the MRTP Act were sought to be done away with.

The new industrial policy of 1991 may be the starting point of a new phase in FDI in India. The most welcome feature of the policy is its emphasis on reduction of bureaucratic interference in commercial matters.

Continuing with its policy to further liberalize the FDI sector, the Indian government has announced another set of sector-specific initiatives to attract larger volumes of foreign investment. The government realizes the fact that domestic resources alone may not be adequate to sustain the required expansion in infrastructure for development. Thus, it has followed a strategy to create incentives for FDI. India, today, has an extremely liberal regime for FDI in terms of entry norms.

There has been a rapid, yet calibrated, move towards de-regulation and liberalization, which has resulted in India becoming a favourite destination for foreign investment. The mood is upbeat and the signals strong. Undoubtedly, India has emerged as one of the most vibrant and dynamic of the developing economies.

The reform process has de-regulated the economy and stimulated domestic and foreign investments, taking India firmly into the forefront of investment destinations. The government, keen to promote investment in the country, has radically simplified and rationalized policies, procedures and regulatory aspects. Foreign investment is welcome in almost all sectors, except those of strategic concern (for instance, defence and atomic energy). A series of incentives has been announced in 2006 to promote investments.

Doing business became easier in India in 2005–06. The reforms reduced the time, cost and hassle for doing businesses in India to comply with legal and administrative requirements, placing the country in the top 20 reformers worldwide. However, the World Bank's Doing Business in 2008 database shows that among the South Asian economies in case of 'ease of doing business' India belongs to the lowest position.

The study adds to the empirical work by extending the coverage of the study to recent data, particularly during 1974–2008, which is significant as a period characterized by substantial inflows of FDI to countries in South Asia as well as a period of extensive reforms, particularly in policies related to trade, industry, fiscal and public sector enterprises and privatization.

On the other hand, the estimated coefficient for FDI is negative and statistically insignificant. The result indicates that FDI is negatively correlated to the economic growth of India and it has not yet been established as a significant determining factor for the economic growth of the country till now. When the coefficient is insignificant, no inference can be drawn from the result under the used data set and the model. It cannot be said that FDI has a positive or negative impact on economic growth for India. The result is also ambiguous for India.

Concluding Observations

FDI is not only a strategic option for a country, but also a key factor in the national economic development. Developing countries, which are not participating in the process of globalization, or those having poorer policies compared to other countries, run the risk of becoming comparatively less competitive in the global economy. Most countries attempt to attract foreign investors through liberalization of investment environment, fiscal reforms and a package of incentive offers. FDI can transform a country's economic scenario within shortest possible time. It is not merely access to funds but also provides transfer of technical know-how and management expertise.

It is evident in the study that there are some interrelated administrative barriers that result in inferiority in policy formulation and implementation, competitive drawbacks, poor quality of skills and infrastructure, ineffective institutions, and below average governance which dampen potential of FDI.

There is not any cross-country empirical study on South Asia and India to see the relationship using OLS regressions with time series data. In most of previous studies only a specific group was tested, for instance, only developing or developed countries, MENA, SAARC or OECD countries, or large samples including a large number of countries with dummy variables for the different groups of countries using panel data and estimation processes like VAR, SUR, LSDV. The result was combined and integrated. However, this study has tried to emphasize the importance of independent data and independent country in a more systematic way.

On the other hand, the estimated coefficient for FDI is negative and statistically insignificant. The result indicates that FDI is negatively correlated to the economic growth of India and it has not yet been established as a significant determining factor for the economic growth of the country till now. When the coefficient is insignificant, no inference can be drawn from the result under the used data set and the model. Thus, it cannot be said that FDI has a positive or negative impact on economic growth for India. The result is also ambiguous for India.

Strategic and Policy Recommendations for India

In India, internal competition was unduly restricted, as was the inflow of foreign technologies. Protected Indian enterprises are now as mature as they will ever be and now need the stimulus of foreign competition and access to foreign technologies to become efficient and competitive. Past restrictions on foreign entry may have outlived their usefulness as an aid to local 'infant' enterprises, certainly in the larger economies with long industrial histories.

There is clearly a need for more liberalization in India to remove the more inefficient of past interventions and make industries more export-oriented. In this context, a liberalization of FDI regulations can be a very useful input into the more general liberalization of trade and domestic competition. However, this is not the only lesson that India could learn among South Asian countries. The other is that the process of liberalization, including that on FDI, has to be controlled and integrated with a set of efficient interventions.

More general factors affect all prospective host economies: political stability, a sound macroeconomic framework, welcoming attitudes to foreign investment, adequate skills, low business transaction costs, good infrastructure and the like. Given these factors, it is still useful to India to implement promotional policies to attract investors, particularly as competition for FDI mounts and investors become choosier. The information for basing investment decisions is not perfect and subjective perceptions matter. Good marketing can make a difference (of course, only if other conditions are in place). And, it is possible for India to create conditions that make investments more viable, rather than simply marketing what they already have. This may simply involve removing constraints to foreign affiliate operations. But it may also involve creating new skills, infrastructure or support institutions.

How much promotion is needed depends on the kind of FDI and the basic attractions of a host economy. A large and dynamic economy like India needs to promote itself less than a small and less dynamic one like Bangladesh and Sri Lanka (e.g., the bulk of the massive inflows into China are not the result of active FDI promotion). And promotion can only go so far. If the economic base is weak or unstable, no amount of persuasion will attract large and sustained FDI inflows. So, India has to select its promotional activities for FDI on the basis of its needs and kinds of FDI. It has to create new infrastructure, new skills and supportive institutional facilities.

The main ways India can seek to attract FDI and the key sensitive issues are stated below:

(i) Reducing obstacles to FDI by removing restrictions on admission and establishment, as well as on the operations of foreign affiliates. The key issues here are how investment is to be defined for liberalizing entry or offering protection (direct and portfolio capital flows may be treated differently) and what kind of control should be exercised over FDI admission and establishment.

(ii) Improving standards of treatment of foreign investors by granting them non-discriminatory treatment vis-à-vis domestic or other foreign investors. The key issue here is what degree of national treatment should be granted to foreign affiliates once they are established in a host country.

(iii) Protecting foreign investors through provisions on compensation in the event of nationalization or expropriation, on dispute settlement and on guarantees on the transfer of funds. A key issue here is how far the right to expropriate or nationalize extends (especially to what extent certain regulatory actions of governments constitute takings of foreign property). Another is the acceptability of the kind of dispute settlement mechanisms available to foreign investors and countries. Third is what restrictions, if any, are acceptable on the ability of governments to introduce capital controls to protect the national economy.

(iv) Promoting FDI inflows through measures that enhance a country's image, provide information on investment opportunities, offer location incentives, facilitate FDI by institutional and administrative improvements and render post-investment services. The key issues here relate to the use of financial, fiscal or other incentives (including regulatory concessions) and the actions that home countries can take to encourage FDI flows to host countries.

Bibliography

Agosin, M.R. and Ricardo Mayer, 2000. 'Foreign Investment in Developing Countries: Does it Crowd in Domestic Investment?', UNCTAD Discussion Paper No. 146, UNCTAD, Geneva.

Agosin, R., 1985. 'Trends and Issues in FDI', *CTC Reporter*, New York, 19 March 1996.

Alam, M.S., 1998. 'Foreign Direct Investment in Bangladesh: An Overview of its Prospects and Realities', *Finance India*, Delhi, Vol. XII, No. 2.

Asian Development Bank (ADB), 2003. *Key Indicators of Developing Asia and Pacific Countries*, Hong Kong: Oxford University Press.

——, 2010, 2004, 2003, 1998, 1997. *Asian Development Outlook*, Hong Kong: Oxford University Press.

Aswathappa, K., 1990. *Essentials of Business Environment*, New Delhi: Himalaya Publishing House, pp. 45–57.

Athukorala, P. and J. Menon, 1995. 'Developing Countries with Foreign Investment: Malaysia', *Australian Economic Review*, Vol. 1, pp. 9–22.

Athukorala, P.P.A.W., 2003. 'The Impact of Foreign Direct Investment for Economic Growth: A Case Study in Sri Lanka', International Conference on Sri Lanka Studies, Full Paper Number 092.

Balasubramanyam, V.N. and V. Mahambare, 2003. 'FDI in India', *Transnational Corporations*, Vol. 12, No. 2, UNCTAD.

Balasubramanyam, V.N. and D.R. Sapsford, 2007. 'Does India Need a Lot More FDI?', *Economic and Political Weekly*, Vol. 42, No. 17, pp. 1549–55.

Baliamoune-Lutz, M.N., 2004. 'Does FDI Contribute to Economic Growth? Knowledge About the Effects of FDI Improves Negotiating Positions and Reduces Risk for Firms Investing in Developing', *Business Economics*, Vol. 39, No. 2.

Baniak, Andrzej, Jacek Cukrowski and Jan Herczynski, 2002. 'On Determinants of Foreign Direct Investment in Transition Economies', GDN Workshop, Prague, December.

Barro, Robert J., 1991. 'Economic Growth in a Cross Section of Countries', *Quarterly Journal of Economics*, Vol. 2, No. 106, pp. 407–33.

Bashir, A.M., 1999. 'FDI and Economic Growth in Some MENA Countries: Theory and Evidence', paper presented at MENA Annual Meeting in Conjunction with the ASSA.

Bashir, Abdel-Hameed M., 2002. 'Foreign Direct Investment and Economic Growth in Some MENA Countries: Theory and Evidence,' Grambling State University Working Paper 2002.

Bashir, Abdel-Hamid M., 1998. 'Foreign Direct Investment and Economic Growth in MENA Countries: Theory and Evidence', paper presented at the ERF Third Conference, Tunisia, August 31–September 2.

Bengoa, M. and B. Sanchez-Robles, 2003. 'Does Foreign Direct Investment Promote Growth? Recent Evidence from Latin America', Universidad de Cantabria, Working Paper 2003.

Bhagwati, J.N., 1978. *Anatomy and Consequences of Exchange Control Regimes*, New York: Balinger Publishing.

Blomstrom, M. and A. Kokko, 1996. 'The Impact of Foreign Investment on Host Countries: A Review of the Empirical Evidence', NBER and CEPR, December.

——, 2003. 'The Economics of Foreign Direct Investment Incentives', NBER Working Paper 9489.

Blomström, M., A. Kokko and M. Zejan, 1999. *Foreign Direct Investment: Firm and Host Country Strategies*, New York: St. Martin's Press.

Borensztein, E., J. De Gregorio and J.W. Lee, 1995. 'How Does Foreign Direct Investment Affect Economic Growth?', NBER Working Paper No. 5057.

——, 1998. 'How Does Foreign Direct Investment Affect Growth?', *Journal of International Economics*, Vol. 45, No. 1, pp. 115–35.

Bosworth, B. and S. Collins, 1999. 'Capital Flows to Developing Economies: Implications for Saving and Investment', Brookings Papers on Economic Activity.

Bruee, K., 1983. 'Foreign Direct Investment is a Sequential Process', in John H. Dunning (ed.), *The Theory of Transnational Corporation*, Vol. 1, New York: Transnational Corporation and Management Division, Department of Economic and Social Development, UN.

Buckley, P.J. and M.Z. Brooke, 1992. *Studies in International Business*, London: St. Martin's Press.

Campos, Nauro F. and Yuko Kinoshita, 2003. 'Why Does FDI Go Where It Goes? New Evidence from the Transition Economies', IMF Working Paper, IMF.

Capolupo, Rosa, 2008. 'The New Growth Theories and their Empirics after Twenty Years', Economics Discussion Papers 2008–27, Kiel Institute for the World Economy.

Carkovic, M. and R. Levine, 2002. 'Does Foreign Direct Investment Accelerate Economic Growth?', University of Minnesota Working Paper, May.

Caves, R.E., 1982. *Multinational Enterprise and Economic Analysis*, Cambridge: Cambridge University Press.

Chakraborty, C. and P. Basu, 2002. 'Foreign Direct Investment and Growth in India: A Cointegration Approach', *Applied Economics*, Vol. 34, No. 9, pp. 1061–73.

Chakraborty, C. and P. Nunnenkamp, 2006. 'Economic Reforms, Foreign Direct Investment and its Economic Effects in India', Kiel Working Paper No. 1272, The Kiel Institute for the World Economy, Germany.

Chary, S. Narasimha and V. Gangadhar, 2006. 'Foreign Direct Investment: A Study of India and China', *The Indian Journal of Commerce*, Vol. 59, No. 4, pp. 52–61.

Chatterjee, Sanchita, 2003. 'How is FDI Related to Economic Development?', CUTS Briefing Paper No. 2.

Chaudhuri, S., 1995. 'Government and Transnationals: New Economic Policies since 1991', *Economic and Political Weekly*, Vol. XXX, Nos 18–19, May 6–13, p. 999.

Chitrakar, Ramesh C., 1994. *Foreign Investment and Technology Transfer in Developing Countries: Motivating Factors and Financial and Economic Performance in Nepal*, UK: Ashgate Publishing Limited, pp. 53–60.

Chowdhury, A. and G. Mavrotas, 2003. 'FDI and Growth: What Causes What?', World Institute for Development Economics Research of the United Nations University (UNU/WIDER), Working Paper, September.

Chugan, P.K., 1997. 'Foreign Collaborations and Export Performance: A Case of MNC's Affiliates and Local Enterprises in Indian Automobile Ancillary Industry', *The Indian Journal of Economics*, Vol. LXXVII, No. 306, pp. 373–89.

Correa, Carlos and Nagesh Kumar, 2003. *Protecting Foreign Investment: Implications of a WTO Regime and Policy Options*, New Delhi: Academic Foundation, pp. 5–22.

Dasgupta, D. and D. Ratha, 2000. 'The Role of Short-term Debt in Recent Crises', *Finance and Development*, Vol. 37, December, pp. 54–57.

Davidson, W.H., 1980. 'The Location for Foreign Direct Investment Activity: Country Characteristics and Experience Effects', in John H. Dunning (ed.), *The Theory of Transnational Corporation*, Vol. 1, New York: Transnational Corporation and Management Division, Department of Economic and Social Development, UN, pp. 312–23.

De Long, J. Bradford and Lawrence H. Summers, 1991. 'Equipment Investment and Economic Growth', *Quarterly Journal of Economics*, Vol. 106, pp. 407–502.

De Mello, L.R., 1997. 'Foreign Direct Investment in Developing Countries and Growth: A Selective Survey', *The Journal of Development Studies*, Vol. 34, No. 1, pp. 1–34.

DeRosa, Dean A., 1998. 'Foreign Trade and Investment Policies in Developing Asia', *Asian Development Review*, Vol. 16, No. 2.

Dhakal, D., Saif Rahman and Kamal P. Upadhyaya, 2003. 'Foreign Direct Investment and Economic Growth in Asia', *Indian Journal of Economics and Business*, Vol. 6, No. 1.

Dritsaki, M., C. Dritsaki and A. Adamopoulos, 2004. 'A Causal Relationship between Trade, Foreign Direct Investment and Economic Growth for Greece', *American Journal of Applied Sciences*, Vol. 1, No. 3, pp. 230–35.

Dunning, J.H., 1981. 'Explaining the International Direct Investment Position of Countries: Toward a Dynamic or Developmental Approach', *Weltwirtschaftliches Archiv*, Vol. 11, No. 1, pp. 30–64.

——, 2002. 'Determinants of Foreign Direct Investment: Globalization Induced Changes and the Role of FDI Policies', Annual Bank Conference on Development Economics in Europe, Oslo.

Durham, J., 2004. 'Absorptive Capacity and the Effects of Foreign Direct Investment and Equity Foreign Portfolio Investment of Economic Growth', *European Economic Review*, Vol. 48, No. 2, pp. 285–306.

Dutt, K.A., 1997. 'The Pattern of Direct Foreign Investment and Economic Growth', *World Development*, Vol. 25, No. 11, pp. 1925–36.

Economic Survey, 2005–06, 2006–07, 2007–08, 2009–10, 2010–11, Ministry of Finance, Government of India, New Delhi.

Edwards, S., 1990. 'Capital Flows, Foreign Direct Investment, and Debt-Equity Swaps in Developing Countries', Working Paper Series, Cambridge, MA: National Bureau of Economic Research.

Enders, Walter, 2004. *Applied Econometric Time Series*, 2nd Edition, New York: John Wiley and Sons.

Evans, Paul, 1998. 'Using Panel Data to Evaluate Growth Theories', *International Economic Review*, Department of Economics, University of Pennsylvania and Osaka University Institute of Social and Economic Research Association, Vol. 39, No. 2, pp. 295–306.

Fan, X. and Paul M. Dickie, 2000. 'The Contribution of Foreign Direct Investment to Growth and Stability: A Post-Crisis ASEAN-5 Review', *ASEAN Economic Bulletin*, Vol. 17, No. 3, p. 312.

Feldstein, M., 2000. 'Aspects of Global Economic Integration: Outlook for the Future', NBER Working Paper No. 7899.

Flexner, N., 2000. 'Foreign Direct Investment and Economic Growth in Bolivia, 1990–1998', Economic Policy Division, Central Bank of Bolivia.

Fontagne, L., 1997. 'How Foreign Direct Investment Affects International Trade and Competitiveness: An Empirical Assessment', Centre d'etudes Prospectives et d'Informations Internationales, Working Paper 97/17, pp. 9–38.

Frey, B., 1984. *International Political Economics*, Oxford: Basil Blackwell.

Fried, Joel and Igor Livshits, 2005. 'Foreign Direct Investment and Economic Growth: Empirical Analyses on Twenty OECD Countries'.

Gandhi, P. Jegadish, 2005. *A Decade of Economic Reforms in India: Two Critical Commentaries*, edited by Ajit Kumar Sinha, New Delhi: Deep and Deep Publications.

Garibaldi, Pietro, Nada Mora, Ratna Sahay and Jeromin Zettelmeyer, 2001. 'What Moves Capital to Transition Economies', Vol. 48, Special Issue, IMF Staff Papers, International Monetary Fund.

Geest, W. van der (ed.), 2004. 'Sri Lanka's Trade Expansion During Economic Reform', in O.H. Chowdhury and W. van der Geest (eds), *Economic Policy Reform and Trade Performance in South Asia*, Dhaka, Bangladesh: The University Press Limited, pp. 14–30.

Globerman, S., A. Kokko, Mattias Revelius and Mikael Sami, 1996. 'MNE Response to Economic Liberalization in a Developing Country: Evidence from India', *Journal of Economic Development*, Vol. 21, No. 2, pp. 163–83.

Gordon, H. Hanson, 2001. 'Should Countries Promote Foreign Direct Investment?', UNCTAD G-24 Discussion Paper Series No. 9.

Goyal, S.K., 1995. 'TNCs and the Third World: Need for a Realistic Policy Framework', *Abhigyan*, p. 38.

Granger, C.W.J. and R.F. Engle, 1987. 'Cointegration and Error Correction: Representation, Estimation and Testing', *Econometrica*, Vol. 55, No. 2, pp. 251–76.

——, 1991. *Long-run Economic Relationships: Readings in Cointegration, Advanced Text in Econometrics*, Oxford: Oxford University Press.

Greenaway, D. and D. Sapsford, 1994. 'What Does Liberalization Do for Exports and Growth?', *Weltwirtschaftliches Archive*, Vol. 130, pp. 152–74.

Greene. W.H., 2011, *Econometric Analysis*, Prentice Hall, 7th Edition.

Gregorio, De J., 2003. 'The Role of Foreign Direct Investment and Natural Resources in Economic Development', Central Bank of Chile, Working Paper No. 196.

Grosse, R. and J.N. Behrman, 1992. 'Theory in International Business', *Transnational Corporations*, Vol. 1, No. 1, pp. 93–126.

Gujarati, D.N., 1995. *Basic Econometrics*, 4th Edition, New York: McGraw-Hill.

Hassan, K.M., 2003. 'FDI, Information Technology and Economic Growth in the MENA Region', University of New Orleans, Working Paper 2003.

Hodgson, J.S. and M.G. Herander, 1983, *International Economic Question*, Prentice Hall.

Holland, Dawn, Magdolna Sass, Vladimir Benacek and Miroslaw Gronicki, 2000. 'The Determinants and Impact of FDI in Central and Eastern Europe: A Comparison of Survey and Econometric Evidence', *Transnational Corporations*, Vol. 9, No. 3.

Hymer, S., 1960. 'On Multinational Corporations and Foreign Direct Investment', in John H. Dunning (ed.), *The Theory of Transnational Corporations*, Vol. 1, New York: Transnational Corporation and Management Division, Department of Economic and Social Development, UN, p. 23.

——, 1976. *The International Operation of National Firms*, Cambridge: MIT Press.

Ikiara, M.M., 2003. 'Foreign Direct Investment (FDI), Technology Transfer and Poverty Alleviation: Africa's Hopes and Dilemma', ATPS Special Paper Series No. 16, Nairobi, Kenya.

Intelligence Economic Unit of Indian Institute of Public Opinion, 1993. 'Monthly Commentary on Indian Economic Conditions', Vol. XXXV, No. 3, pp. I–XI.

Iqbal, Alam B., 2006. 'FDI: A Tool for Economic Development', *Foreign Trade Review*, Vol. XLI, No. 2, pp. 62–79.

Iqbal, Badar A., 1997. *Japanese Foreign Direct Investment in South Asia: A Case of India*, New Delhi: Mittal Publications, pp. 161–80.

Jason Lewis, J., 1998. 'Factors Influencing Foreign Direct Investment in Lesser Developed Countries', *The Park Place Economist*, Vol. VIII.

Joze Mencinger, J., 2003. 'Does Foreign Direct Investment Always Enhance Economic Growth?', *Journal of Kyklos*, Vol. 56, No. 4, pp. 491–508.

Kathuria, Vinish, 1998. 'Technology Transfer and Spillovers for Indian Manufacturing Firms', *Development Policy Review*, Vol. 16, pp. 173–92.

Khawar, M., 2005. 'Foreign Direct Investment and Economic Growth: A Cross-Country Analysis', *Global Economy Journal*, Vol. 5, No. 1, pp. 1–10.

Kishor, N., 2003. 'Foreign Direct Investment in the Post Globalized Era: India's Strategy and Prospects', *Business Perspectives*, Vol. 5, No. 2, July–December.

Kojima, K., 1975. 'International Trade and Foreign Investment: Substitutes or Complements', *Hitotsubashi Journal of Economics*, Vol. 16, pp. 1–12.

Krugman, P., 1990. *Rethinking International Trade*, Cambridge: MIT Press.

Kumar, N., 1994. *Multinational Enterprises and Industrial Organization: The Case of India*, New Delhi: Sage Publications.

——, 2002. *Globalization and the Quality of Foreign Direct Investment*, New Delhi: Oxford University Press.

Kumar, Nagesh and Jaya Prakash Pradhan, 2002. 'Foreign Direct Investment, Externalities and Economic Growth in Developing Countries: Some Empirical Explorations and Implications for WTO Negotiations on

Investment', RIS Discussion Papers No. 27/2002, New Delhi: Research and Information System for the Non-aligned and Other Developing Countries.

Kyaw, S., 2003. 'Foreign Direct Investment to Developing Countries in the Globalized World', Working Paper, paper presented at the DSA Conference 2003, University of Strathclyde, Glasgow, 10–12 September.

Lal, Deepak, 1975. *Appraising Foreign Investment in Developing Countries*, London: Heinemann.

Lall, S. and P. Streeten, 1977. *Foreign Investment, Transnational and Developing Countries*, London: Macmillan.

Lall, S., 1993. 'Foreign Direct Investment in South Asia', *Asian Development Review*, Vol. 11, No. 1, pp. 102–19.

Lensink, Robert and Oliver Morrissey, 2001. 'Foreign Direct Investment: Flows, Volatility and Growth in Developing Countries', *DESG*.

Lipsey, R.E., 1999. 'The Location and Characteristics of US Affiliates in Asia', NBER Working Papers 6876, National Bureau of Economic Research, Inc.

Liu, X., Peter Burridge and P.J.N. Sinclair, 2002. 'Relationship between Economic Growth, Foreign Direct Investment and Trade: Evidence from China', *Applied Economics*, Vol. 34, No. 11, pp. 1433–40.

Lucas, R.E., 1988. 'On the Mechanics of Economic Development', *Journal of Monetary Economics*, Vol. 22, pp. 3–42.

Makki, S.S. and A. Somwaru, 2004. 'Impact of Foreign Direct Investment and Trade on Economic Growth: Evidence from Developing Countries', *American Journal of Agricultural Economics*, Vol. 86, No. 3, pp. 795–801.

Mamun, A.A., 2003. 'Globalization and Foreign Direct Investment: Policies, Strategies, Status and Challenges for Bangladesh', *BIBM Bulletin*, Vol. 6, Nos 1 and 2.

Mankiw, N.G., D. Romer and D. Weil, 1992. 'A Contribution to the Empirics of Economic Growth', *Quarterly Journal of Economics*, Vol. 107, pp. 407–38.

Marino, A., 2000. 'The Impact of FDI on Developing Countries Growth: Trade Policy Matters', ISTAT (National Institute of Statistics), Italy, Working Paper 2000.

——, 2001. 'FDI, Development and the Distribution of International Capital Flows', ISTAT (National Institute of Statistics), Italy, Working Paper 2001.

Markusen, J.R. and Anthony J. Venables, 1997. 'Foreign Direct Investment as a Catalyst for Industrial Development', NBER Working Paper No. 624, Cambridge, Mass.

Martinussen, J., 1997. 'Neo-Marxist Theories of Underdevelopment and Dependency', in *Society, State and Market: A Guide to Competing Theories of Development*, London: Zed Books, pp. 85–100.

Meyer, H.W.J., 2003. 'Information Use in Rural Development', *The New Review of Information Behaviour Research*, Vol. 4, pp. 109–26.

Meyer, Klaus E., 2003. 'Foreign Direct Investment in Emerging Markets', Unpublished Project Working Papers, Copenhagen Business School, pp. 3–4.

Moore, M., 1993. 'Determinants of German Manufacturing Direct Investment: 1980–1988', *Weltwirtschaftliches Archiv*, Vol. 129, pp. 120–37.

Nagesh, K., 1996. 'India: Industrialization, Liberalization and Inward and Outward Foreign Direct Investment', in J.H. Dunning and Rajneesh Narula (eds), *Foreign Direct Investment and Governments*, New York: Oxford University Press, pp. 348–78.

Nunnenkamp, Peter and Julius Spatz, 2002. 'Determinants of FDI in Developing Countries: Has Globalization Changed the Rules of the Game?', *Transnational Corporations*, Vol. 11, No. 2.

OECD, 1983. 'Incentives and Disincentives and the International Investment Process', Paris.

——, 1987. 'International Investment and Multinational Enterprises: Recent Trends in International Direct Investment', Paris.

Oman, C., 1993. 'Trends in Global FDI and Latin America', in C.I. Bradford (ed.), *Mobilising International Investment in Latin America*, Paris: Organisation for Economic Co-operation and Development.

Ozawa, T., 1992. 'Foreign Direct Investment and Economic Development', *Transnational Corporations*, Vol. 1, No. 1, pp. 129–49.

Pant, M., 1989. 'A Financial Model of the Multinational Corporation', *Indian Economic Review*, Vol. XXIV, No. 2, p. 207.

——, 1993. 'Export Performance, Transnational Corporations and the Manufacturing Sector: A Case Study of India', *Indian Economic Review*, Vol. XXVIII, No. 1, pp. 41–54.

——, 1995. *Foreign Direct Investment in India: The Issue Involved*, New Delhi: Lancer Books, pp. 161–80.

Patarasuk, W., 1991. 'The Role of Transnational Corporations in Thailand's Manufacturing Industries', *Regional Development Dialogue*, Vol. 12, No. 1, Spring, UNCRD, Nagoya, Japan.

Paul, Justin, 2006. *Business Environment: Text and Cases*, New Delhi: Tata McGraw-Hill Publishing Co. Ltd., pp. 359–63.

Pfefferman, G.P. and A. Madarassy, 1992. 'Trends in Private Investment in Developing Countries', International Finance Cooperation, Discussion Paper No. 14, Washington, DC.

Pradhan, Jaya Prakash, 2004. 'FDI Spillovers and Local Productivity Growth: Evidence from Indian Pharmaceutical Industry', MPRA Paper 17080, University Library of Munich, Germany.

Prebisch, Raúl, 1950. 'The Economic Development of Latin America and its Principal Problems', reprinted in *Economic Bulletin for Latin America*, Vol. 7, No. 1, pp. 1–22.

Reza, S. and M.A. Rashid, 1997. 'Foreign Direct Investment: Problems and Prospects', in M.G. Quibria (ed.), *Bangladesh Economy in Transition*, Dhaka: University Press Limited.

Ruffin, J.R., 1993. 'The Role of Foreign Investment in the Economic Growth of the Asian and Pacific Region', *Asian Development Review*, Vol. 11, No. 1, pp. 3–19.

Sahoo, P., 2006. 'Foreign Direct Investment in South Asia: Policy, Trends, Impact and Determinants', ADB Institute Discussion Paper No. 56, p. 6.

Sapsford, D.R. and V.N. Balasubramanyam, 2003. 'Globalisation and the Terms of Trade: The Glass Ceiling Hypothesis', in H. Bloch (ed.), *Growth and Development in the Global Economy*, Cheltenham: Edward Elgar, pp. 157–69.

Saramma, A.D., 2005. 'Economic Reform and its Effects on Foreign Direct Investment in India', in Ajit Kumar Sinha (ed.), *India Towards Economic Super Power*, New Delhi: Deep and Deep Publications, pp. 312–14.

Sharma, S. and R. Sharma, 2003. 'Globalization, Foreign Direct Investment and Development', *Business Perspectives*, Vol. 5, No. 2.

Singer, H.W., 1950. 'U.S. Foreign Investment in Underdeveloped Areas: The Distribution of Gains between Investing and Borrowing Countries', *American Economic Review*, Papers and Proceedings, Vol. 40, pp. 473–85.

Sinha, S., 1994. 'Financial Structure of Foreign Controlled Companies in India', *Indian Journal of Finance and Research*, Vol. IV, No. 1.

Sury, Niti, 2004. *Foreign Direct Investment: Global and Indian Aspects*, New Delhi: New Century Publications, pp. 132–36.

Teece, D.J., 1986. 'Transaction Cost Economics and the Multinational Enterprise: An Assessment', *Journal of Economic Behavior and Organization*, Vol. 7, No. 1, pp. 21–45.

Townsend, I., 2003. 'Does Foreign Direct Investment Accelerate Economic Growth in Less Developed Countries?', St. Olaf College, Northfield, MN, Working Paper 2003.

United Nations Conference on Trade and Development (UNCTAD), 1999b-WIR99. *The World Investment Report 1999*, United Nations, New York and Geneva: United Nations Publications.

——, 2002-WIR03. *The World Investment Report 2002: Transnational Corporations and Export Competitiveness*, United Nations, New York and Geneva: United Nations Publications, p. 291.

——, 2002. *World Investment Report 2000, 2001, 2002, 2003, 2005, 2006, 2007*, United Nations, New York and Geneva: United Nations Publications.

——, 2002. *FDI in Least Developed Countries at a Glance*, United Nations, New York and Geneva: United Nations Publications.

Varshney, R.L., 1995. 'Multinationals: A Developing Country Perspective', *Abhigyan*, p. 25.

Waldkirch, A., 2002. 'Foreign Direct Investment in a Developing Country: An Empirical Investigation', Oregon State University, Working Paper 2002.

Wallace, Cynthia (ed.), 1990. *Foreign Direct Investment in the 1990s: A New Climate in the Third World*, Dordrecht: Martinus Nijhott Publishers.

Wang, Z. and N. Swain, 2000. 'The Determinants of Foreign Direct Investment in Transforming Economies: Empirical Evidence from Hungary and China', *Weltwirtschaftiches*, Vol. 129, pp. 359–81.

Wei, S.J., 2000. 'How Taxing is Corruption on International Investors?', *Review of Economics and Statistics*, Vol. 82, No. 1, pp. 1–11.

Williamson, J., 1990. 'What Washington Means by Policy Reforms', in *Latin American Adjustment: How Much has Happened*, Washington: Institute for International Economics.

Willmore, L.N., 1986. 'The Comparative Performance of Foreign and Domestic Firms in Brazil', *World Development*, Vol. 14, No. 4, pp. 489–502.

Wong, J. and H. Khan, 1991. 'Transnational and Industrialization in Singapore', *Regional Development Dialogue*, Vol. 12, No. 1, Spring, UNCRD, Nagoya, Japan.

World Bank, 1999. 'Foreign Direct Investment in Bangladesh: Issue of Long-run Sustainability', Washington, DC.

Index